# *The Adventurous Fish Cook*

# *The Adventurous Fish Cook*

*George Lassalle*

M

First published 1976 by Macmillan London Limited
in association with Pan Books Limited

This edition published 1982 by
PAPERMAC
a division of Macmillan Publishers Limited
4 Little Essex Street London WC2R 3LF
and Basingstoke

Associated companies in Auckland, Dallas,
Delhi, Dublin, Hong Kong, Johannesburg,
Lagos, Manzini, Melbourne, Nairobi,
New York, Singapore, Tokyo, Washington
and Zaria

ISBN 0 333 32416 1

Printed in Great Britain by
BUTLER & TANNER LTD
Frome and London

For
Caroline,
Georgie, Patrick and Harriet,
and, for old times' sake,
E.D. and C.K.

This edition for Anne Cavendish

# Contents

# Acknowledgements

To Elizabeth David for permission to quote from *Italian Food*, *A Book of Mediterranean Food* and *Spices, Herbs and Seasonings in the English Kitchen* (all in Penguin)

To Alan Davidson for three recipes from *Mediterranean Seafood* (Penguin)

To Miriam Carlton (formerly Mohamed) for her Fish Curry;
Nita Denton for two cocktail specialities;
Allan Pote for his Paella;
Shirley Foulkes for her Smoked Trout Pâté;
Diana Foot of New South Wales for the recipe for Rock Cod;
Luke Wilson of Toronto, Canada, for advice and information and
Kyle Cathie for additional assistance and patience beyond the call of duty

# Measurements and metrication

The weights and measures used throughout this book are based on British Imperial standards and the nearest workable metric units to keep the recipes in the right proportions.

*International measures*

| measure | UK | Australia | New Zealand | Canada |
|---|---|---|---|---|
| 1 pint | 20 fl oz | 20 fl oz | 20 fl oz | 20 fl oz |
| 1 cup | 10 fl oz | 8 fl oz | 8 fl oz | 8 fl oz |
| 1 tablespoon | $\frac{5}{8}$ fl oz | $\frac{1}{2}$ fl oz | $\frac{1}{2}$ fl oz | $\frac{1}{2}$ fl oz |
| 1 dessertspoon | $\frac{2}{5}$ fl oz | no official measure | | |
| 1 teaspoon | $\frac{1}{5}$ fl oz | $\frac{1}{8}$ fl oz | $\frac{1}{6}$ fl oz | $\frac{1}{6}$ fl oz |

*Conversion of fluid ounces to metric*

4 tablespoons ($2\frac{1}{2}$ fl oz) = 70 ml (0·7 dl)
2 tablespoons ($1\frac{1}{4}$ fl oz) = 35 ml
1 tablespoon ($\frac{5}{8}$ fl oz) = 18 ml
1 dessertspoon ($\frac{2}{5}$ fl oz) = 12 ml
1 teaspoon ($\frac{1}{5}$ fl oz) = 6 ml
(all the above metric equivalents are approximate)

*Equivalents*

1 UK (old BST standard) cup equals $1\frac{1}{4}$ cups in Commonwealth countries
4 UK tablespoons equal 5 Commonwealth tablespoons
5 UK teaspoons equal 6 New Zealand or 6 Canadian or 8 Australian teaspoons
1 UK dessertspoon equals $\frac{2}{3}$ UK tablespoon or 2 UK teaspoons
In British cookery books, a gill is usually 5 fl oz ($\frac{1}{4}$ pint), but in a few localities in the UK it can mean 10 fl oz ($\frac{1}{2}$ pint)
Other non-standard measures include:
Breakfast cup = approx 10 fl oz
Tea cup = 5 fl oz
Coffee cup = 3 fl oz

# Author's note

As with collecting stamps, English watercolours or (God forbid) Goss china, you have to adventure some distance into any field of cookery before it begins to grab you. I hope this book makes it possible – or even easy – for those who are inexperienced in fish cookery to adventure to a point where they will see clearly the obvious advantages of cooking fish at home as opposed to eating it in restaurants or buying it from fried fish shops, battered to death and cooked in dubious oil.

I have also tried to suggest, without in any way withholding the respect due to the great traditions of *haute cuisine* and regional cookery, that marriages between a particular fish and one great sauce were not made in heaven, and that we can today afford to make free with such sauces and liberate them to serve with excellent – and cheaper – fish.

A good deal of space has been given to fish soups and fish pies, in which my reading suggests that many cooking traditions (particularly the English) are deficient, and if this book achieves nothing more than to persuade those who read it to experiment for themselves in these largely unexplored fields, I shall be content.

I have also stressed the need to set up a personal relationship with the ordinary or extraordinary fishmonger. For, unless we give the fishmonger our support by letting him know we need him, he will vanish completely from the scene and we shall all be condemned to the supermarket shuffle to the freezer.

For overseas readers, I have devised a simple method – based on the texture and qualities which characterize different types of fish available in this country – which should enable them to apply the recipes in this book to fish with similar characteristics in their own countries. This is outlined on pages 113–15.

All the recipes in this book are based on quantities for four people unless otherwise specified. All oven temperatures are preheated.

# Introduction to the new edition

I am delighted to write a foreword to this third edition of *The Adventurous Fish Cook*, and would like at once to express my sincere gratitude for the kindness with which it has been received in its two previous incarnations.

It is with special, if slightly guilty, pleasure that, harrowed by reports of the worst winter Britain has experienced for many years, I write this from a Mediterranean island. In 1976, when this book was first published, I had absolutely no idea that one year later I would be leaving England to take up residence in Cyprus. 1977 was a year of exceptional excitement for me: it was forty years since – as described in the book – I had begun to cook on the island of Agios Nikolaos, and I had given up all hope of ever again living on the shores of the Mediterranean, a nostalgic longing for which is so evident in *The Adventurous Fish Cook*.

As a cook, I found 1977 an *annus mirabilis* in other respects too. It was the year of Michel Guérard's *Cuisine Minceur* – a latter-day form of the medieval 'plenary indulgence', enabling us to commit all the sins of gourmandise without incurring the severe penalties usually imposed by natural justice: obesity and exploding arteries.

1977 was also the year in which Mrs Elizabeth David fell on the Philistine bakers, smiting them hip and thigh with her sturdy book, *English Bread and Yeast Cookery*. In a rational world, you would think that a book of this kind would stop the rot. But . . .

This brings me directly to the two motives which, apart from my strong desire to foster a healthy piscivorous and home-cooking habit in the nation, originally impelled me to write this book. First, I wanted to add one small voice to those resisting the take-over of the country by the Convenience, Fast and Fake Food Industries (CFFFI, for short). Second – and as an integral part of the same campaign, particularly from a fish lover's point of view – I wanted to urge the need to win public support for that seriously endangered species, the 'friendly neighbourhood fishmonger'. That battle needed to be joined on both these issues has, alas, been amply confirmed during the past six years.

As regards the first, New Year tidings came with Messrs Foulger and Routledge's publication of the result of their researches in *The Food Poisoning Handbook*. It reported that *a.* 23 million working days are lost each year as a result of food poisoning; *b.* 70 per cent of establishments inspected are found to be contravening health regulations; *c.* notified cases of food poisoning form only a fraction of the true total; *d.* risks have been multiplied by 'the increase in high-protein convenience food, the widespread and often abused use of modern food preservation methods and the rapid expansion of take-away snack food trade'. The authors also cite the growth of the catering trade as a contributory factor.

This is poisoning on an epidemic, not to say epic, scale, and news of it has been followed by that of the Government's recent decision to relax the regulations concerning the adulteration of the minimum meat content of convenience foods such as sausages of all kinds, and pork, steak-and-kidney, and veal-and-ham pies. This has no doubt galvanised the CFFFI into adopting new and insidious forms of research – an adulterators' charter indeed!

As regards the second cause dear to me in this book – the preservation of the fishmonger – a recent item in *The Times* both pleased and disturbed me. It referred to a conference of the National Federation of Consumers' Associations, called to discuss a controversial report criticizing the marketing methods of the British fish industry and revealing the ominous fact that '*a generation of housewives under the age of 30*' was '*largely unfamiliar with fresh fish*'. This ignorance was blamed on the 'rapid decline in *retail outlets*'.

I don't know whether Britain reeled when it heard this news. I myself was at the time stirred by a hope that powerful bodies were busy trying to protect the fish lover's interests, but also profoundly depressed by the gloomy vision of innumerable (how large, numerically, *is* a whole generation of housewives in the United Kingdom?) young women whose only conception of fish is based on the frozen, plastic-wrapped, breadcrumbed or battered, ready sauced or buttered slabs, oblongs, cubes and cylinders of fish in the grey-to-yellow spectrum band officially designated 'white'. (I trust these deprived ladies will not be unescorted when they have a first terrifying encounter with a live lobster or a giant crab, or, when swimming, they come face to face with a yawning monkfish or meet an octopus eyeball to eyeball. Dear God! – or *Kyrie Eleison*, as we say in my local vernacular.)

I was also not happy that a controversial report, completed some five months earlier, had only just come up for discussion in the presence of a minister of state from the 'Min. of Ag. and Fish'. But it was with real sorrow that I noted that our 'friendly neighbourhood fishmonger', skilled in handling his delicate and perishable stock, honest and friendly enough to hold together a faithful band of steady customers and vigilantly conscientious in maintaining the high standards of hygiene essential in a wet fish shop, had been neutered and degraded to the rank of a mere '*retail outlet*'.

However, it was not until I reached the final lines of this item that hope almost died in me. The moment had come when the minister was to speak. What had I expected from him? A new *Marseillaise*? A Churchillian call for 'action this day'? I imagined the chairman rapping with his gavel, the hubbub dying away until only the blown nose, the bronchitic cough and the viral sneeze – those homely British noises – competed with the sound of plaster falling from the damp walls of the conference hall.

The minister rose. 'There is', he began – his right hand under his jacket covering his heart as proof of sincerity – 'no room for,' he continued – but then paused for gravity and emphasis. What was coming – surely it would make the hall resound? But his momentary hesitation was over – now he pulled from the sky with his left hand the word for his purpose. It was 'complacency'.

The night after I read that item I had strange dreams about the fishmonger's plight. At one moment I was in White's, and from an armchair a voice was droning in a matter-of-fact tone.

'Of course, you know, in a great sporting nation such as ours, we've got to take the country gentleman's point of view into account. My friends in the country tell me fishmongers aren't like pheasants, and there are few grounds for preserving 'em. Slow to breed, costly to rear, you can't even shoot 'em, and even if you could, they wouldn't provide much fun for the guns – I mean, you couldn't miss 'em, could you? And just think what a hullaballoo there'd be from every crank and do-gooder in the country if you proposed to eat 'em!'

But even this vision paled before the one that succeeded it: the long, rain-soaked queue outside Madame Tussaud's, all waiting to see the new simulacrum – the Last of the Fishmongers, juxtaposed between Crippen and Sweeney Todd; the latter, of course, the patron saint of food adulterators.

For this edition I have added a short chapter, by way of postscript, dealing with fishy matters in the Eastern Mediterranean. I have made some suggestions for their adaptation to British conditions . . . and they may also, I hope, serve to spark off nostalgic memories for some of my readers and inspire sunny kitchen fantasies in others.

The John Dory

# Introduction

It is still, I believe, true to say – Madame Prunier said it in 1938 – that most fish cooked and consumed in British homes is either boiled, fried or grilled. It is served traditionally with bottled sauces – varied now, perhaps, with instant, packet sauce mixes. Thousands of cookery books have poured from the presses, in ever heavier and glossier formats, since the first appearance, in 1950, of Mrs David's *A Book of Mediterranean Food*, which led to the great cookery-book explosion. I believe that those who have most benefited from this vast extension of culinary instruction have been not those of us who cook at home, but that new happy breed, the restaurateurs; these may fairly be described as pullulating in our cities, towns and villages, backed by the food chemists and manufacturers who produce, in instant, pre-packaged and often synthetic form, 'batches' of 'classic' dishes and sauces – and their survival positively depends on their deterring people from ever buying fresh fish at the fishmonger's and daring to prepare and cook it in their own kitchens to the accompaniment of genuinely home-made sauces and stocks.

This book is written partly as a protest against this baneful and accelerating trend in the pollution of our domestic environment, but there are other reasons which seem to me compelling for writing a new book on the subject. Firstly, the poverty of the English gastronomic tradition in this branch of cookery, as reflected by the small number of fish recipes to be found in seventeenth-, eighteenth- and early nineteenth-century cookery books. This gap in an otherwise rich culinary tradition begs to be filled, and I have accordingly included here, alongside the many delicious established dishes of French and other foreign origins, a number of recipes which I have 'invented' (or perhaps 'evolved' is a better word) in English conditions, and which, so far, have stood the test only of discriminating friends. Secondly, in recent years, the choice of fish available to the British shopper has expanded dramatically. Some of these fish are formidable in appearance and need persuasive introduction. The fish sections of most current cookery books do not give much space to such varieties as garfish, flying fish, monkfish and the like, and in the course of this book I have tried to give these newcomers the attention they deserve.

My final reason for writing this book is a personal one. I must confess that I have been a fish fanatic since my early days, and I have been meddling in the cooking of fish for some forty years; I say 'meddling' because much of my experience has been acquired, and my practice carried out, in other people's kitchens. Only recently have I been able to settle down at leisure to collate that experience and reduce it to a form in which, I hope, it will be of use to others.

One does not become a fanatic about anything, let alone fish, without going through a period of prolonged frustration. How my addiction came about can best be explained by describing two events at widely separated periods of my life.

I first fell in love with fish at the age of thirteen, in a village called Twelve Crows Nest on the eastern edge of Loch Corrib in Connemara. There I was taught to get up at dawn and, before Mass and breakfast, catch a tinful of daddy-long-legs for the day's fishing on the loch. As breakfast was either a brown trout caught the day before or an inch-thick lump of fat bacon swimming in its own grease, the incentive to a day's fishing was overwhelming.

We would set out – the priest, the old gillie and I – at about nine-thirty, equipped with rods, artificial flies and lures, the big tin of now buzzing 'daddies' and a bigger tin of sweet brown bread. Half a dozen Guinness bottles were left to swish around in the bilge. In such circumstances, miracles could be expected to happen, and that year the sun shone every day, though in a chequered sort of way, the threat of rain only rarely being fulfilled, and then not for long. The old gillie baited our lines with the live daddies, and the priest and I flogged the lake in front of us as we drifted slowly backwards, broadside on. Suddenly the trout would begin to jump and every strike would lose a daddy or take a fish. They were small – none as large as a pound in weight – but we seldom took less than a dozen at a go when they were rising. Then, for perhaps an hour, there'd be no sign. We would be trolling, our lines streaming out behind the boat, baited with glittering, twisting silver minnows. We would be into the Guinness and brown bread, and suddenly the ratchet would scream and . . . We never saw what the old cook did to them, but our catch would come to us smoking hot and barred brown and black. The taste of the exquisite pink flesh (we consumed them seasoned only with butter and a little salt) is with me still. By the end of a week, I was totally committed – and doomed thereafter to ten long years of growing frustration before I would experience any comparable gastronomic thrill.

It was indeed almost exactly ten years later, in Greece (in the middle 'thirties, between two minor revolutions), when I was staying on the islet of Aghios Nikolaos in the narrow waters between Euboea and Boeotia, that I first began to cook. The one-armed cook, Ervin, a refugee from Hitler's Brownshirts, was frequently unable to attend to his duties and on these occasions, sacred to Bacchus, I managed, with the assistance of two peasant boys, to provide not only the regional diet for the island's nine resident labourers, but also tolerable meals for the frequent guests of its lovable and eccentric owner. Ervin's repertoire was limited (he had previously been an electrical engineer at Siemens), and on the rich and heavy side for the heat of a Greek summer. The guests ranged from young German *Wandervögeln* to near-apoplectic American profs of Eng Lit; from minor diplomats to touring English dilettanti. They were animated, one and all, by an intense curiosity to confirm Athenian gossip of bizarre happenings on Aghios Nikolaos. I naturally tried to spare this motley flow of Private Eyes the rigours of Prussian cooking and, with the aid of a battered Mrs Beeton, I started my apprenticeship. Supplies of fresh vegetables, fruit and wine were brought in by rowing boat from the large mainland village of Khalia (literally, rubbish dump) while meat and groceries involved a weekly trip to the nearest big town, Khalkis. But our immediately available larder was the sea all around us which teemed with fish, the best of which, for our purposes, were the red and grey mullets – the latter being of exceptional size. *Zargana* (garfish of the green bones), *caponi* (gurnard) and many other varieties – apart from octopus, squid and sepia – were plentiful. For all of these we hunted by night, four to a boat, with wide-shaded acetylene lamps overhanging the stern, and armed with ten-foot trident-topped poles and long iron swords (these were for the garfish). When the dynamiters were out, we would rush towards the sound of the explosion to hijack their catch. On the first of these expeditions, we hijacked a number of stunned red mullet; these were of about the same size as my Loch Corrib trout. We cooked them just as they were, scales and all – after rubbing them with oil – on a large, flat, iron griddle, over the wide opening of a wood-fired range; after turning them three times, at three-minute intervals, the skins were almost charred, but still intact, even though the scales had been jumping off throughout the cooking. Hungrily I opened my fish down the back, and the aroma which came up at me almost sent me into shock. It was the experience of Loch Corrib all over again, but with something added which was not just the gamy flavour which has earned the mullet the title of woodcock of the sea. I had eaten mullet many times before in the tavernas of Athens, but never any as large or as fresh. Perhaps my overwhelming reaction to this particular fish was quite subjective, brought on by the excitement of my first night-fishing expedition and the tremendous hunger it generated. The fact remains that that red mullet closed all the exits from an obsession which I have never since wished to escape.

It is obvious that the two peaks of gastronomic experience recorded above have to do with absolutely fresh fish, personally taken from the water, and grilled. This established in my mind one axiom of good fish cookery: that, for really fresh fish, grilling is the ideal method to use. I have since learned – though such refinements were far from my mind on those two apocalyptic occasions – that the addition of a savoury butter or a small sauce might have even further enhanced my pleasure. Since Aghios Nikolaos, there have been many stages in the widening of my experience and practice – many of them connected with wartime years in the Middle East, during which I was shuttled from Cyprus to Iraq, from Iraq to Egypt, from Egypt to Istanbul, and thence – to my immense delight – back to Greece. Later, on my return to the austerities of England and when running a rather bizarre guesthouse on the Kent coast, I was forced to learn the hard way that cardinal rule of catering: that the cost of the food provided should in no circumstances exceed the financial contributions of the customers. But that is another story. My only strictly culinary gain here was in the acquisition of those new disciplines required for cooking for larger numbers of people.

Of recent years, I have become deeply interested in the elaboration and refinement of sauces. (Is this the sign of a jaded palate? I do not really think so, for the interest has been repaid by the entranced and meditative expressions I have observed on the faces of friends confronted by new experiences.) The contriving of sauces – the alchemy of the kitchen – has led me to a new gastronomic satisfaction: that of the creator as opposed to that of the mere partaker.

The desire of the addict to communicate his addiction to others made it inevitable in the long run that I should want to write a book. This may not be a good – but it is certainly a powerful – reason for doing so.

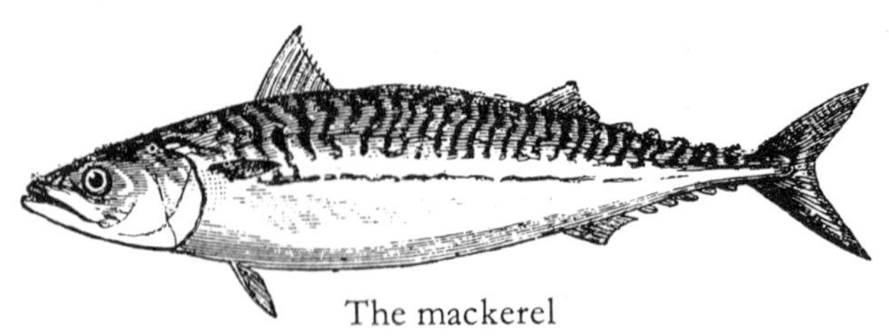

The mackerel

# The fish you can buy

Most of our finest white fish, such as sole, turbot, halibut, whitebait and eels, are available all the year round to those who can afford them. Fortunately for the fish-lover whose budget will only occasionally allow these luxuries, a number of fish in a lower price range can also be found in the larger fishmongers' shops throughout the year. Haddock, the mullets (red and grey), cod and codling, plaice, whiting, coley and conger are nearly always in supply, as, in the shellfish range, are prawns and shrimps.

Other fish are only seasonally available fresh, and even when in season may not always be easy to find. Although scallops should have a seven-month run through the winter (from October), the bulk of the catch in this country is now either exported to the Continent or contracted for in advance by big hotels and restaurants, not to mention the frozen-food industry. The meagre ration left for the private shopper must be competed for, and in this climate of shortage only a close relationship with your fishmonger will ensure you a regular supply – at, of course, a stiff price. In this country, mussels follow the oyster pattern, and should be available from September to the end of April; however, suppliers of the finest mussels tend to wait for the Teignmouth harvest, which is sometimes late in reaching the market. Here, again, unless you cultivate your fishmonger, hotel and restaurant demand tends to absorb the clean-shelled, even-sized varieties, leaving only the seaweed-shaggy and barnacle-infested surplus for the private shopper. The cleaning of these is a time-consuming and exhausting task.

A cheerful side to the picture is the increasing volume of Mediterranean and transatlantic varieties of fish now appearing in the fishmongers' shops, partly as a result of ethnic changes in the population. Although the seasonal availability of these is not reliably predictable, the supply being dependent on weather and other factors beyond control, they are appearing more and more commonly in the larger shops in many areas. Such fish as fresh tunny, sardines and anchovies, bonito, garfish, octopus, squid and cuttlefish should be looked for on visits to the fishmonger. When shopping, we should also take account of those fish which, though plentiful in British waters, were not thought to be commercially worth while in the past for one reason or another. Such fish as monkfish and tope (porbeagle) are now sold openly on their merits, and the dogfish has at last been released from its tawdry 'rock salmon' disguise.

From time to time, the press gives cheering news; fish farming, though still in its early stages, may well help to redress the balance in favour of the private individual. We are told that the oyster may again become the 'food of the people' it once was. The intensive farming of lobsters may help to restore this princely crustacean to the fishmonger's slab at a possible price. The hotel and restaurant demand for small lobsters which will divide into two expensive portions cannot fail, in the long run, to be exterminatory; perhaps lobster farming will be able to satisfy this voracious demand, and once again we shall see large lobsters in the shops. Trout farming already has a long and successful history and is being rapidly developed. But one warning note must be struck in connection with all fish farming, with regard to the chemical and artificial foods employed to induce rapid growth and standardization of size. Bearing in mind what the battery system has done to the taste of the chicken, it is to be hoped that the fish farmers will have regard as much for the quality and the natural taste as for the quantity and size of the seafoods they produce.

Whatever we may look forward to in the future, the present situation regarding the seasonal availability of fish caught in British waters is given below. Fish caught in other waters are included, but marked with an asterisk to indicate that their availability is too erratic to chart with certainty. It should be stated that nearly every variety of seasonal seafood can be bought deep-frozen at all times of the year. The fact that all the recipes in this book are for fresh fish does not imply a condemnation of frozen fish.

In the seasonal availability chart which follows I have tried to make a broad distinction between fish of a firm texture and fish of a softer texture, as this is one of the earliest and most important lessons a fish cook has to learn.

## *Seasonal availability of fish*

x=availability; ★=availability may be erratic; (f)=firmer textured fish; (s)=less firm

| | Jan | Feb | Mar | Apr | May | June | July | Aug | Sept | Oct | Nov | Dec |
|---|---|---|---|---|---|---|---|---|---|---|---|---|
| ★Anchovy | x | x | x | x | x | x | x | x | x | | | |
| Angler-fish (f) | x | x | x | x | x | x | x | x | x | x | x | x |
| Bass (f) | x | x | x | | | x | x | x | x | x | x | x |
| Bloater (s) | | | | | | | | | x | x | x | x |
| ★Bonito (f) | x | x | x | x | x | x | x | x | x | x | x | x |
| Bream (f) | x | x | x | | | x | x | x | x | | | |
| Brill (f) | x | x | x | x | x | x | x | x | x | x | x | x |
| Buckling | | | | x | x | x | x | x | x | x | x | |
| Carp (f) | x | | | | | | | | | | x | x |
| Clams | | | | | | x | x | x | x | | | |
| Cockles | | | | | | x | x | x | x | | | |
| Cod, codling (s) | x | x | x | x | x | x | x | x | x | x | x | x |
| Cod roe | x | x | x | x | x | | x | x | | | x | x |
| Coley (s) | x | x | x | x | x | x | x | x | x | x | x | x |
| Conger eel (f) | | | x | x | x | x | x | x | x | x | | |
| Crab | x | x | x | x | x | x | x | x | x | | | |
| Crawfish | | | | | x | | | | x | | | |
| Crayfish | x | x | | | x | x | x | x | | | | |
| ★Cuttlefish | x | x | x | x | x | x | x | x | x | x | x | x |
| Dab (s) | | | | | | | | | x | x | x | x |
| Dogfish (f) | x | x | x | x | x | x | x | x | x | x | x | x |
| Eel (f) | x | x | x | x | x | x | x | x | x | x | x | x |
| Elvers | | | x | | | | | | | | | |
| ★Garfish (f) | x | x | x | x | x | x | | | x | x | x | x |
| Grayling (f) | | | | | | | | | x | x | x | x |
| Gurnard (f) | x | x | x | x | x | x | | | | x | x | x |

x = availability; ★ = availability may be erratic; (f) = firmer textured fish; (s) = less firm

| | Jan | Feb | Mar | Apr | May | June | July | Aug | Sept | Oct | Nov | Dec |
|---|---|---|---|---|---|---|---|---|---|---|---|---|
| Haddock (f) | x | x | x | x | x | x | x | x | x | x | x | x |
| Hake (s) | x | x | x | x | x | x | x | x | | | x | x |
| Halibut (f) | x | x | x | x | x | x | x | x | x | x | x | x |
| Herring and kipper (s) | | | | x | x | x | x | x | x | x | x | |
| John Dory (f) | x | x | x | x | x | x | x | x | x | x | x | x |
| Ling (s) | | | | | x | x | x | | x | x | x | x |
| Lobster | | | x | x | x | x | x | x | x | x | | |
| Mackerel (s) | x | x | x | x | x | x | x | | | | | x |
| Monkfish (f) | x | x | x | x | x | x | x | x | x | x | x | x |
| Mullet, grey (s) | x | x | x | x | x | x | x | x | x | x | x | x |
| red (f) | | | | | | x | x | x | | | | |
| Mussels | x | x | x | x | | | | | x | x | x | x |
| ★Octopus | x | x | x | x | x | x | x | x | x | x | x | x |
| Oysters | x | x | x | x | | | | | x | x | x | x |
| Perch (f) | | | | | | x | x | x | x | x | x | x |
| Pike (f) | x | x | | | | | | x | x | x | x | x |
| Pilchards (s) | | | | x | x | x | x | x | x | x | x | |
| Plaice (s) | x | x | x | x | x | x | x | x | x | x | x | x |
| Pollock | x | x | x | x | x | x | x | x | x | x | x | x |
| Prawns | x | x | x | x | x | x | x | x | x | x | x | x |
| Salmon (f) | | | x | x | x | x | x | x | x | x | | |
| Salmon trout (f) | | x | x | x | x | x | x | x | | | | |
| Sardines (s) | | | | x | x | x | x | x | x | x | x | |
| Scallops | x | x | x | x | | | | | x | x | x | x |
| Scampi (imported) | x | x | x | x | x | x | x | x | x | x | x | x |
| Shad | x | x | x | x | x | x | x | x | x | x | x | x |
| Shrimps | x | x | x | x | x | x | x | x | x | x | x | x |
| Skate (f) | x | x | x | x | | | | x | x | x | x | x |
| Smelts (f) | x | x | x | x | x | | | | | x | x | x |
| Sole: all types (f) | x | x | x | x | x | x | x | x | x | x | x | x |
| Sprats (s) | | x | x | | | | | | | x | x | x |
| ★Squid | x | x | x | x | x | x | x | x | x | x | x | x |
| Sturgeon (f) | x | x | x | | | | x | x | x | | | |

x = availability; ★ = availability may be erratic; (f) = firmer textured fish; (s) = less firm

| | | | | | | | | | | | | |
|---|---|---|---|---|---|---|---|---|---|---|---|---|
| Tench (s) | | | | | | | | | | x | | |
| Tope (f) | x | x | x | x | x | x | x | x | x | x | x | x |
| Trout (f) | | | x | x | x | x | x | x | x | | | |
| ★Tunny (f) | x | x | x | x | x | x | x | x | x | x | x | x |
| Turbot (f) | x | x | x | x | x | x | x | x | x | x | x | x |
| Whelks | x | x | x | x | x | x | x | x | x | x | x | x |
| Whitebait (s) | x | x | x | x | x | x | x | x | x | | | |
| Whiting (s) | x | x | x | x | x | x | x | x | x | x | x | x |
| Winkles | x | x | x | x | x | x | x | x | x | x | x | x |

SCALLOP FISHING.

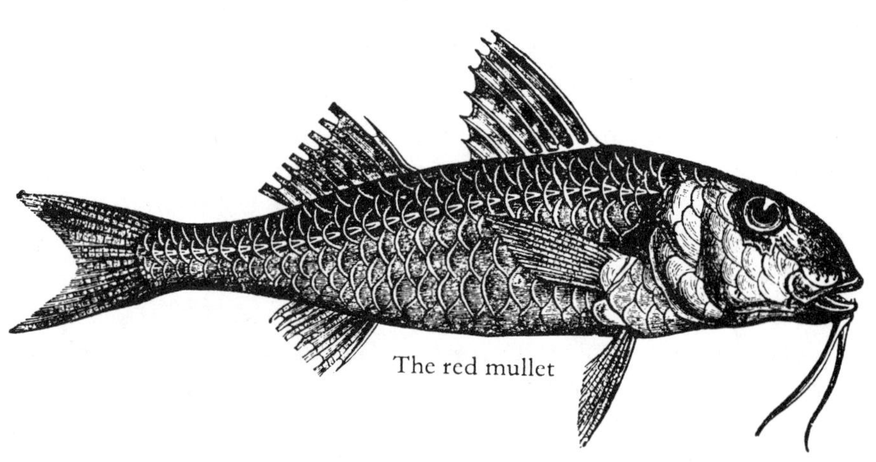
The red mullet

# Kitchen equipment

The best and most instructive description of an efficient, happy kitchen is to be found in the first chapter of Elizabeth David's *French Country Cooking* under the heading '*Batterie de Cuisine*'. At the time when that book was written, most ironmongers were still stocked with thin, rubbishy pans totally unsuited to good cooking of any kind, and combing the London street markets for good, heavy copper or iron pans and old earthenware cooking pots became a national sport. (In the course of searching for such treasures, I once stumbled on two unopened wax-sealed bottles of black truffles, dating, I suppose, from the Edwardian period. Alas, 'wax-sealed' or not, the truffles were a great disappointment, having lost almost all their flavour.) Today, good, heavy, flat-bottomed pans can be bought in any large department store, in all sizes, shapes and materials. The choice of material is a matter of personal taste, but size, shape and depth play an important role in making fish cookery the pleasure it ought to be. Much of the *angst* in fish cookery comes from the need to handle fish quickly and deftly when it is cooked – as when transferring it from pan to dish. A pan which by its depth or shape makes it awkward to get the fish slice underneath the fish (or too narrow a fish slice for too big a fish) can turn the simplest of operations into a tragi-comic performance.

Most of the recipes in this book are based on the quantities required to serve four (or five – I have a tendency to err on the generous side) people, and I have found the following list of pots and pans more than adequate to this purpose.

**Fish kettle and turbotière** Although cooking in metallic foil has gone some way towards ousting the fish kettle, the latter is still essential for the proper poaching of salmon and other large, whole round fish. With its two-handled perforated tray enabling you to lift the whole fish out of the *court-bouillon* when cooked without breaking it up, the kettle can also serve as a *bain-marie** for keeping sauces warm or very gently cooking. The *turbotière*, for poaching large flat fish such as turbot, halibut or brill, is even more adaptable as a *bain-marie*, its shape enabling it to take a wide range of saucepans. Both of these can be bought in tin-lined copper, aluminium or tin. The tin-lined copper kettle makes a very pretty ornament on the kitchen wall, but in practice I prefer the aluminium kind, which is lighter and easier to handle and clean.

**Asparagus kettle** This is a strong, aluminium-lidded pan which goes far towards solving all poaching problems with smaller fish. The one I use is 30×20×14 cm (12×8×5 in) deep. Like the fish kettle, it has a two-handled perforated tray, but with the added advantage that the tray can be adjusted to lie at different angles to the base. This makes it possible for you to poach your fish with their tail ends out of the *bouillon*, thus preventing them from becoming overcooked. This pan will take four average-size round fish of up to 450 gr (1 lb) in individual weight.

**For grilling** Apart from the grill incorporated in your gas or electric cooker, you should ideally have a large, round griddle, 30 cm (12 in) in diameter. This is a solid iron plate with an iron basket handle for lifting. A two-handled, folding wire-mesh clamp in which fish can be held and turned while grilling is also desirable.

**For frying** For frying any fish, I personally like a pan larger than is strictly necessary, but I make an exception in the case of deep frying. The pan I use for this purpose is 20 cm (8 in) wide and 10 cm

*A *bain-marie* is simply a 'bath' of hot water in which small saucepans can be stood to keep their contents just warm or very slowly cooking as required. The bottom half of a double saucepan is a *bain-marie* for the single saucepan that sits in it.

(4 in) deep, with, of course, a wire-mesh basket. Those who do a great deal of deep frying of quite large fillets, or of vast quantities of chips, will probably need a larger pan. I must confess that I do little deep frying myself and mostly use my pan for frying small garnishes such as crabmeat (or other forcemeat) balls to accompany soups or other dishes. As for chips, they are the one form of potato *not* to serve with deep-fried fillets of fish.

For shallow frying, I have two long-handled, slope-sided, heavy iron pans, one 30 cm (12 in) in diameter, the other rather smaller – 25 cm (10 in). A two-handled oval aluminium dish 35 cm (14 in) across serves me well for *sauté* or *meunière* dishes, and will comfortably accommodate sufficient fish for four people. Both these pans can also be used for poaching fish.

Three small (one very small) frying pans hang around my kitchen, and are in constant use for frying parsley or mixing quick, last-minute accompaniments to various dishes.

**For steaming** You should have two double saucepans with lids, the base of one upper pan being perforated.

**For stocks** I find two identical aluminium pans of 2·4-litre (4-pint) capacity adequate for all stock- and soup-making purposes. I also have a similar pot of 4·8-litre (8-pint) capacity for cooking large quantities of rice or spaghetti and for making big fish stews on party occasions.

**For sauce making** The ideal is four different-size saucepans, one double, holding 1·2 litres (2 pints), the other of the following capacities: 6 dl (1 pint), 1·2 litres (2 pints), and 2·4 litres (4 pints). You will also need several wooden spoons and a small, fine wire whisk.

**Vegetables** In this department, I survive with two old enamelled iron pans, which have somehow managed to remain uncracked, each with a capacity of 2·4 litres (4 pints).

**Miscellaneous** Supporting your metal stalwarts, various glazed earthenware soufflé, casserole, pie and *gratin* dishes – square, round, and oval, of different sizes, and mostly with lids – will perform multiple duties. In addition, I find a number of small dishes, some with handles, some with lids, very useful for serving sauces, garnishes and so on. Mixing bowls, from 2·4-litre (4-pint) size down to very small – 3-dl ($\frac{1}{2}$-pint) capacity – are essential, and take up little room since they fit snugly one into the other.

Most of the above – and more – will already be found in most kitchens where cooking is treated as a serious matter. The following ancillary equipment, cutlery and gadgets are all things I personally could not possibly do without:

perforated fish slices of several sizes
palette knives of various widths
a pair of sharp-ended kitchen scissors
several very sharp attenuated steel knives
large sandwich tongs (most useful, these, for lifting small whole fish and fillets)
a large draining spoon, for lifting anything you want out of a liquid and for skimming
a good large colander, and a smaller one
several strainers of wire, from a wide down to a very narrow gauge
a good large mortar and pestle
a good heavy half-moon chopper for herbs and vegetables, and a well-seasoned hardwood chopping bowl with which to use it
a basting brush
a garlic squeezer
a stainless-steel grater, with grids of varying width

Most kitchens nowadays contain gadgets like grinders and blenders which have taken much of the tedium out of preparing sauces, and I assume in this book that such gadgets are available. If you do not happen to possess such electric aids, you will have to revert to the old-fashioned mincing machine (which I still use quite often) or resort to pounding in your mortar. The 'Mouli' series of shredding and purée-making instruments are still available. I use my own quite often for old times' sake.

An absolutely essential item in the kitchen is a good coarse-grinding mill for black pepper – one that will release at a twist not dust, but a shower of chunky particles.

For making pastry to cover pies or for rolling out *panadas*, you will need a pastry board and rolling pin.

You should have a large block of wood, stone or marble, at least 40 cm (16 in) square and 3·75 cm (1½ in) thick, for handling your fish when preparing it for cooking, and for other cooking operations.

Always to be kept in stock are rolls of kitchen paper, and metal foil for 'paper-bag' (*en papillote*) cooking.

Last, but not least, you need a pair of scales, a measuring jug or cup, and a clock.

THE COMMON ANGLER, OR FISHING FROG.

1 barbel; 2 perch; 3 trout; 4 grayling; 5 tench; 6 chub; 7 bream; 8 roach; 9 dace; 10 crayfish; 11 gudgeon; 12 bull trout (young); 13 loach; 14 miller's thumb; 15 ruffe or pope; 16 bleak; 17 minnow

# Choosing and preparing fish

## CHOOSING FISH

I have heard a rumour that some fishmongers, when trade is bad and their weary and dull-eyed stock has to go on show for one more day before it is consigned to the swill tubs, inject into the fish a mysterious elixir which, after a spray from the hose, restores them to their pristine beauty and freshness. I am sure that no such elixir exists, but all the same feel prompted to suggest that the regular fish-eater should choose his fishmonger before choosing his fish. Of no professional body of men can it more truly be said than of fishmongers that you can tell a good one by his friends. A fishmonger without friends is a desperate man indeed, open to every temptation offered by the brilliant advances of chemical and deodorant research. Therefore, if it is possible in your district, do a little shopping around, noting the general atmosphere of each fish shop and the relations between the fishmonger, his assistants and his customers. If the atmosphere is happy, business brisk, and it is apparent from the conversation that the customers are regular, accord the fishmonger your allegiance for a probationary period. From the start, give him to understand that you will be more than just a Friday customer; then put yourself in his hands. There is no better way of ensuring that the fish you buy will be as fresh as the logistics of the fishing industry make possible. From a good beginning, many benefits will flow. When certain fish are in short supply, such as scallops, sea-bream, bass or skate, he will keep some for you under the cold counter, and eventually you will be able to telephone your order with complete confidence, until, of course, one day he lets you down. When this happens (naturally, the blame will lie with an underling or apprentice), have the courage to upbraid him in no uncertain terms – but out of earshot of his other customers – and all will be well again . . . until the next time.

Meanwhile, it is possible for you to acquire the ability to judge the freshness of a fish yourself. The tests for freshness in fish are visual, tactile and olfactory. Visual evidence should be enough; the symptoms of decline are much the same as in human beings: sunken, lack-lustre eyes, paleness of the gills and general dulling of the scales, or flaccidity of the skin and loss of colour (particularly noticeable in mackerel). A fish worth buying should be firm to the touch and, if picked up by the middle, should not immediately flop over and try to touch its tail. The parallel with human beings ends here, as there is no such thing as *rigor mortis* in the case of fish. Testing by the nose is difficult unless you have been accustomed to handling fish regularly and know what sort of aroma should or should not be present in this or that fish. A skate, however fresh, has a distinct but very slight ammoniac scent from which many might recoil. White fish must smell of fish and, at the same time, of the sea. My own method of testing is to hold my breath and bend my head down very close to the fish; there I release breath and take a good sniff. If the fish is not for me, an inbuilt conditioned reflex jerks my head back. However, this kind of testing is not calculated to endear you to the fishmonger if carried out in the presence of other customers.

In the ordinary course of events, your fishmonger will scale, decapitate, clean, fillet and skin your fish for you as requested. Nevertheless, you should be able to perform these simple tasks yourself. Notes on the procedures are given below, but if the task is left to the fishmonger, see that you get what you have paid for: that is, the head, the bones and, in the case of white fish, the skin, as these are essential ingredients for fish stocks and *fumets*. When buying scallops, ask for unopened ones, or at least see that you take away with you the concave upper shell, which is useful not only for *Coquilles St Jacques*, but for many other small *au gratin* dishes. Normally these are reserved for hotels and restaurants supplied by the fishmonger, but there is no earthly reason why you should not insist on having your scallop in its two shells.

## CLEANING AND PREPARING FISH

### *Scaling*

Fish are scaled upwards, from tail to head. If you are using a knife, it should not be too sharp or it will tear the skin. Scale fish as swiftly as possible, under running water, being careful to see that all foods in the vicinity are covered – fish scales fly off in all directions and are difficult to retrieve.

### *Cleaning*

Unless you wish to retain the head of your fish, remove it with a diagonal stroke of your knife, slanting from the back of the head to the underside of the fish. As you remove the head, some of the insides of the fish may come away with the gills. In all the normal types of fish with which you are likely to deal, the gills are located under the flaps behind the head, which open and shut as the fish 'breathes' under water. The gills themselves are bright red in colour and are a complicated system of myriads of bloodfilled capillaries which extract oxygen from the sea and expel excess salt and waste products. They are easy to locate and remove. Slit the underside of the fish and scrape out all intestines. Wash away all blood and dry the fish well on kitchen paper.

Many cooks, myself among them, like sometimes to retain the heads of round fish for the 'look of the thing'. In this case, the gills must be cut away and all traces of blood removed. In recipes where stuffings are required, it is useful to have the stomach of the fish unslit. The fish should then be cleaned through a slit made in the neck, using a long-handled pickle fork or a spoon.

In the case of certain fish (notably the red mullet) the preservation of the liver is important. This can be located near the thickest complex of blood vessels (the heart) of the fish, partially surrounding the intestine at the front end of the fish. The intestine should be removed and discarded, if possible without disturbing the liver.

### *Filleting*

**Flat fish** Lay the cleaned fish on a board. With a sharp knife and starting at the head, cut the fish down to the bone, and draw the knife right down the line of the bone to the tail. Then, with flattened blade, work the fillet away from the bone, taking care that your blade is held close to the bone. Turn your fish and repeat.

**Round fish** Starting at the head, cut deeply down to the bone and draw the knife down to the tail. Work the fillet away from the bone on one side and when free of the bone, cut the fillet from the head. Cut the bone through at the tail, and work the bone free of the flesh of the other fillet. Detach the fillet from the head. Herring, mackerel, haddock and other round fish can be filleted in another way, as follows. Press the cleaned fish, open side down, on to a board and with mallet, rolling pin or bottle, strike it smartly on the back all along the line of the bone. Turn the fish over and it will be found comparatively simple to remove the main bone, together with many of the smaller bones, in one operation.

### *Skinning*

Make a light incision across the skin where it joins the tail and ease the skin away from the flesh for about 2 cm (1 in). Using salt, a cloth or kitchen paper to give you a firm grip, pull the skin up and off towards the head. Turn the fish and repeat this process. With round fish it will, of course, be necessary to split the skin along the length of the spine.

To skin an eel, the eel should first be suspended on a strong hook by a string tied firmly round the head beneath the gills. With a sharp knife, cut the skin all round beneath the string and pry the skin loose from the flesh for about 6 mm ($\frac{1}{4}$ in) all round. The loose skin should then be gripped on both sides, pulled sharply downwards and drawn off. A pair of damp cotton gloves, the thumb and fore-finger dipped in salt, are useful here.

## CLEANING AND PREPARING SHELLFISH

### *Scallops*

If you can get your scallops whole, open them by placing them, hollow shell down, in a warm oven. They will open in a few moments. Be careful to reserve any liquor that has gathered in the deep shell. To clean, remove with a knife the ragged, yellowish-brown skirt and the black intestinal thread which goes from behind the main white cylinder of muscle to the base of the coral tongue.

## *Mussels*

After many long hours spent struggling to scrape clean the shaggy and barnacle-laden variety of mussels which appears in September, I have learned to be patient and to wait for the arrival in the shops of the smoother, more shapely later crop. Even so, their preparation should be a painstaking task. After scrubbing the shells thoroughly and pulling out as much as you can of the wiry beard which usually projects to some extent from the slightly concave edge of the shell, you should give them a final run through, one by one, before cooking. Any that are even slightly open and that do not snap shut as you handle them should be discarded. Any which seem to be heavier than the rest should be severely tested for mud, sludge or even tar: knead the shells strongly with your fingers. If any substance oozes out, discard. In about forty quarts of mussels bought last year, I found only two of these muddy ones; they are fortunately rare, but on that account always to be borne in mind.

I have kept mussels in perfect condition for up to three days, in a pail of sea-salted water, liberally sprinkled with white flour, on an outside window ledge; *but as a rule, they should be cooked on the day of purchase or gathering.*

## *Crab*

Crab is mostly bought ready-cooked and, if you shop early, the steam rising from them will reassure you that they are freshly so. The fishmonger will open them for you and remove the inedible parts, which are the lungs (attached to the bony body of the crab) and the sac (attached to the top of the big shell). All the rest is edible. Watch the fishmonger open the crab, so that you can, thereafter, open one for yourself at home. Make it an axiom *never* to buy a crab that has any crack or hole in its shell, as this means that the soft meat within will be watery and overcooked and also that there is a possibility of contamination. Also, never buy a crab that has not been opened in your presence.

Opening small crabs is easy, but there is a knack to it. First, twist off all legs and claws. Hold the crab firmly, upside down (narrow end towards you). Exert pressure on the body with your thumbs (pushing away from you) and the body should lift out easily. With larger crabs it is sometimes necessary to force a blunt or rounded table-knife between the shell and the body to create a gap. This will give a better purchase for your thumbs, but it is no use denying that it is sometimes a struggle. When the body has been separated from the main shell, it leaves behind some of its own thin shell which should be neatly broken off up to the clearly marked groove on the main shell. This will make the shell tidy as a dish for your dressed crabmeat.

Buying crab by size is a chancy business. As a rough rule of thumb, weigh two of equal size, one in each hand, and buy the heavier of the two. A crab weighing from 450 to 675 gr (1–1½ lb) is sufficient for one person as a main course, or will make up to four good crab cocktails.

### *Lobster and crawfish*

These should be laid face down on a hard surface and cut swiftly with a sharp, heavy knife from the head to the centre of the tail. Separate the halves and remove the (easily recognizable) 'sac' from the head, and also remove the grey-black thread of intestine running into the tail. If your cutting has been accurate, you will find fragments of this thread in each half. If not, the thread may lie embedded and invisible in one side. Probe for it and remove it. See also pages 144-5.

### *King prawns, crayfish (scampi, Dublin Bay prawns)*

The intestine in the tail of these crustacea should be removed. It may often be drawn out whole, if you seize the centre section of the tail and pull sharply. If this fails, cut in from underneath to remove it.

## CLEANING AND PREPARING CEPHALOPODS

### *Octopus*

I have not yet met the fishmonger who will prepare this for me, and the simple instruction to cut out the beak, the eyes and the organs of the head, including the ink sac, is not sufficient encouragement to tempt the uninitiated to have a go. The exact geography of these organs in the head is difficult to describe and the surgery involved is necessarily messy. I propose therefore to remove the psychological obstacles to inclusion of octopus in your regular diet of seafood – at a stroke. Simply remove and discard the head by cutting through (well below the eyes) the 'webbing' of flesh which unites all the tentacles. Beat the tentacles with a steak-beater, mallet or brickbat until all 'spring' has gone from them. Remove the scaly pads which cover the suckers – though most of these will have jumped off during the beating. In the case of any octopus with tentacles of more than 30 cm (12 in) long, the tentacles will require blanching and skinning. They will then be ready to cook. A very small baby octopus – tentacles under 10 cm (4 in) long – can be cooked whole, head and all.

## *Squid, cuttlefish*

The bag (the purse-shaped body) of the squid and the cuttlefish contains a spine which can easily be found with the fingers and pulled out or cut away. (At the very apex of the bag, which can be turned inside out for cleaning, a deposit of sand or shell debris is often present and should be removed.) Like the octopus, both the squid and the cuttlefish have beaks and ink sacs. In their case, too – until familiarity has bred affection – I would suggest that you use only the tentacles and the bag. Large specimens should be blanched and have the outer skin removed. As with the octopus, if the tentacles are under 10 cm (4 in) long, the fish should be cooked whole. With both squid and cuttlefish, the ink from the sac can be an important ingredient of certain recipes, so, if possible, detach this sac from the head with a knife or with your fingers. Squid and cuttlefish, even when large, require no beating; but they do need long, slow cooking.

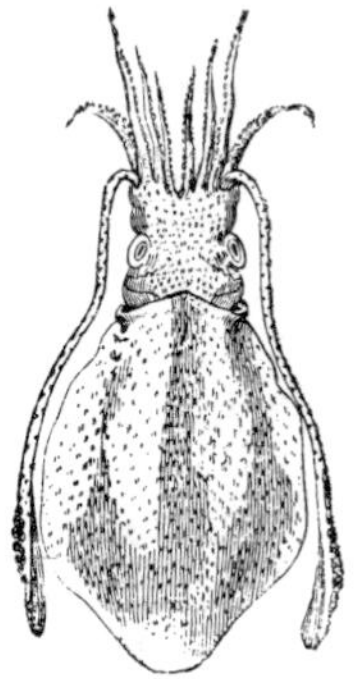

THE CUTTLE-FISH.

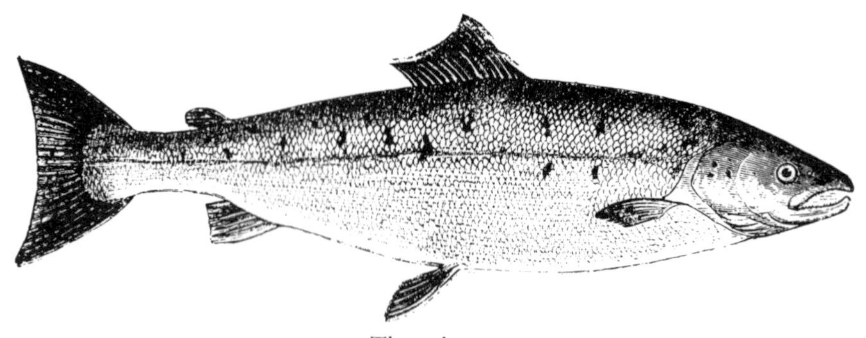

The salmon

# Methods of cooking

The flesh of most fish will be perfectly cooked when it has reached a temperature very much below the boiling point of water (100°C/212°F). However, this lower temperature (60–65°C/140–150°F) must be reached throughout the whole body of the fish, and for a short but variable time which will depend on age, size, texture and previous treatment (freezing, curing, marinating). Theoretically, therefore, if you are cooking a whole fish in, say, a stock or *court-bouillon,* you ought to be able to attain perfection by starting with your *bouillon* cold, gradually raising the heat by stages at each of which the inner temperature of the fish must level up to the outer, and finally, having reached the variable optimum (60–65°C/140–150°F), holding it there for that short – but variable time. *Voilà!* Your fish is perfectly cooked.

In actual practice, however, you would have wasted a great deal of time, and although your fish would be cooked, you would simply have turned it from an originally fresh fish into a cooked stale one. I emphasize the fact that fish is cooked at a comparatively low temperature in order to eradicate from the mind the slightest idea of *boiling* as a method of cooking fish other than crustacea or molluscs (lobsters, crab, clams etc). Even the cephalopods such as octopus and squid should only be very gently simmered for as long as it takes to make them tender. Boiling should only be employed in the making of stock (*court-bouillon*) or sauces. If we eliminate the idea of using it for other purposes, we shall have removed the chief cause of spoiled and overcooked fish, and the consequent demoralization of the cook.

It is important to learn at an early stage to distinguish between the firm-fleshed and the soft-fleshed fish. The former – which include sole, turbot, halibut, brill, conger – can just survive a small margin of overcooking, but in the case of the latter – plaice, cod, whiting, hake, herring, mackerel – the slightest overcooking spells disaster.

It follows from what I have been saying that there are stages in the cooking of fish when the concentration of the cook must be complete, moments when the slightest distraction can mean the ruin of a meal. If the telephone rings at such a moment, either ignore it or remove your fish from the fire and make your conversation short, even peremptory. The risks of overcooking have been much increased by the imposition of natural gas, which it is often impossible to control down to the level required for poaching or simmering. To some extent, however, this problem can be solved by the use of asbestos mats.

**Grilling** is cooking by direct exposure to the fire of your electric, gas or charcoal grill. Radiant heat from the glowing elements or coals plays the essential part in the internal cooking of the fish.

To assist the internal cooking process, any fish weighing more than 225 gr (8 oz) should be scored with shallow diagonal cuts to let the heat penetrate nearer the main bone. A problem can arise here with the larger, fatter fish of, say, 40 cm (16 in) or over. They are not really large enough to cut into steaks for grilling, and a shallow scoring of the sides will not accomplish the cooking of the flesh near the bone before the outside of the fish is overcooked or badly burned. Keeping these larger fish farther away from the source of heat and reducing the fierceness of the grill (which will extend the cooking time) provide one solution. Another – and, although I am aware of strong prejudice against it, my own habitual practice with fish of this intermediate size – is to score them heavily down to the bone on the side which is to be put to the fire first. When the fish is turned, the other side is then scored down to the bone – care being taken that these cuts are made *between* the cuts on the other side. The advantages of this method are (a) that not so many of the internal juices are lost as by cutting into steaks, and (b) that you can serve your fish whole on a dish – its wounds prettily dressed with Parsley Butter and thin segments of lemon.

All fish requires basting while grilling, and once the grilling has started, the cook must stay at the stove until the process is complete.

A form of grilling can be carried out on a solid, oiled iron griddle (a large, heavy iron frying pan can stand in for this). It should be heated to a very high temperature, short of being red-hot. This method is much used on the Continent, and is excellent for the almost instant cooking of small fry (sprats, fresh sardines, small herrings, anchovies and so on), particularly those of an oily nature. Larger fish require frequent basting and turning on the griddle, and more successful results will usually be achieved if the fish is left unscaled.

When using gas or electric grills, time must be allowed for the grill to become really hot before you begin to cook.

When grilling, it is important to have the proper utensils for the lifting, turning and basting of fish. These essential aids are listed on pages 25–9.

**Deep frying** involves immersing your fillet or whole fish – previously coated with flour, egg and breadcrumbs, or batter – in oil heated to a temperature of 160–170°C/312–325°F. Olive oil or a good nut oil should be used, and correct temperature can be gauged by dropping a small piece of bread into the oil. If it rises to the surface immediately and assumes a light brown colour, the oil is ready to receive your fish. If it rapidly turns black, the heat must be reduced.

**Shallow or pan frying** For this most common method of frying, only olive oil, butter or a combination of the two should be used. Your oil and/or butter should be sufficient to come up to the level of half the thickness of the fish.

**Frying à la meunière** Quick, light frying of fillets in really hot butter is the method here. When the fish is cooked on both sides, it is removed from the pan – to which more butter is added and then swirled around till foaming. The juice of half a lemon is then introduced, together with a tablespoonful of finely chopped parsley. This mixture is then poured over the fish, which has been kept hot in a heated serving dish.

**Poaching** As far as fish is concerned, this means cooking by total immersion in a seasoned fish stock or *court-bouillon*. The stock should then be brought briskly to the point at which its surface just begins to show lateral disturbance (in other words, it is moving round rather than bubbling upwards!). Now the heat should be reduced (sometimes it can even be turned off) to prevent the dreaded *boiling*, which, as has been previously affirmed, is not a proper method of cooking fish.

Poaching times for fish from
450 gr to 4 kg (1–9 lb) weight

| | | |
|---|---|---|
| 450 gr | (1 lb) | 6 minutes |
| 675 gr | (1½ lb) | 7 minutes |
| 1 kg | (2¼ lb) | 10 minutes |
| 2 kg | (4½ lb) | 14 minutes |
| 3 kg | (6¾ lb) | 18 minutes |
| 4 kg | (9 lb) | 28 minutes |

Times given cannot in all circumstances be taken as scientifically accurate. Too many imponderables are involved (e.g. age and freshness of fish; whether frozen or chilled). However, if the times given above are adhered to when poaching fish, there will be little danger of overcooking. For any given weight of fish, poach for the suggested time and inspect your fish to see if the flesh will just come away from the bone.

**Baking** is cooking in the oven with butter – either with or without a small amount of liquid. Frequent basting is required. The whole fish (or fillets or cutlets) should be turned once during the process.

*En papillote* Here the fish is cooked in the oven, either hermetically sealed in paper or foil, or placed in a small, totally sealed vessel which exactly fits it. By this method the fish actually cooks in its own juices and steam.

**Steaming** There are two kinds of cooking we refer to as steaming. In one, the fish is put into the upper part of a double saucepan with a tightly fitted lid and a perforated base. Water is then put into the lower part of the double pan and boiled, the steam rising and passing through the perforations in the base of the upper pan to surround the fish and cook it.

In the second kind of 'steaming', no steam reaches the fish, as the upper part of the double saucepan does not have a perforated base. This method is slow but effective. By using it, you will retain all the juices of the fish.

**Braising** This is a method akin to baking in the oven, but in braising the fish is accompanied by a certain amount of stock and by vegetables which have been previously chopped and lightly browned in butter. The secret of braising is to use the smallest covered dish which will hold your fish and the other ingredients.

**Cooking au gratin** This term covers two different processes. In the first, fish already cooked, or very nearly so, is masked with a sauce, the ingredients of which (such as butter and cheese) are susceptible to rapid browning under a grill or in a hot oven. In the second, uncooked fish is combined in a dish with a sauce which must itself thicken and cook simultaneously with the fish and its juices. This creates nice problems of timing and oven temperature if we are to synchronize a golden-brown surface on a well-cooked sauce with a fish which is perfectly cooked – and only just so.

**Smoking** Simple smoking is a short-term method of preserving fish when no refrigeration is available. In town, shopping from day to day, one is not often burdened with a superfluity of fish. In the country, however, economies can be made by buying on the coast in modest bulk and 'laying down', so to speak, by curing and smoking, fish not to be eaten immediately.

For efficient smoking, all that is required is a shed, cupboard, old refrigerator or inverted jumbo-sized barrel which can be adapted for use as a smoking chamber. An old tarpaulin boat cover, converted into a sort of tent with the aid of poles or garden implements, can also be effective. At the bottom of whatever contraption you favour, a small fire should be started, preferably with charcoal or peat. Pine cones and needles, oak chips or other hardwood sawdust should then be thrown on this fire to produce the necessary smoke. Twigs and leaves of herbs such as thyme, rosemary, fennel or eucalyptus can be included. To a rod fixed across the top of your contraption the fish to be smoked should be attached by the head.

Simple smoking of uncured fish can be carried out in from three to six hours, depending on the size of your fish, during which time the smoking chamber should be kept filled with smoke and the fire kept well damped down to prevent heat arising from it. In a hot Greek summer, this simple process enabled me to keep fish for three days, in a none-too-cool larder, without any sign of deterioration.

You can also now buy small smoking boxes, in which you can comfortably smoke three or four fish the size of a mackerel. The smoking is done with oak chips and instructions are provided.

**Curing before smoking** There are many degrees of curing, salting and dry-salting fish as a prelude to smoking. For sea fish, one of the simplest processes, in coastal areas, is to let the cleaned and split fish lie in sea water for several hours before drying and hanging up to smoke. Otherwise, a brine should be prepared in the following proportions (the total amount depending on the amount of fish to hand):

6 dl (1 pint) water
450 gr (1 lb) crushed rock salt
100 gr (4 oz) brown sugar
1·5 dl (¼ pint) wine vinegar
1 teaspoon saltpetre

Small fish should be steeped in this mixture for at least 3 hours, and then washed quickly and dried with a cloth before smoking. Larger fish – 450 gr (1 lb) upwards – should be left steeping a further hour for each 225 gr (8 oz) weight.

For small fish, such as herrings or sprats, I have found that 'dry-salting', using the same mixture as given above, but omitting the vinegar and the water, is a fairly foolproof method, which produces a delicious 'closed kipper' sort of result, with just that touch of sweetness so often lacking in the shop-bought kipper. The process should take some 4 hours (in the case of sprats) to 6 hours (for herrings). Scale, clean and dry the herrings without removing the heads; leave the sprats entire. Rub the dry-salting mixture into the fish with the hands, paying particular attention to the inside of the cleaned fish. Press the fishes close together and leave them covered for half an hour. Repeat the process at widening intervals during the next few hours. Rinse and dry the fish well before putting them in to smoke for 4 hours. Trout and mackerel can also be most successfully dry-salted along the lines described for herrings.

It is possible to experiment widely with your curing mixtures, making them more or less sweet according to taste.

SHRIMPERS.

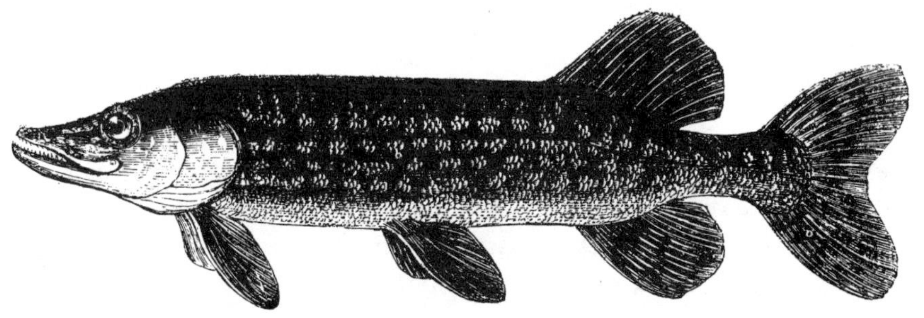

The pike

# Vegetables, herbs and spices

In the following subjective notes on an important aspect of fish cookery, no attempt at botanical classification has been made.

In my own cooking, I have recently come more and more to favour the dominant use, in a sauce, of a single herb or spice when this is of very distinctive flavour. This does not mean that only one single herb or spice should be used in any given sauce – as is the case with mint sauce and horseradish cream – but that, against a well-chosen background of certain essential flavours, one herb or spice should be allowed to predominate. I feel that it is along these lines that we should go in search of an individual style in fish cookery.

The essential flavouring agents, a selection of which should always appear in the background (though one of which, used in strength, may be chosen to dominate in a given sauce) are the following.

**1** Of the first importance, I name the aromatic onion family – onion, shallot, leek, garlic, chive, spring onion. At least one of these should appear either as a background – in stocks for sauces or *courts-bouillons* for poaching fish – or as a final flourish in a strong sauce, when grated, chopped or crushed, in the raw state. However pungent, the members of the onion family never seem to mask the flavour of the fish, but rather to enhance it. (This is particularly evident in the case of mussels, scallops and the cephalopods – octopus, squid and so on.) The onion, then, is an indispensable ingredient of almost all fish dishes – and makes marvellous 'onion' sauce in its own right.

**2** Just as essential is parsley. So perfectly does this unique herb meld with the flavour of fish that it is surprising not to find it sprouting from the sands and shingles of our beaches. Use parsley first and last – on the stalk in stock, fried as a garnish, its heads finely chopped in a sauce. 'Sprinkle with chopped parsley and serve' is a standard phrase, and rightly so, in almost every fish recipe. The broad-leafed variety, imported from Cyprus, lasts longer when cut than the curlicue English kind, but there is little to choose between them in flavour.

**3** Celery and celery leaves are a natural ingredient of all stocks for soups, sauces and *courts-bouillons*. Raw celery, grated or liquidized, also has many parts to play in the last-minute strengthening and freshening of simple sauces, soups and fish pies.

**4** Fennel (and fennel seed) and dill should be used *pianissimo* as background elements, but in strength they too make splendid sauces in their own right. (Not everyone can accept the flavour of fennel in strength. As a boy I was once frightened by a seed cake in a cricket pavilion,* and for long after had an aversion to anything faintly resembling aniseed. This aversion vanished some years later with my first taste of Pernod.) Fennel twigs are used as a bed on which to grill sea-bass and other whole fish, and the smoke produced imparts a delicious smell to the kitchen, if not to the fish itself.

**5** Carrot provides yeoman background service in the stock pot and also, finely grated, has its uses in varying the final flavour of soups, sauces, pies and *au gratin* dishes.

Permutations of these five herbs and vegetables provide the fish cook with a great many ways of 'orchestrating' the background to his sauces. Other herbs which figure prominently in fish cookery are the following.

*Elizabeth David rightly points out that the seeds used in the cake which frightened me as a boy were *caraway*, as opposed to *dill* or *fennel*. There is, however, some affinity of flavour which accounts for my fighting shy of the latter herbs until converted by Pernod. A similar aversion to liquorice is associated in my mind with a diabolical childhood medicine called Gregory powder.

**Bay leaf** To be used with economy in all stocks. Even a quarter of an average-size leaf wins through to the end product. It can, however, be used in strength for sousing and pickling herring, mackerel, tunny, salt anchovies and in other marinades.

**Thyme** Combined with bay leaf, parsley stalks, tarragon or basil, it is an essential ingredient of the *bouquet garni*, for use in general cookery and in many sauces. Used liberally, it makes an excellent 'one-herb' sauce – although at least one member of the onion family should be present in the background.

**Tarragon** What I have said about thyme applies equally to tarragon, which is every bit as eligible as mint to provide a single flavour. Tarragon can be incorporated into mayonnaise and many other sauces.

**Basil** Possibly, after parsley, the most useful of all herbs. It makes a wonderful 'one-herb' sauce. It should be stirred into the sauce at the last stage of its making, and the sauce should then be allowed to stand for at least half an hour before serving. Basil can also be incorporated into mayonnaise.

**Marjoram** has a strong, spicy flavour and can be used instead of thyme, with which it is comparable.

**Sage** should only be used in the smallest of quantities in stuffings and *quenelles*. Like the clove, when used to excess, it will take over from all other flavours. It is therefore not for use in soups, sauces or, of course, in stocks.

**Rosemary** is not quite so overpowering as sage, but tends to acquire a stale flavour during cooking.

**Capers and nasturtiums** are frequently used in both hot and cold sauces. They are especially good in mayonnaise.

**Horseradish** is not, strictly speaking, a herb, but is one of the best flavourings for sauces for all kinds of fish. Horseradish, extensively used in the eighteenth century and much neglected in the twentieth, figures largely in the recipe section of this book.

**Mustard** is traditionally used in sauces to go with herrings, mackerel and other fish rich in oil. To me, horseradish is greatly superior in flavour and makes a much better sauce for these and other fish.

**Elder flowers and berries** Very subtle in taste. Where grapes are used in a sauce, elder helps to bring out their flavour.

Of all the spices, *pepper* is the one most valued in my kitchen; the flavour of the freshly and coarsely ground black peppercorn never palls. Never mind the black specks in the white sauce – I would as soon object to the speckling on the breast feathers of a thrush. White, finely ground pepper I hardly ever use, though it makes excellent sneezing powder.

Of other spices, *mace*, *nutmeg* and *juniper berries* are important. *Coriander*, *cardamom*, *turmeric*, *saffron* and many others play their part in the permutations and combinations of sauce making. Green unripe peppercorns, which can now be bought in tins, are expensive and consequently not for everyday use; but, crushed and added at the last moment to the plainest of sauces, they are magical.

Almost as if I had purposely kept the best wine to the last, I now come to some of the most frequently called-for and valuable ingredients of fish cookery, without which the repertoire would be severely restricted.

**Tomato** The tomato has many uses in both the background and the foreground (tomato sauces) of fish cookery, though it should not be allowed to infiltrate every dish we cook. For thickening sauces strong in flavour without benefit of eggs, flour or cream, it is unique. Tomato paste should always be kept in store, though too frequent use can become a bad habit. The tomato tends to dominate Italian and other regional traditions, not entirely to their advantage.

**Sweet peppers** (pimentos) Strongly flavoured and dangerously addictive to anyone with heady Mediterranean memories, they are marvellous with crab, lobster, mussels, rice dishes and pies. Blanched, seeded and finely diced or sliced, their bright red and green colours match their brilliant flavour which could never be mistaken for anything else.

**Mushrooms** The ultimate question with a good field mushroom, full of the flavour of the rather *louche* soil from which it magically springs, is whether to pick it early in button form, or to return later to find it open and perhaps riddled with busy maggots. For the cultivated mushroom, I have nothing but praise, if only for the reason that what was, in my young days, a rare treat, is now an all the year round staple article on everyone's shopping list. In button form, fresh from the wholesaler, cultivated mushrooms have almost the flavour of their country cousins, but they lose it quickly thereafter. As will be seen later, mushrooms can be used in many ways, in pies, sauces and *au gratin* dishes. A purée of raw button mushrooms can electrify the palate, but should only be used in the right context. When chanterelles or other types of edible fungus come our way, we must be prepared to use them to the best advantage.

**Chervil, watercress and spinach** Apart from its qualifications as an understudy for parsley in a crisis, chervil can be used with considerable effect in fish soups and for other purposes. Watercress and spinach are both versatile and are certainly more often called for.

**Olives** In a category on its own, the olive – more especially the large, dark Kalamata olive – is the basis of one or two sauces splendidly perverse in taste and velvety in texture and colour.

**Lemons** Of the lemon I need say little. It is, in fact, a sauce on its own, pure and simple, and there is hardly any form of fish dish which is not improved by it. With its compeers, the onion and parsley, it forms an incomparable trinity of the fish kitchen.

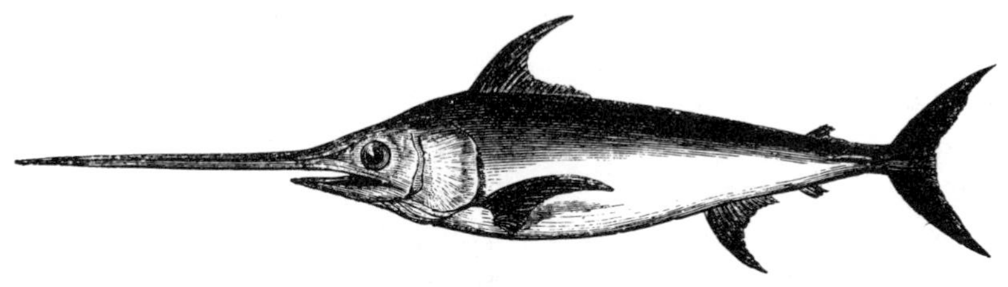

THE SWORD FISH.

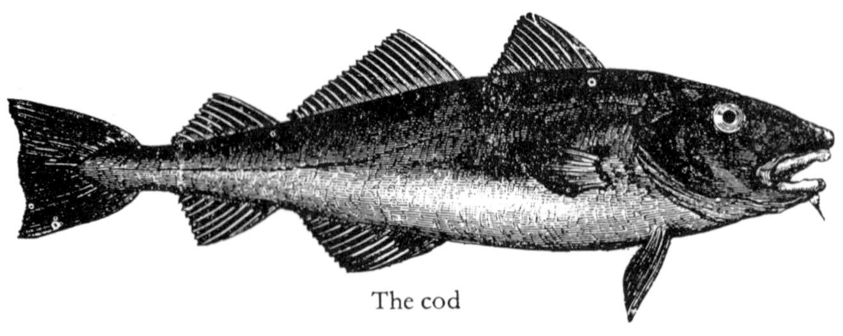

The cod

# Sauces for fish

The French tradition excels in its repertoire of rich sauces for fish. In modern terms and in a country which less than thirty years ago came out of a long period of strict rationing with vastly improved health, it is something of a dietetic anachronism. We may yet live to see a Government warning attached to the more elaborate dishes on the menus of our expensive restaurants – no doubt with the same effect on the eating habits as such warnings have had on the smoking habits of the country. Danger has always been a spice to the pursuit of pleasure and it is one of the basic human liberties that we should be allowed to 'dig our own graves with our teeth'. In our calorie-conscious, coronary-haunted age, there is still no dearth of candidates for martyrdom. They can be seen in all the Grand Hotels and restaurants of the world, gaily munching their way towards what, in Edwardian days, used to be called apoplexy.

For those of us whose diet consists mainly of fish, the process of self-immolation can be a much slower one. And if we exercise a little self-control in the choice and quantity of the sauces with which we eat our fish, the dramatic end may be postponed indefinitely, to ripe old age – when who cares anyway? But the necessary control can only be exercised at home, in our own kitchens.

How are we to reverse the present dreadful trend? The rage – and it is nothing less – for eating out is a baleful symptom of the revolutionary times in which we live, uneasily counting our anxieties and our credit cards as once we told our blessings and our beads. There is a great deal to be said for an occasional visit to a restaurant of unimpeachable repute to indulge in a *Lobster Thermidor* or a *Délices de Sole Marquise de Polignac*, if we – or our friends – can afford it. However, the number of such restaurants outside great cities is extremely limited. As I have said, we have the right to dig our own graves with our teeth; it is quite another thing to have them dug for us by food chemists and the swarm of inferior but pretentious restaurateurs who now infest the catering system of the country as a whole. The widespread misuse of the nomenclature of the French *cuisine* for simulated dishes, confected with adulterated and processed ingredients bearing no relation to the distinguished originals, eludes the provisions of the Trade Descriptions Act. Pollution of this kind is no new thing. In essence it is a form of pilfering for profit, comparable to the watering of milk or wine, the stretching of flour with dust, sugar with fine sand, horseradish with sawdust. It is pilfering in the sense that, in the pursuit of profit, it erodes quality and educates the inexperienced to false standards. If it can be proved to be hygienic, this is only in the sense that no self-respecting bacteria would consent to be present in its products.

It was some time in the late 1940s that my attention was first drawn to such practices. While staying with friends (I was convalescent at the time) in a country cottage someone had kindly lent me, I came across a book after reading which I have never felt any affection towards caterers. The occasion itself glows for me in the elation spread by a splendid *cassoulet* of bacon bones, beans and herbs, slowly cooked to a point at which the bacon bones almost disintegrated. After this, comforted by generous cups of vintage Algerian wine, we settled down before the fire with such books as we could find. One among my own selection was small folio in size, bound in blue cloth, with gilt lettering. My memory not serving me exactly, '*Hotel Cooking Manual*' must be taken as a paraphrase of title and legend. Above this appeared the exhortation 'To be kept in the office safe at all times!' and below, 'Not to be allowed out of the manager's possession'. It may be imagined with what excitement we anticipated the disclosure of all the quintessential mysteries of hotel *cuisine*. 'But,' said a puzzled friend, 'why the manager only, and not the cook?' 'Perhaps he was a manager/cook,' I said. 'They do, I suppose, go together in old family hotels, handed down from generation to generation.' 'No, no,' said someone. 'Then it would be proprietor and not manager – and what manager, if he were also proprietor, would instruct himself in gilt lettering to keep his cookery secrets in his own safe? And why a *printed* book at all? Surely a most expensive way of doing things, what with the paper shortage and everything.' 'A limited edition,' I suggested, 'for members of the family and a few chosen friends sworn to secrecy.' But I was wrong there. It was not only unlimited, but not even a first edition. This implied large numbers of such books in existence, moving mysteriously from safe to manager and back again. But where or why . . . ?

What we had lighted on was, in fact, a cook counterfeiter's manual, issued to its managers by a well-known chain of hotels and restaurants. I have a clear memory of two specific items, which will serve to convey its tone. One was a detailed instruction on how to make imitation French sauces, using *ersatz* materials. The other was an advisory paragraph on how to meet the emergency of a sudden influx of casual customers when there was insufficient food in the kitchen to feed them. On no account should such customers be turned away. There followed detailed instructions as to how to perform a miracle of the loaves and fishes and turn food already prepared to feed twenty hotel residents into a banquet for forty.

For over twenty-five years I have tried to find another copy of this book, which misguided scruples prevented me from 'borrowing' at the time. Not one copy has ever appeared on the street markets I frequent, and no secondhand book dealer has ever been able to trace one for me. Perhaps each manager is buried or cremated with his book beside him. Perhaps the book was produced in wartime and continued in use only in the immediately postwar period of shortages. The fact that it was not a first edition and that it was printed on good-quality paper depressingly suggests more venerable prewar origins. If this is so, we should ask ourselves how, if it still exists, this system of clandestine instruction has evolved since the 1940s. Do such books still circulate, now probably in the twentieth edition, and fat with appendices extending the frontiers of their insidious expertise?

Ages before the loss of gastronomic innocence recorded above, when I first started cooking on the Greek island of Aghios Nikolaos,

I had no idea how to set about making a sauce. On consulting Mrs Beeton (1899 – a very pretty dictionary version of the original), I saw that butter, flour and eggs came frequently into the picture. At that time, in that place, fresh butter was unobtainable and the tinned variety so rancid as to suggest it had originally been rations captured in some old Balkan war. Whenever, therefore, Mrs Beeton said butter, I used olive oil and many a sauce that seemed good to me at the time came out of it. I still find such sauces good and recipes for making them will be given later in this section, even though by including them I may find myself excluded from that great kitchen-in-the-sky to which all good cooks are said to go. For one thing, sauces of this kind go very well with the coarser, strong-tasting fish and for another, there are a number of people for whom, on medical or dietary grounds, butter and dairy products are forbidden, while olive oil is not.

This introduction to sauce making would not be complete without a clear restatement of one of the main principles of fish cooking, that no sauce should be so powerful or so plentiful as to obliterate the flavour or smother the texture of the fish with which it is to be served. As to the flavouring of sauces, I believe that my hankering after the 'single flavour' (see page 45) does not conflict with this principle. Regarding quantity, I have tried throughout this book to limit the quantity per person to 1·5 dl ($\frac{1}{4}$ pint). Most sauces are rich and calorie-laden ingredients of a meal and dietary considerations alone should impose self-restraint in this respect.

But it is time we got down to the elements of sauce making. I begin with the very simplest of basic sauces, quick to make, and perfectly suitable for grilled, poached, baked or fried fish of any kind. Also, this sort of 'lazy' sauce is a good introduction to fish cookery for beginners who have the idea that sauce making must always be a complicated business.

## *Chameleon Sauces*

Sauces of this kind were a regular, though undeveloped, feature of eighteenth- and nineteenth-century English cooking. As a class, they might be called relishes, like Worcester sauce, mushroom ketchup and the famous *garum* of antiquity.

**Chameleon Sauce** (Basic Recipe)
Mix together in a bowl the following ingredients:

1 teaspoon prepared English mustard
1 shallot *or* small onion, grated
4 tablespoons wine vinegar
juice ½ lemon
1 teaspoon sugar (brown or white)
1 heaped tablespoon parsley, finely chopped
¼ teaspoon salt
generous shower freshly milled black pepper
Stir all together and leave to stand so that the onion and parsley have time to impregnate the whole sauce.

This simple sauce is rightly named, being capable of any number of variations in flavour and character. By substituting for mustard any other powerfully flavoured ingredient in sufficient strength, we obtain a completely different sauce. Amongst others, I have successfully used the following alternatives to for mustard:

1 heaped tablespoon capers, pounded
1 level dessertspoon horseradish, finely grated
2 tablespoons purée* of celery heart and leaves
2 tablespoons purée of sweet green or red peppers
2 tablespoons purée of fresh raw button mushrooms (substituting wine for vinegar and eliminating sugar)
2 tablespoons purée of watercress leaves
2 cloves garlic, crushed or very finely chopped
*see Glossary.

The constants in this sauce, whatever the dominant flavour, are always at least one member of the onion family, plus parsley, lemon juice, vinegar, sugar, salt and pepper (a small quantity of cayenne can be substituted for black). It is the constants which make this sauce eminently suitable for fish.

This sauce (or, rather, this whole range of sauces, of which only eight examples are given here) can be served hot or cold as a kind of relish. Only a teaspoonful or two will be required by each person. Of course, common sense is required. If, for instance, anchovy essence or pounded anchovy is chosen as 'dominant', then the salt will be omitted; and if you choose garlic, you need not necessarily include other members of the onion family.

I have deliberately chosen to begin with this type of sauce for three reasons. Firstly, it makes an 'instant' and confident fish cook of the beginner. Secondly, it illustrates perfectly the principle of the 'one-flavour sauce' to which I have already referred under 'Vegetables, herbs and spices'. Thirdly, it is a good point of departure from which to make a logical approach to the richer and more involved sauces of *haute cuisine*.

For instance, we can enrich the sauce in two basic ways:

**1 Improved Chameleon Sauce**

Simply by stirring 2 tablespoons olive oil into the original Chameleon Sauce ingredients, we make quite a sophisticated sauce of a mock-vinaigrette type (see page 71). This can be served either hot or cold.

**2 Butter Sauce**

The addition of 50 gr (2 oz) butter to the original Chameleon Sauce, heated over a low flame, makes an excellent butter sauce. The butter should be well beaten into the sauce, which should not be allowed to boil.

If we now want to enrich the sauce further, we have the choice of binding with either egg yolk or flour.

## *Binding a sauce with egg yolk*

Add to 1 yolk in a bowl 1 tablespoon of the Improved Chameleon Sauce, hot but *not boiling*, and beat well together. Stir the mixture into the remaining sauce, and continue to beat over low heat, preferably in a double saucepan, until the sauce thickens. For the small quantities involved here, this should not take longer than 8 minutes.

The yolk of a hard-boiled egg may also be used to bind sauces. In this case, pound the egg yolk in a mortar and slowly pour the sauce over it, beating thoroughly throughout the process.

At this point we have already come a long way from our original fluid 'relish' type of sauce, and we are already carrying out processes which are used in the making of many of the finest sauces of the *haute cuisine*.

## *Binding a sauce with flour*

To illustrate the process of binding and thickening with flour, we need a little more elbow-room than our humble Chameleon Sauce allows; we now leave it, since it has served its introductory purpose.

If we want to bind or thicken any liquid with flour, we can do it in four different ways – the amount of flour used depending on the quantity of liquid to be thickened.

### 1 Plain flour method

Simply spoon a small quantity (about 1·5 dl or $\frac{1}{4}$ pint) of the liquid into the flour and mix until smooth. Dilute a little further and then add the mixture to the liquid. Bring to the boil in a saucepan and simmer until as thick as required. You now have a plain, naturally white sauce, free of butter, fat or oil. What it tastes like will depend on the concentration of flavours in your stock or *court-bouillon*.

### 2 Kneaded butter (beurre manié) method

Knead together in a basin equal quantities of butter and flour until smooth. Bring the stock to the boil in a saucepan, keep it simmering and drop into it small pieces of the butter-and-flour mixture, stirring all the while as the *beurre manié* dissolves into the *bouillon*, which thickens in the process. With this method of binding (known as *liaison*), we find ourselves at the heart of a controversy, some authorities saying that the kneaded butter should be stirred into the liquid before this has reached simmering point and should not be allowed to simmer thereafter. In practice I find it best to simmer my sauces while stirring for at least 5 minutes after all the fragments of *beurre manié* have completely dissolved, a process which, in my experience, usually takes from 8 to 10 minutes. The final addition of a dessertspoon of fresh butter folded into the sauce off the fire just before serving greatly enhances sauces made by this method.

### 3 Roux method

Melt in a saucepan 1 tablespoon butter and stir into it until smooth 1 tablespoon flour. Allow to cook over a low heat for 1 minute, stirring all the while. (For a white sauce, the mixture should be allowed to take only the faintest tinge of colour; for a brown sauce, it should be allowed to assume a nutty tone although not to become singed.) This mixture is a *roux*, a term in universal use for which we have no English equivalent. Remove the *roux* from the fire and gently pour in the hot (but not boiling) stock, stirring vigorously. Return to heat and stir on until the sauce reaches simmering point, at which moment it will thicken quickly. Add further stock until the desired consistency is reached, and allow to simmer for 15–20 minutes, stirring to avoid any sticking or burning. Your sauce is now ready for further enrichment or thickening with egg yolk, cream or fresh butter, according to recipe or inclination.

I have given above roughly equal measures of flour and butter for both the *beurre manié* and *roux* methods of binding sauces, but we shall be dealing with more precise quantities shortly when we tackle the recipes for individual sauces.

**4 Oil and flour method**

The same procedure as that described above for the butter and flour *roux* method should be followed in the case of binding with oil and flour. Sufficient plain flour should be added to, say, 3 tablespoons of oil to make a thick paste (but not a dough) in which all the oil is seen to be completely absorbed. Hot stock is then stirred steadily into it. When, at simmering point, the mixture suddenly thickens, pour on more stock until the desired consistency is reached. Simmer, while stirring, for 15 to 20 minutes.

These oil-based sauces, whether hot or cold (when they still flow, though butter-based sauces may solidify), are eminently receptive to purées of sweet peppers, leeks, onions, garlic, black olives, celery, watercress and chervil (see Glossary).

Some taboo, like that which discourages attempts to interbreed between species, inhibits the use in these oil sauces of dairy products, despite the fact that they respond to enrichment with egg yolks and cream. But they are completely at home with all kinds of wine, from a dry white to Marsala or port.

## *Court-bouillon*

A *court-bouillon* is the traditional name for a savoury stock in which fish of all kinds is poached. Just enough *court-bouillon* to cover the fish should be used; the amount required, therefore, will depend on the size of the vessel in which your fish is poached, and on how cosily the fish fits into it.

Here are three recipes for stocks. The first is a *court-bouillon* for poaching fish; numbers 2 and 3 are both excellent for making sauces and soups. In each case, to 1·2 litres (2 pints) water add the following ingredients:

**Court-bouillon 1**

1 stick celery, chopped
2 onions, chopped
the white of 1 leek, chopped
a sprig of thyme
1 teaspoon chopped tarragon
½ bay leaf
2 or 3 parsley stalks
1 teaspoon salt
6 black peppercorns, crushed
juice ½ lemon
1·5 dl (¼ pint) white wine (optional)

**Court-bouillon 2**

225 gr (8 oz) white fish trimmings
1 carrot, grated
1 stick celery, roughly chopped
2 onions *or* shallots, chopped
2 or 3 parsley stalks
½ bay leaf
1 teaspoon salt
6 black peppercorns, crushed
1·5 dl (¼ pint) white wine

**Court-bouillon 3**

225 gr (8 oz) small whiting
a sprig of fennel
the white of 1 leek, chopped
2 onions *or* shallots, chopped
1 teaspoon basil, chopped
2 or 3 parsley stalks
1 teaspoon salt
6 black peppercorns, crushed
1·5 dl (¼ pint) white wine

In each case, bring to the boil, simmer for 40 minutes, strain and set aside for use. It will be noted that certain elements (namely onion, parsley, black pepper, salt) are present in all three stocks, the other ingredients of which may be varied to suit the needs of a particular dish. This applies especially to stocks for soups and sauces, where the inclusion in the stock of, say, one small red mullet or a few mussels can alter the whole character of the end result.

**Fumet**

If, after the fish has been poached in it, the *court-bouillon* (now enriched by the juices of the fish) is reduced by boiling from, say, 9 dl (1½ pints) to 3 dl (½ pint), then we are in the presence of a *fumet* – that is to say an enriched and concentrated stock. This can be used for making sauces, added to sauces already made – or simply used as a sauce on its own.

I now give detailed recipes for six basic sauces and a selection of sauces which stem from each.

## *1 Velouté de Poisson*

50 gr (2 oz) butter
50 gr (2 oz) flour
9 dl (1½ pints) fish stock

In a saucepan, melt the butter and stir in the flour to make a white *roux* (see page 56). Pour in your stock (hot but not boiling), bring to the boil while stirring and allow to cook for 20 minutes. This will make a fairly thick *velouté*; if a thinner sauce is required (e.g. for use in enriching soup), another 1·5 dl (¼ pint) stock should be used. If the sauce is not for immediate use, stir until cool, pour over it a small amount of melted butter to prevent skin forming, cover and set aside to be gently reheated, stirring all the while, when required.

## *Sauces derived from the Fish Velouté*

**Sauce Aurore** (a rosy tomato sauce)
3 tablespoons Rich Tomato Sauce (see page 66)
6 dl (1 pint) fish *velouté*
25 gr (1 oz) butter

Stir the rich tomato sauce into the *velouté* and then add the butter. Using fresh tomato sauce is a good idea from the point of view of flavour and also because tinned tomato paste (a possible substitute) does not always give the sauce the bright colour which its name ('rosy-fingered dawn') demands.

**Sauce Bercy** (a white wine sauce)
1 tablespoon shallot, chopped
3 tablespoons white wine
3 dl ($\frac{1}{2}$ pint) fish *velouté*, made with a concentrated fish stock
25 gr (1 oz) butter
1 dessertspoon parsley, finely chopped *or* 1 teaspoon basil, finely chopped

Cook the chopped shallot in the wine until the latter is reduced by half, and then stir into the *velouté*. Finish by stirring in the butter and the parsley or basil.

**Sauce Marinière** (a mussel sauce)
Make a *Sauce Bercy*, as above, and stir in the liquor in which mussels have been cooked (see *Moules Marinière*, page 153), reduced to a volume of 1·5 dl ($\frac{1}{4}$ pint). Add 8 poached mussels, removed from their shells.

**Sauce Poulette** (a rich sauce)
1 onion, finely chopped
1 glass wine
3 dl ($\frac{1}{2}$ pint) fish *velouté*
2 egg yolks
25 gr (1 oz) butter
pinch of nutmeg
juice $\frac{1}{2}$ lemon
1 tablespoon parsley, chopped

In a small, heavy saucepan, cook the onion in the wine until the latter is reduced to a bare tablespoonful and add to the *velouté*. Beat the egg yolks with 1 tablespoon of sauce (hot but not boiling), and stir into the rest of the sauce on a low heat. Finish by adding the butter, nutmeg and lemon juice, and fold in the parsley just before serving.

The egg yolks are not intended to thicken but merely to enrich the sauce, which should therefore be kept hot – but not hot enough to cook. This sauce is excellent for turbot, brill and sole, but also for general use with all white fish.

**White Wine Sauce**

3 tablespoons white wine
3 dl ($\frac{1}{2}$ pint) fish *velouté* made with a concentrated fish stock
1 egg yolk
2 tablespoons double cream
25 gr (1 oz) butter

Add the white wine to the *velouté* and cook gently, stirring the while, for 15 minutes. Allow to cool. Beat the egg yolk and the cream thoroughly together and combine with the sauce. Cook on a very low heat until the sauce thickens a little. Fold in the butter.

**Sauce Normande** (a sauce flavoured with shellfish)
If, when making a *velouté* for the above recipe, you have a *Sauce Normande* specifically in mind, the stock used should be fortified by the addition of a few shellfish. The original recipe calls for oysters, but because of their present prohibitive prices, I suggest the alternative of mussels, clams or scallops.

Now, for *Sauce Normande*, you will need 3 dl ($\frac{1}{2}$ pint) concentrated *fumet* from the fish you are cooking, and the reduced cooking juices of oysters, mussels, clams or scallops (if these have not been included in the *velouté*). It is possible to use tinned clam juice here; it gives very good results. Add the *fumet* and shellfish juices to the Basic White Wine Sauce, stir well together, and cook slowly for 12 minutes, stirring continuously. Sprinkle with parsley. If you have cooked shellfish to obtain their juices, use them to garnish your dish.

**Sauce Régence**
The addition of 1 tablespoon finely chopped mushrooms *and/or* 1 teaspoon chopped truffle *or* truffle essence turns *Sauce Normande* into *Sauce Régence*.

**Sauce Cardinal** (a lobster sauce for fish)
3 dl ($\frac{1}{2}$ pint) fish *velouté*
2 tablespoons white fish *fumet*
25 gr (1 oz) lobster meat
25 gr (1 oz) lobster coral (*or* coral from the female crab)
50 gr (2 oz) butter
2 or 3 fennel leaves, finely chopped
1 teaspoon chives, chopped
1 teaspoon truffle essence *or* mushroom ketchup

Add to the *velouté* first the *fumet* and then the lobster meat and lobster or crab coral pounded up with the butter, the fennel and chives and the essence or ketchup. Simmer all together over a low heat for a few minutes, stirring all the time.

Many restaurant cooks are unable to resist the temptation to match up to the cardinal's hat by adding a few drops of cochineal.

**Sauce Mornay** (a cheese sauce)
2 tablespoons white wine
6 dl (1 pint) fish *velouté*
100 gr (4 oz) grated Gruyère cheese
50 gr (2 oz) butter
freshly ground black pepper

Add the wine to the *velouté* and cook gently for 5 minutes, stirring all the time. Let the sauce cool down to well below boiling point and then stir in the cheese gradually, until it has all dissolved and amalgamated with the sauce. Fold in the butter and sprinkle with pepper. (If your sauce is intended for poached fillets, the very much reduced poaching liquid should be added to the sauce with the wine.) This sauce can be enriched by binding with egg yolks and by the addition of cream, but I recommend the simpler version above.

You will find it rewarding to experiment with many different cheeses when making this sauce, and also with the addition of other ingredients, such as grated onion, chopped celery, mustard, chopped watercress and so on. The combinations are endless, and this is one of the most valuable sauces in fish cookery.

The sauce can also be made with a *béchamel* base (see page 64), and using an equal mixture of Parmesan and Gruyère cheese.

**Sauce Gratin**
This, as its name suggests, is excellent for covering fillets or whole small fish to be nicely browned in a hot oven or under the grill.
25 gr (1 oz) mushrooms, chopped
25 gr (1 oz) shallots, chopped
50 gr (2 oz) butter
6 dl (1 pint) fish *velouté*
50 gr (2 oz) tomato purée
1 tablespoon parsley, finely chopped

Sauter the mushrooms and shallots well in half the butter. Add to the fish *velouté* and cook for 5 minutes, stirring all the time. Add the tomato purée and the chopped parsley, and amalgamate well with the sauce. Fold in your remaining butter.

Tinned tomato purée can be used, but try occasionally to make your own from fresh, skinned and deseeded tomatoes, reduced to the required consistency with butter and a little garlic, or prepared in the blender (see Glossary).

**Chaudfroid Sauce**

As its name implies, this sauce can be served either hot or cold. When cold, it becomes a stiffish, semi-transparent jelly which is useful for coating cold fish or for using in moulds of minced fish, made up from the remains of yesterday's rather grand dinner (at which perhaps we overestimated the *gourmandise* of our guests). It can also be used in *hors-d'oeuvres* and cocktail savouries.

The classic recipes for this sauce involve some eight hours' stirring, spread over two days. Lacking a scullion, I have resigned myself to an excellent second-best. A strong skate stock is used, as this fish has excellent 'jelling' properties and there is no need to use gelatine to get the desired effect.

*for the stock:*
225 gr (8 oz) skate on the bone
a few parsley stalks
½ stick celery, chopped
the white of 1 leek, chopped
1 shallot, chopped
6 dl (1 pint) water
2 egg whites
shells of 2 eggs
3 dl (½ pint) fish *velouté* sauce

Chop up the skate and put it with the vegetables in the water. Boil steadily for about 1 hour until reduced to 1·5 dl (¼ pint) liquid. Clarify this *fumet* by bringing it to a brisk boil and putting into it the beaten whites of 2 eggs and their pounded shells. Boil for 3–4 minutes, then strain through a fine-meshed sieve. Add to your *velouté* sauce and cook for a few minutes, stirring well. Remove from the fire, and stir from time to time as the sauce cools.

We have not by any means exhausted the possibilities of the fish *velouté*; however, the recipes given show its adaptability in compound sauces of all kinds. Other variations, not mentioned here, will crop up later.

I will now move on to the *Béchamel* and a selection of the sauces derived from it.

## *2 Sauce Béchamel*

This sauce is similar to the *velouté*, but is made with flavoured milk instead of fish stock.

50 gr (2 oz) butter
50 gr (2 oz) flour
9 dl (1½ pints) milk
1 medium onion, finely chopped
*bouquet garni* of thyme, parsley and bay leaf
¼ teaspoon salt
½ teaspoon freshly ground black pepper

In a saucepan, melt the butter and add the flour to make a *roux*; pour on the milk slowly, stir well and bring to simmering point. Put in all the other ingredients and cook gently for 30 minutes. Remove *bouquet garni*.

To each man his own *béchamel*, and so it has been for more than three centuries. Most of us have been making *béchamel* for years without knowing it. Variations in the flavouring of the milk are to be encouraged.

## *Sauces derived from the Béchamel*

### Cream Sauce

1·5 dl (¼ pint) double cream
4·5 dl (¾ pint) *Sauce Béchamel*

Add the cream to the *béchamel*, bring to simmering point and cook slowly for 1–2 minutes, stirring all the time. This, without any further enrichment of eggs or butter, is the basis for a splendid range of single-flavour sauces such as the following examples.

**Fennel Sauce**

Add to the Cream Sauce 2 tablespoons washed and pounded fennel leaves. Allow the sauce to simmer gently for a few minutes while stirring.

**Parsley Sauce**

To the Cream Sauce add 1 tablespoon lemon juice and 3 tablespoons washed and pounded or chopped parsley.

**Spanish Onion Sauce**

Add to the Cream Sauce a squeeze of lemon juice and 2 tablespoons of the juice of a large Spanish onion, obtained as follows. Slice the onion finely in rings. Lay the rings on the sloping sides of a deep plate. Lightly dust with fine sugar and leave in a warm place for 1 hour. At the end of that time, you should be able to collect 2 tablespoons of juice from the well of the plate. For full impact on the palate, this sauce should not be cooked further after the onion juice has been added. Zowie!

**Green Peppercorn Sauce**

To the Cream Sauce, add 1 dessertspoon pounded green peppercorns, and allow the sauce to stand and keep hot – but not to cook – for 15–20 minutes. This sauce deserves a good sole or thick steak of turbot.

And so on . . . with chopped garlic (1 teaspoon), leek (2 tablespoons), chives (2 tablespoons), watercress (2 tablespoons), horseradish (1 dessertspoon), basil (1 dessertspoon), tarragon (1 dessertspoon), in the quantities given.

Single-flavour sauces of this kind marry well as follows:

| | |
|---|---|
| leek<br>chive<br>watercress | with all good poached<br>white fish such as cod,<br>haddock, coley and plaice |
| garlic | with mackerel, grey mullet and eel |
| horseradish | with mackerel, gurnard, garfish and skate |
| tarragon<br>basil | with river fish: pike, perch,<br>tench and carp |

As will be seen, there is wide scope for experiment with this *béchamel*-based cream sauce.

**Sauce Nantua** (crayfish sauce)
50 gr (2 oz) Crayfish Butter (see page 79)
3 dl ($\frac{1}{2}$ pint) *Sauce Béchamel*, enriched with 3 tablespoons thick cream
8 or 9 small scampi or Dublin Bay prawns

Dissolve the Crayfish Butter in the *béchamel* over a low heat. Stir well together. The word 'Nantua' always implies a garnish of small crayfish.

**Sauce Soubise** (onion sauce)
3 medium onions, finely chopped
50 gr (2 oz) butter
3 dl ($\frac{1}{2}$ pint) *Sauce Béchamel*

Cook the onions in the butter until very soft. Pass the mixture through a Mouli or a sieve and add to the *béchamel*. If you wish to, you can enrich the sauce with 25 gr (1 oz) butter and 2 tablespoons cream.

This is another sauce which provides a wide range of opportunities for further development – even within the onion family alone. Try the following. With the onion, cook the whites of 3 thick leeks, finely chopped. Or, at the end, add 1 tablespoon chopped chives and a small clove of garlic, crushed. Add to each of these variations on the onion theme in turn 1 tablespoon celery heart, finely chopped, and 1 dessertspoon lemon juice.

**Rich Tomato Sauce**

Perhaps the best development from the *Sauce Soubise* is the delicious rich tomato sauce which we create by adding to it 2 tablespoons tomato purée and 1 dessertspoon finely chopped basil. This sauce goes particularly well with fish of coarser texture (such as monkfish, dogfish, conger), but is also suitable for general use.

**Newburg Sauce**

I mention this here because *béchamel* is involved in the making of Lobster Newburg; the full recipe for this dish is given in the section on the lobster (page 145). The method used in making this dish can, with slight variations, be effectively employed in cooking other kinds of crustacea, shellfish and firm white fish.

With the *béchamel*, as with the fish *velouté*, we have an indispensable tool for the construction of compound sauces. Further uses for it will occur elsewhere in this book.

## *3 Sauce Hollandaise*

4 tablespoons wine vinegar *or* 2 tablespoons lemon juice and
  2 tablespoons wine vinegar
12 peppercorns
2 egg yolks
100 gr (4 oz) unsalted butter
salt

Boil the vinegar with the peppercorns and reduce to a bare tablespoon of liquid; strain into another saucepan and allow to cool. Now, with a whisk, beat in your egg yolks and, on a very slow fire, add, little by little, half the butter, stirring vigorously all the time. When the egg shows signs of thickening, remove the pan from the heat and gradually add the remaining 50 gr (2 oz) butter, stirring all the while, until the mixture acquires the texture of thick double cream.

This beautiful sauce should not be kept waiting, but will survive if kept warm in a double saucepan on a low heat and beaten up from time to time.

## *Sauces derived from the Hollandaise*

The simple opulence of this egg- and butter-rich sauce need not inhibit us from giving it a variety of flavours of our own choice. Such variations need only be incorporated into the *hollandaise* as the final stage of the operation.

For instance, 2 tablespoons concentrated purée of tomatoes, stirred into a completed *hollandaise*, produces *Sauce Victoria*, though, for this sauce, the vinegar used in the initial stages of the *hollandaise* should be tarragon-flavoured.

However, we need not slavishly follow established recipes in exploring the *hollandaise* further, and any of the following additions to the original recipe should be tried as occasion suggests:

$\frac{1}{4}$ teaspoon pounded saffron, infused in a little boiling water
1 tablespoon juice of the Spanish onion (see page 65)

1 teaspoon made mustard, slightly diluted
1 teaspoon horseradish cream
1 teaspoon pounded juniper berries, infused in a little boiling water
1 small clove garlic, pounded and infused in a little boiling water
1 teaspoon green peppercorns, pounded and infused in a little boiling water
small quantities of any of the following in purée form: basil, tarragon, chervil, fennel, celery

The *hollandaise* is a sauce for universal use with all kinds of fish, though by custom it is associated in the public mind with lobster, salmon, trout, sole and turbot. It can be served with hot or cold dishes, makes an excellent accompaniment to shellfish and to simple fish soups (1 dessertspoonful added to each bowl). But perhaps the most famous scion of the *hollandaise* family is the *Béarnaise*, named after Henri IV of France.

**Sauce Béarnaise**

This tarragon-flavoured sauce can be made with either butter or oil. In either case the technique is similar to that for *hollandaise*. When oil is used, it makes a marvellous cold sauce for use with cold dishes and fish salads.

2 shallots, finely chopped
1·5 dl ($\frac{1}{4}$ pint) vinegar (tarragon-flavoured if possible)
3 egg yolks
100 gr (4 oz) butter *or* 5 tablespoons olive oil
1 tablespoon tarragon, chopped
freshly ground black pepper, a generous scattering
$\frac{1}{2}$ teaspoon salt

Boil the finely chopped shallots in the vinegar until they are almost a purée and only 2 or 3 tablespoons vinegar remain in the pan. Strain and allow to cool down, then beat into the mixture the 3 yolks of egg and, gradually, over low heat, the butter or oil. When the sauce has acquired the texture of thick cream, fold in the tarragon, liberally sprinkle with black pepper and season with salt.

The *Béarnaise* method using oil also lends itself to a number of excellent one-flavour sauces for use hot or cold. It should be tried with caper, horseradish, chervil, watercress, parsley, garlic, leek and celery. In each case, 1 tablespoon of the selected herb, finely chopped, should be cooked with the shallots in plain wine vinegar, which is then reduced, strained and thickened with egg and oil; 1 further tablespoon of the chosen herb is folded in as a final stage. Common sense, I hope, will suggest that in the case of horseradish or garlic, the quantity should be reduced to 1 teaspoon in the vinegar and 1 teaspoon in the final mixture.

## *4 Mayonnaise*

2 egg yolks
1 dessertspoon wine vinegar
¼ teaspoon salt
¼ teaspoon freshly ground black pepper
3 dl (½ pint) olive oil

In a bowl, beat the egg yolks well together with half the vinegar and the salt and pepper. Then, drop by drop, beat in the oil – *very* slowly at first, until the mixture thickens. Continue the process, letting the oil drip faster until it is all absorbed. Fold in the rest of the vinegar.

This is the *sauce mayonnaise* at its very simplest. A more common recipe includes 1 teaspoon English mustard, which is mixed with the vinegar and the yolk of egg and seasonings before adding the oil. 1 dessertspoon lemon juice may be substituted for the wine vinegar.

When making a mayonnaise, you should make sure all the ingredients are at room temperature. If, for any reason, the mayonnaise fails to thicken or starts to curdle in its later stages, drip it slowly on to an egg yolk in another basin, whisking all the while. If this fails, cut your losses and start again.

Traditionally, mayonnaise is served with cold dishes of the finest fish such as crustacea, but this should not deter you from experimenting with hot or cold, poached or grilled, white fish of all kinds.

## *Sauces derived from Mayonnaise*

**Aïoli** (garlic mayonnaise)
In addition to the ingredients required for mayonnaise (see above) you will need 10 small cloves of garlic.

Pound the garlic to a fine paste and beat together with the egg yolks and half the lemon juice or vinegar. Pour in the olive oil, drop by drop, beating the mixture with a wooden spoon until all the oil is absorbed and the sauce thick. Add remaining lemon juice or vinegar. Season with salt and pepper.

**Sauce Rémoulade**

3 dl ($\frac{1}{2}$ pint) mayonnaise
1 teaspoon French mustard
1 anchovy fillet, pounded
1 heaped tablespoon of the following, chopped finely together: gherkin, parsley, capers, tarragon and basil

Work the mustard and the anchovy, pounded to a paste, into the mayonnaise. Fold in all the herbs.

My partiality for horseradish has tempted me to use it instead of mustard in this sauce and, to my mind, it is an improvement. The great Escoffier shared my enthusiasm for horseradish, as witness the following recipe.

**Mayonnaise Escoffier**

3 dl ($\frac{1}{2}$ pint) mayonnaise
1 teaspoon fresh horseradish, finely grated
1 teaspoon parsley, chopped
1 teaspoon chervil, chopped
1 teaspoon chives, chopped

Simply fold all the ingredients into the mayonnaise.

I have added chives to the original recipe, as I think it improves the sauce when eaten with fish.

**Sauce Tartare**

To 3 dl ($\frac{1}{2}$ pint) made mayonnaise, add 1 teaspoon of each of the following, finely chopped: chives, capers, parsley, gherkins, green olives. Season with pepper. Substitute, if you wish, 1 teaspoon finely chopped green sweet pepper for the olives. This is a version I myself prefer.

**Sauce Verte** (green sauce)

To 3 dl ($\frac{1}{2}$ pint) made mayonnaise, add 1 teaspoon of each of the following, finely chopped and pounded: watercress, chervil, blanched young spinach leaf, fresh tarragon and chives. Fresh basil can be substituted for the tarragon. It makes for a fresher-tasting sauce.

We now come to our fifth basic sauce, which is not so much a sauce as a method of producing quick sauces for fish already cooked and dished which must not be kept waiting.

## 5 *Sauce Soi-même*

This type of sauce is named to imply that its quality and flavour derive from the reduced stock in which the fish itself has been poached, and to which it has imparted much of its juices and flavour. The clearest example of a *soi-même* is a sauce made from the flavoured liquor in which mussels have been cooked until open. *Beurre manié* in which the proportion of butter to flour is at least 2:1 is stirred into this savoury stock, which is then only very gently simmered for a moment or two before serving. When cream is added to mussels cooked in this way, they appear on the menu as *Moules Bonne Femme*.

When this method is applied to the wine stock in which freshwater fish has been poached, the sauce (with the addition of a binding of egg yolks as described on page 55, cream and lemon juice) becomes *Sauce Conotière*.

The method is simplicity itself and here again, we open up another rich field for the beginner. Such sauces, even if not enriched with eggs, butter and cream, are never negligible or to be despised.

In dealing with our next basic sauce, I have to refer back to the simple relish type of Chameleon Sauce at the beginning of this chapter. I said then that the moment we improved one of these relishes with olive oil, we were in fact making a sophisticated version of a mock-vinaigrette sauce.

## 6 *Sauce Vinaigrette*

2 tablespoons wine vinegar
6 tablespoons olive oil
salt and pepper

This, in all its simplicity, is the true basic vinaigrette which makes a delicious dressing for all green and other salads, and is not to be despised as an accompaniment to grilled, fried or poached fish. But we are still at liberty to create as many variations as we wish by adding herbs, seasonings, condiments of our choosing; provided the proportion of oil to vinegar (i.e. 3:1) is roughly maintained, we shall be making a true vinaigrette sauce. We may, therefore, turn any Chameleon Sauce into a true vinaigrette by reducing the amount of vinegar in the recipe to 2 tablespoons and stirring into it 6 tablespoons olive oil.

## *Six exceptional sauces and relishes*

Before going on to savoury butters, I give recipes for six very interesting sauces and two relishes which do not fall into any of the categories of sauce described above.

### Sauce Gribiche

4 yolks of hard-boiled eggs
1 teaspoon horseradish cream *or* English mustard
½ teaspoon salt
½ teaspoon black pepper
3 dl (½ pint) olive oil
1 dessertspoon wine vinegar
1 teaspoon each of the following, finely chopped: parsley, gherkins, capers, chives, tarragon

Put the egg yolks, the horseradish or mustard and the salt and pepper into a mortar and pound all together into a paste. Now add the oil, drop by drop, until the sauce thickens and all the oil is absorbed. Stir in the vinegar, and fold in all the finely chopped herbs. A perfect sauce for lobster, salmon, pike and for general use.

### Special Tomato Sauce

1 kg (2¼ lb) fresh tomatoes
1·5 dl (¼ pint) white wine
juice 1 lemon
2 cloves garlic
3 fillets anchovy, pounded
50 gr (2 oz) butter
1 tablespoon olive oil
1 tablespoon parsley, finely chopped
1 dessertspoon basil, chopped
freshly ground black pepper
1 teaspoon horseradish cream

Plunge the tomatoes into boiling water for 15 seconds. Remove, allow to cool and peel off the skins. Chop and pound the tomatoes and put into a saucepan with the wine and lemon juice. Cook vigorously until reduced to a thick purée. In another pan, sweat 1 chopped clove of garlic, with the finely pounded fillets of anchovy, in the butter and oil. To this add the reduced tomato purée and the parsley. Cook, stirring, until the tomato is further reduced and begins to get really thick. Remove from fire and stir in the finely chopped basil and the remaining clove of garlic, pounded to a paste with black pepper and the horseradish cream. Let the sauce cool down, cover and allow to stand for at least an hour before using. This sauce can be served hot or cold. If to be served with a hot dish, it should be made very hot but not allowed to boil.

This is one of my favourite sauces for shellfish – especially mussels, served in the shell with a teaspoonful added to each. But it also goes well with many other kinds of fish. A tablespoonful added to a bowl of simple fish soup transforms it into something special.

**Cream and Butter Sauce**

4 tablespoons water
1 shallot, chopped
freshly ground black pepper
salt
100 gr (4 oz) unsalted butter
1·5 dl (¼ pint) double cream

Boil the first 4 ingredients and reduce the liquid to a bare dessertspoonful. Strain and put it into a saucepan in which you have your butter, melted. Beat together. When butter is hot, begin slowly to add the thick cream. Allow the mixture to bubble, until *liaison* is complete. Season with salt and pepper.

This sauce is excellent for fish whose flesh inclines to be dry, such as pike, large salmon or halibut; but it is also good for general use.

**Sauce Caroline** (a lemon and wine sauce)

This delicious sauce is a distant relative of the *Bigarade* or Orange Sauce usually associated with duck.

2 tablespoons wine vinegar
2 tablespoons dry white wine
2 teaspoons sugar
2 tablespoons lemon juice
1·5 dl (¼ pint) fish *fumet*
1 dessertspoon parsley, finely chopped
1 dessertspoon basil, finely chopped

Put the vinegar, the wine and the sugar into a small, heavy saucepan and allow to boil vigorously until the mixture shows signs of caramelization, but do not allow to brown. Add at this point 1 tablespoon lemon juice and the concentrated fish *fumet* (this *fumet* should already have been fully seasoned with salt and pepper). Bring to the boil and again reduce the liquid down to the point of caramelization, but do not allow to turn brown. Withdraw from the fire, add the remaining lemon juice and stir vigorously. Using a brush, coat the grilled or poached fillets with the sauce and sprinkle them with the very finely chopped parsley and basil.

A teaspoon of the juice of a Spanish onion (see page 65), mixed with the lemon juice added in the final stage, gives an interesting variation.

This sweet-and-sour glazing sauce is a favourite of mine. It is quick to make and goes especially well with small sautéed or poached fillets of monkfish. It is also good as a coating for skate, as a change from *beurre noir*. Poached fillets of white fish, whole prawns, segments of eel or lobster, coated with *Sauce Caroline* and then put under a hot grill for a few seconds to brown, are beautiful to look at and strangely enhanced by this simple process.

**Beurre Blanc**

2 shallots, finely chopped
1·5 dl ($\frac{1}{4}$ pint) white wine and white wine vinegar in equal quantities
225 gr (8 oz) unsalted butter
salt
freshly ground black pepper

In a small, heavy saucepan cook the chopped shallots in the wine and vinegar mixture and reduce to 2 tablespoons. Strain, allow to cool, and then beat in the butter, nut by small nut, over very low heat until all the butter is absorbed and the sauce is of the consistency of shiny whipped cream. Taste and season with salt and pepper.

A most delicate sauce for general use with all good white fish – particularly good with turbot, brill or salmon trout.

**Portobello Sauce**

This sauce, based on a combination of black olives and the ripe flesh of the avocado pear, is capable of many variations. It is rich, strongly flavoured and perhaps not for the serious weight-watcher. Depending on the proportions of the main ingredients, the colour varies between a velvety brown and a macabre purplish black. This funereal garb is at the last minute relieved by the addition of a tablespoon of finely chopped red sweet pepper.

12 large, black Kalamata olives
1 small, ripe avocado pear
2 cloves garlic
4 anchovy fillets
juice ½ lemon
1·5 dl (¼ pint) dry red wine
1·5 dl (¼ pint) olive oil
1 teaspoon freshly ground black pepper
2 egg yolks
1 tablespoon red sweet pepper, finely chopped

Stone the olives and pound them with the flesh of the avocado, the 2 cloves of garlic and the anchovy fillets. Add the lemon juice and the wine and put through the blender. Now put the mixture in a small, heavy saucepan, add the olive oil and cook for 7 or 8 minutes, stirring well. Season with the freshly ground black pepper. (It was in this form that I first used this sauce, putting a few drops into each of a hundred mussels served in the half-shell, with memorable results. However, the sauce was not fully bound, and on a subsequent occasion I decided to effect the binding with egg yolks.) To the well-beaten egg yolks in a mixing bowl, add the *cooled* mixture, gradually beating with a wooden spoon. To serve hot, put the mixture in a double saucepan or a *bain-marie* and stir over a gentle heat until the sauce is hot enough. Garnish with the finely chopped red pepper.

For those addicted to the olive and to garlic, this sauce makes an excellent dip to be eaten with chunks of real bread, but its main duty lies with the more powerfully flavoured fish such as skate, conger, dogfish and other members of the shark family (monkfish, porbeagle). I have used it with tunny, squid (*calamari*) and octopus. A septuagenarian friend of mine claims that this sauce has aphrodisiac properties . . .

**Rouille**

*Rouille* is a relish which provides a powerful punch-line in the finishing of fish soups and stews.

3 large cloves garlic
2 large red sweet peppers
2 anchovy fillets
the crumb of 1 small white loaf, soaked in milk and squeezed dry
3 tablespoons olive oil
1·5 dl ($\frac{1}{4}$ pint) good fish stock
black pepper

Chop and pound the garlic, sweet peppers and anchovy to a paste. Add the bread crumb. Work in the olive oil and add the fish stock. Season with freshly ground black pepper.

Substituting 1 tablespoon paprika for the sweet peppers produces a quickly made 'mock-*rouille*' which has its own modest virtues and makes a successful dip.

**Pickled Walnut Relish**

4 pickled walnuts
2 cloves garlic
1 egg yolk
pinch of ground ginger
1 teaspoon horseradish cream
3 tablespoons olive oil

Drain, dry and pound the pickled walnuts with the garlic. Beat in the egg yolk, add the ginger and horseradish and stir all well together. Now pour on the olive oil, slowly, beating until all the oil is absorbed.

This can be served with cold fish, fish salads and fish curries. It is particularly good with cold mackerel and with smoked trout.

**Green Peppercorn Relish**

1 tablespoon green peppercorns
3 fillets salted anchovy
2 tablespoons wine vinegar
3 tablespoons olive oil

Pound the green peppercorns and anchovy fillets together until smooth. Add the wine vinegar and stir in the oil. Allow to stand for 1 hour before using.

Very simple to make, this relish has a unique flavour, excellent with all types of fish or for enlivening fishcakes, pies, salads and soups.

## SAVOURY OR COMPOUND BUTTERS

Savoury or compound butters are small and delicious sauces in their own right. They are excellent with poached, fried or grilled fillets or whole fish. They are also most usefully employed as last-minute garnishes for fish soups of all kinds and for the enrichment of other sauces. In addition, they provide an almost unlimited choice with which to vary *canapés*, *hors-d'oeuvres* and cocktail savouries.

Compound butters form the basis of a number of simple cream sauces for the cook in a hurry. (The butters can be stored in the deep freeze for use when required.) Simply melt the compound butter in a saucepan over a low heat, and beat into it 1·5 dl (¼ pint) cream. As there are at least thirty compound butters in the French repertoire, this leaves the field fairly wide open to even the laziest and most retrograde of home cooks.

For every 100 gr (4 oz) butter required (this is ample for 4 to 5 people), 2 tablespoons herbs or other ingredients will, in almost every case, be found sufficient. In the following brief recipes, this proportion of butter to other ingredients will be adhered to unless otherwise stated.

Compound butters are simple and quick to make, with one or two exceptions – such as Montpellier Butter (see below) – which no one will want to make every day. Many and various though they are, all compound butters go well with any kind of fish.

The simplest method of making any of these compound butters quickly is to melt the butter over a very low heat, chop up the herbs or other ingredients (not too finely) and pass everything through a blender. When thoroughly blended, pour into a dish and leave to solidify. This is one sphere of cookery in which the electric blender fully justifies its cost and the trouble of mounting, dismounting and thoroughly cleaning.

**Basic recipe:**
**Parsley Butter** (*Maître d'Hôtel* Butter)

I give this recipe here, out of order, because the process used in making it applies to butters made with the following: capers, fennel, tarragon, basil, chervil, chives, celery.

Knead 2 tablespoons finely chopped parsley with 100 gr (4 oz) butter. Season with $\frac{1}{2}$ teaspoon lemon juice, salt and freshly ground black pepper.

This butter is a universal standby for all good white fish – poached, grilled or fried – and for soups, sauces and so on.

**Anchovy Butter**
3 anchovy fillets are pounded to a paste and blended with the butter. Add a little black pepper, the pounded flesh of 1 large, soft black olive and a little grated onion.

**Black Peppercorn Butter**
1 teaspoon freshly ground black peppercorns is mixed in with the butter and 1 teaspoon grated onion.

**Caviare/Lumpfish Roe/Salmon Roe Butter**
Black or red lumpfish roe can be used. Pound 1–2 tablespoons roe with the butter; add 1 teaspoon lemon juice and black pepper – no salt. For any good white fish – grilled, fried or poached.

**Chivry Butter**
Use 1 teaspoon of each of the following, finely chopped: fresh tarragon, chervil, chives, onion. Knead with the butter, seasoning with salt and black pepper. For garnishing sauces, *canapés*, *hors-d'oeuvres*.

**Colbert Butter**
Parsley Butter (see above) enriched with a little strong jelly made from a reduced veal-bone stock. For fried, stuffed fish (*à la Colbert*) and for general use.

**Crab Butter**
*White:* 1–2 tablespoons white crabmeat, pounded with the butter and seasoned with a little lemon juice and red pepper (cayenne). *Red:* coral from the female crab, treated as above. *Brown:* use the

body meat of the crab, pounded with 1 teaspoon finely chopped chives. Proceed as for white crabmeat.

**Crayfish Butter**

Pound 1–2 tablespoons cooked and shelled crayfish meat. Incorporate into butter and pass through a sieve. Season with salt and black pepper.

**Garlic Butter**

Pound 3 cloves garlic, 1 dessertspoon chopped parsley and 1 finely chopped shallot. Knead with the butter. For general use – if you like garlic.

**Green Butter**

Pound a few leaves of uncooked spinach to extract their juices and colour. Amalgamate juices with the butter. Season with salt and black pepper. For use in white sauces, and for garnishing soups.

**Green Peppercorn Butter**

Pound 1 dessertspoon green peppercorns and amalgamate them with the butter. Marvellous with all fried, grilled and poached fish. Try it, melted, with mussels – a drop or two to each one.

**Herring or Bloater Roe Butter**

Add to the pounded roe 1 teaspoon anchovy essence, 1 teaspoon grated onion. Combine with the butter and season with black pepper and salt.

This is excellent for *hors-d'oeuvres* and *canapés*, but also goes with most grilled and poached fish. Bloater roes, hard or soft, are a great delicacy, but it is becoming increasingly difficult to find a bloater when you want one.

**Lemon Butter**

1 teaspoon of the finely grated outer rind of the lemon is mixed in with the butter; season with salt and black pepper.

**Lobster Butter**

The lobster coral and roe are pounded with other parts of the cooked lobster, and 1–2 tablespoons of this are incorporated with the butter, salt and black pepper. If shell is pounded up with the lobster trimmings, then the butter must be passed through a sieve. For garnish; for flavour; for adding to sauces and soups.

### Montpellier Butter

You will need 1 chopped teaspoon of each of the following green herbs, finely chopped: parsley, chives, watercress, basil. Pound all together and add 1 clove garlic, 1 shallot and 1 gherkin, all finely chopped and pounded; 1 dessertspoon chopped capers and 2 small, pounded anchovy fillets. Combine the resulting paste with the butter. Add the yolk of a hard-boiled egg and 2 tablespoons olive oil. Blend all well together, seasoning with salt and black pepper. Spread on a plate and allow to set. Excellent for shellfish, hot or cold. A decorative butter for any good grilled fish.

### Mushroom Butter

Chop and pound 3 or 4 raw button mushrooms. Incorporate into the butter, seasoning with a pinch of nutmeg and salt and black pepper.

### Mustard/Horseradish Butter

Work 1 heaped teaspoon prepared English mustard into the butter with 1 teaspoon finely chopped chives. Substitute horseradish for mustard in the above, or use both in conjunction for variety. These are excellent butters for herring, mackerel, tunny and pickled fish.

### Paprika Butter

Work 1 dessertspoon paprika into the butter with 1 teaspoon finely chopped red sweet pepper. Add salt, black pepper and a few drops of lemon juice.

### Pimento Butter

Finely chop or pound 1 dessertspoon pimentos (sweet peppers). Incorporate with the butter, seasoning with a little salt and black pepper.

### Prawn or Shrimp Butter

See method for Crayfish Butter, above.

### Sardine Butter

Pound 2 or 3 tinned sardines to a paste. Add 1 teaspoon anchovy essence or 1 pounded anchovy fillet. Combine with the butter, finishing with a few drops of Worcester sauce *or* vinegar and black pepper.

### Shallot Butter

Combine 2 tablespoons finely chopped and pounded shallots with the butter and add salt, black pepper and a few drops of lemon juice.

### Tomato Butter

Combine 1 tablespoon thick, freshly made (or tinned, in emergencies) tomato purée with 1 teaspoon finely chopped basil and 1 teaspoon finely chopped chives. Amalgamate with the butter.

### Watercress Butter

Combine 1 tablespoon finely chopped and pounded watercress leaves with the butter, and work in 1 teaspoon finely chopped parsley.

THE LOBSTER.

The sprat

The sardine

The whitebait

The anchovy

# Hors-d'oeuvres and savouries

## HORS-D'OEUVRES

In tender youth I used to consider the word '*hors-d'oeuvres*' the most exciting on the menu. Nowadays, however, I go pale at the sound of the trolley approaching, even if it isn't aimed at me personally.

At first sight, the very name suggests the lazy product of the shiftless, who ought to be out of work. There are pleasant exceptions, but many restaurants seem still to be cemented in a convention which dictates the following ritual offerings: one fillet of anchovy *or* whole sardine, half a fillet of Bismarck herring, one dessertspoon coleslaw *or* Russian salad *or* potato salad, one slice hard-boiled egg, one slice tomato *or* beetroot, one olive, one tablespoon baked beans, the whole resting on two very weary outer leaves of lettuce.

I take *hors-d'oeuvre* really to mean the first course served at table, which by its excellence should put everyone in a good humour, sharpen up the appetite and the repartee, and augur (Bacchus aiding) fine things to come.

Personally, all that anyone need do is put before me a couple of dozen Colchester oysters in the deep shell, or 100 gr (4 oz) Beluga caviare, rolled up in thin slices of the pinkest of smoked salmon (memories of Tokatlyan's, Istanbul, 1944, assail me here). To these two happy preludes, *hors concours*, I add a recipe supplied to me by the beautiful wife of one of the foremost authorities on antique watches – Mrs Nita Denton, who purveys *haute* (strictly kosher) *cuisine* delicacies to weddings and bar mitzvahs.

**Solomon's Rolls** (salmon-stuffed salmon)
450 gr (1 lb) fresh Scotch salmon, poached
¼ teaspoon freshly ground black pepper
1 tablespoon mayonnaise (see page 69)
6 spring onions, finely chopped
450 gr (1 lb) smoked salmon, finely sliced
5 lemons
1 crisp lettuce

Skin and fillet the salmon and pound to a paste; add the pepper, the mayonnaise and a squeeze of lemon juice, and continue to pound all together until the mixture is creamy. Add the very finely chopped white of the spring onions.

Place a portion of this creamy mixture at one end of each slice of smoked salmon and roll into good tight cylinders. Serve, with segments of lemon, on crisp lettuce leaves. This quantity serves ten people.

In view of the state of the nation, this contemporary recipe has a certain effrontery I admire. However, we can't always be eating oysters, caviare and salmon, and – apart from smoked trout, eel and mackerel, which are obvious candidates and need little preparation – there are many other delicious first courses we can prepare and serve without ruining the weekly budget. For special occasions a selection of dishes, but often just one, can be chosen from the following categories:

**1** Freshly made fish pâtés
**2** Fish salads
**3** Some kinds of fishcake or dumpling
**4** Dips
**5** Small fish and crustacea
**6** Individual mousses or soufflés
**7** Fish cocktails

## *1 Fish pâtés*

A fish pâté should be served, very cold, in a terrine. It should be eaten with toast or slices of crisp French bread.

**Herring Pâté** (a basic recipe for pâté)
225 gr (8 oz) skinned, filleted and lightly cooked fresh herring
100 gr (4 oz) butter
1 shallot, finely chopped and pounded
1 tablespoon parsley, chopped
½ clove garlic, chopped
3 anchovy fillets, pounded
pinch of cayenne pepper
1 teaspoon freshly ground black pepper
1 dessertspoon Worcester sauce
4 tablespoons fish *fumet* (see page 59)

Blend all the ingredients except the fish *fumet* together into a smooth paste. Stir in the *fumet*, which should be cold and on the point of setting.

Press your pâté firmly down into a terrine. Cover and put in the refrigerator to set. Serve very cold. If it is to be kept for more than 12 hours, seal it with a layer of melted butter before covering.

This recipe works well with all types of white fish, with salmon, trout, and the crustacea. In the case of kippers, bloaters, smoked haddock or smoked cod roe, omit the anchovy fillet and adjust seasoning with salt before putting the pâté into the terrine. Turtle Soup or Crosse & Blackwell's Consommé can replace the *fumet*.

Variations of this recipe can be made by substituting other ingredients for those given above – 1 teaspoon horseradish cream for the anchovy, basil for the parsley, and so on.

**Foulkes' Smoked Trout Pâté**
1 smoked trout
juice 1 lemon
100 gr (4 oz) fresh, unsalted cream cheese
½ teaspoon freshly ground black pepper
½ teaspoon paprika
salt (optional)

Skin and fillet the trout and put the flesh through the blender with the lemon juice. Work in the cream cheese thoroughly. Season with pepper and paprika. Taste for seasoning with salt – and possibly a little more lemon juice. Press into a terrine and put in the refrigerator for a couple of hours. If the pâté is to be kept, seal with melted butter (see under Herring Pâté, above).

I am indebted to a friend for the above recipe. Of the simplest kind, it can be applied to all smoked fish such as salmon, haddock, kipper, cod roe, mackerel and eel.

### Smoked Eel Pâté

225 gr (8 oz) smoked eel
2 anchovy fillets
1 dessertspoon chives, finely chopped
100 gr (4 oz) butter
1 teaspoon lemon juice
few drops only of sherry, Marsala, port *or* Madeira
pinch each of red and black pepper, grated nutmeg, powdered dried thyme

Skin, fillet and pound the flesh of the smoked eel. Add all the other ingredients and pound together into a smooth, thick paste. Press the mixture down into a terrine, cover closely and allow to stand in the refrigerator for at least 3 hours. Serve with brown bread, or toast, and butter. If the pâté is to be kept, seal with melted butter (see under Herring Pâté, above).

### Panic Pâté

225 gr (8 oz) any cooked *or* tinned, drained fish
1 heaped teaspoon *Patum Peperium or* 1 dessertspoon anchovy essence
juice ½ lemon
1 tablespoon Worcester sauce
freshly ground black pepper

Pound and blend all ingredients together into a firm paste. When friends or freeloaders suddenly descend, this pâté can be put together in a few minutes, as a holding operation while you start making the omelette mixture.

Sheer poetry in paste form, *Patum Peperium* or Gentleman's Relish has – thank heaven – survived, albeit in a plastic mac, into these prosaic times, bringing a breath of those palmy days when sandwiches were centimetre-thin and luncheon baskets an essential part of every gentleman's equipment. *Patum* survives, but we must be vigilant or, like so many other well-loved confections, it may gently vanish one day.

Another useful dish in this category is Potted Shrimps (see page 168).

## 2 Fish salads

The fish salad recipe on page 204 – or adaptations of it – can serve admirably as an *hors-d'oeuvre* dish. Another excellent first-course salad is the following.

**Salade Niçoise**

3 tomatoes, peeled and sliced
3 or 4 small potatoes, cooked and diced
French beans, cooked and diced
8 small anchovy fillets
4 tablespoons plain vinaigrette sauce (see page 71)
1 dessertspoon basil, chopped
1 dessertspoon chervil, chopped
1 dessertspoon tarragon, chopped
8 black olives
450 gr (1 lb) fish

Distribute the tomato slices round the edge of a shallow dish. Pile the diced potato and French beans in the middle. Lay on them the anchovy fillets. Stir the vinaigrette and pour it over the whole. Sprinkle the basil over the tomatoes, and the tarragon and chervil, mixed, over the diced vegetables; decorate the dish with the olives.

As it stands, the *Niçoise* salad provides a good, clean background for all white fish, crustacea, shellfish and cephalopods. Tinned tunnyfish is particularly suitable. You can use segments of eel, small fingers of monkfish, dogfish, skate, sole, brill, turbot or halibut; pieces of lobster, scallops or crayfish, or whole shrimps; these should be treated in one of the two ways described below.

*Marinade for Salade Niçoise*

1·5 dl ($\frac{1}{4}$ pint) water
3 dl ($\frac{1}{2}$ pint) vinegar
1·5 dl ($\frac{1}{4}$ pint) white wine
juice 1 lemon
1 small chilli pepper, crushed
1 clove garlic, crushed
1 tablespoon Spanish onion juice
1 stick celery, chopped and bruised
1 bay leaf
1 teaspoon salt
10 black peppercorns, crushed
2 bruised cloves

This is a good, rich (and also variable) marinade. Pack your fish pieces tightly into a small dish so that the marinade covers them. The quantity given here is for 450 gr (1 lb) of fish cut into small pieces.

After marinating for at least 3 hours, drain and lay the pieces in an orderly manner on your *Niçoise*, between the black olives and the anchovies.

*Coating syrup for fish*

As an alternative to marinating the fish for putting into your *Niçoise*, a coating sauce (of the *Caroline* type given on page 73) can be made, using the same ingredients as those used for the marinade above, but adding a teaspoon of sugar and a pinch of cayenne pepper and taking care to remove the hot chilli.

In a saucepan, boil all the marinade ingredients (except the chilli) and reduce the liquid by two-thirds. At this point, strain the liquid into a small, heavy pan and add the sugar and cayenne pepper. Boil and reduce the liquid until it begins to be syrupy and remove from the fire as it begins to froth up prior to caramelization. Pour on to a cold plate and either gently roll the pieces of fish in the syrup or coat them carefully using a brush. Now incorporate them into the *Niçoise*, between the anchovies and the black olives.

## *3 Fishcakes and fish dumplings*

Crabmeat croquettes (see page 131), small fishcakes (see page 188), and small *quenelles*, or dumplings (see pages 158 and 189) come into this category. Those made with shrimp, prawn, lobster or crayfish meat usually find most favour. They can be served with a sauce or, if there is a 'dip' on the table, they can be 'dunked' in it before being eaten.

## *4 Dips*

**Taramasalata** (smoked cod roe dip)

This is a not unworthy successor to the original *taramasalata* of Greek and Mediterranean regions which, certainly in 1945, was still being made from the preserved roe of the grey mullet.

225 gr (8 oz) smoked cod roe
2 cloves garlic, crushed and pounded
100 gr (4 oz) cream cheese
1½ tablespoons olive oil
1 tablespoon lemon juice
freshly ground black pepper
1 dessertspoon chives, chopped

Mix the cod roe, garlic and cream cheese together thoroughly. Slowly fold in the olive oil and then the lemon juice. Sprinkle with black pepper and chives.

**Crab-coral Dip** (a summer dip)
225 gr (8 oz) red coral from the female crab
100 gr (4 oz) Boursin cheese (the 'garlic and fine herbs' kind)
1 tablespoon lemon juice
freshly ground black pepper
½ teaspoon salt
1 dessertspoon parsley, chopped

Pound the crab coral with the Boursin. Fold in the oil and the lemon juice. Season with pepper and salt, and sprinkle with parsley.

A cold *Sauce Béarnaise* (see page 68) made with olive oil makes a splendid dip for cold crustacea. So do *Rouille* (see page 76) and *Aïoli* (see page 69).

## *5 Small fish and crustacea*

In this category, too, a wide choice is available. I suggest smoked sprats or brisling (just heated through), served with mustard or horseradish and segments of lemon; and scampi, prawns, crayfish, (boiled), served with a cold *Béarnaise* (see page 68) or a *Sauce Rémoulade* (see page 70). *Coquilles St Jacques* (see page 166), or other white fish or crustacea *en coquilles*, make excellent *hors-d'oeuvres*.

Here is one of my favourite starters:

**Stuffed Mussels**
Many stuffings can be used, for example, *Sauce Aurore* (page 59), Portobello Sauce (page 74), melted Garlic Butter (page 79), *Sauce Mornay* (page 62); I recommend the Special Tomato Sauce on page

72. The mussels should be opened in the usual way (see page 35) and the juices from them reduced and added to the chosen sauce. Lay the mussels in the half-shell on plates and put 1 teaspoon of sauce into each one. A dozen mussels per person is ample and 3 dl (½ pint) of sauce should be plenty. These can be served hot or cold.

## *6 Fish mousses and soufflés*

Mousses make excellent first courses and this, I feel, is their proper role. The following recipe can be used to make mousses with all kinds of fish.

### Smoked Haddock Mousse

450 gr (1 lb) cooked smoked Finnan haddock
the whites of 2 large eggs
½ teaspoon pepper
a pinch nutmeg
a *soupçon* of powdered bay leaf
4·5 dl (¾ pint) double cream

Skin, fillet and flake the haddock. Pound it to a paste, adding gradually during the process the egg whites and the seasoning. Sieve, cover and place in the refrigerator for 1½ hours. Then stir in the double cream with a wooden spoon. Put the mixture into a mould, stand in a pan of boiling water and poach in a moderate oven (180°C, 350°F, gas 4) for 25 minutes or until properly set. The mould should be big enough to allow for expansion during cooking of up to one-third.

Individual soufflés can be made using a variety of different fish, shellfish and crustacea; see the basic recipe for soufflés on page 203.

## *7 Fish cocktails*

By international convention among restaurateurs, the tiny inhabitants of shellfish cocktails invariably come to the table covered in an insipid pale pink sauce and resting on a thick mattress of old shredded lettuce designed to keep their numbers to a minimum.

I suggest the following variation. Fresh prawns are expensive, but not much more expensive than the tinned variety, which are soft and rather tasteless.

## Prawn Cocktail

4 heaped tablespoons *rocca* (obtainable from Cypriot greengrocers) *or* shredded chervil *or* shredded watercress
1 small green sweet pepper, finely sliced
salt and black pepper
8 large king prawns, shelled
3 dl ($\frac{1}{2}$ pint) *court-bouillon* 3 (see page 58)
a few drops Green Peppercorn Relish (see page 76) *or* Tabasco sauce
juice 1 lemon
4 tablespoons tomato juice
parsley for garnish

Distribute the greenery and green pepper around the bottom and sides of 4 large wineglasses. Sprinkle with salt and pepper. Now slice the prawns (previously boiled for 6 minutes in the stock) very finely lengthwise from head to tail. Embed them in the greenery. Sprinkle over them the peppercorn relish or Tabasco, add the lemon juice and then the tomato juice (fresh is much better; tinned can be used) to just below the rim of the glass. Leave to stand for about half an hour in the refrigerator before serving, garnished with sprigs of parsley.

Delicious cocktails can be made with oysters, crab, poached mussels, poached and chopped scallops – and with any firm white fish (sole, whiting, monkfish, smelts), cooked, diced and flaked – as well as with prawns.

Using the above recipe, substitute for the tomato and lemon dressing: *in cocktails to be served cold:* plain Mayonnaise, *Sauce Rémoulade*, *Mayonnaise Escoffier*, *Sauce Tartare, Sauce Gribiche,* Green Sauce. (Ideally a little jellied fish *fumet* or jellied consommé should be added to the fish before putting in your sauce.)
*for cocktails to be served hot: Sauces Marinière*, *Poulette*, *Normande*, *Bercy Béarnaise*, *Hollandaise* (and its variations), or the following *béchamel*-based sauces: Fennel, Parsley, Green Peppercorn.

## Marinated Kipper Fillets

1 packet kipper fillets
1 onion
1 bay leaf
4 tablespoons olive oil
2 tablespoons white wine vinegar
salt and black pepper
pinch castor sugar
pinch mustard powder

Slice the onion into very thin rings. Remove the skins from the kipper fillets, cut them into 5 cm (2 in) pieces and arrange them with the rings of onion and the bay leaf in a small dish. Make a marinade from the remaining ingredients and pour this over the kippers. Put in the refrigerator to chill for at least 4 hours and serve with brown bread and butter or toast.

## AFTER-DINNER SAVOURIES

The savoury served after the sweet at dinner appears to be a vanishing custom. Nevertheless, for traditionalists and also for those who dislike (or fear) sweets, I give below two old stagers which still appeal to me.

### Sardines on Toast

1 large tin sardines
2 anchovy fillets
juice ½ lemon
a few drops of Tabasco sauce *or* a pinch of cayenne pepper
freshly ground black pepper
1 teaspoon chives, chopped
1 teaspoon parsley, chopped
4 slices bread, toasted on one side only (and with the crusts cut off)

Mash the sardines and the anchovy fillets. Add the other ingredients and work into a paste. Spread this paste on the untoasted side of the bread and grill for 5 minutes.

The bread may, optionally, be rubbed with garlic before being toasted.

### Angels on Horseback

8 oysters
8 rashers very finely cut bacon
4 slices toast, with the crusts cut off

Wrap each oyster in a strip of the thin bacon and skewer together with a cocktail stick. Grill until the bacon is crisp. Remove skewers, and serve 2 per person, on toast.

## COCKTAIL SAVOURIES

### Fish canapés

Unfortunately, fragments of various fish, sicklied o'er with various substances and resting on limp toast are still to be found at official receptions and at cocktail parties serviced by caterers. Why have they survived?

I well remember (when I was working at a foreign embassy in London in the late 1940s) a reception at which a famous caterer had excelled himself with his piping bag and in the construction of every shape known to aspic geometry. Unfortunately, so crowded was the scene that very few people could, without drawing unwelcome attention to themselves, partake of the jewelled morsels. Also, a great deal of the food was so cunningly placed as to be quite out of reach. When I pointed this out to a waiter (supplied by the caterer) he gave me a solemn wink such as one expects to see on the impassive face of a hired mourner at a Connemara funeral, and said 'It's all in the game, sir.' I was too busy then to take the matter further, but later, when all the guests had left and the fragments (of which there were considerably more than twelve baskets) had been packed up and taken away, it occurred to me that a study of the migratory habits of the *canapé* in diplomatic circles might be of some interest. On a subsequent occasion, therefore, I conspired with friends to mark a number of *canapés* with golf tees, embedding them deep in the aspic so that they appeared to be part of the decoration. These peregrinating *canapés* were later sighted at various receptions around London, and for a week or two provided an 'in' joke which relieved the tedium of these pointless functions.

The confection of these miniature masterpieces for the cocktail hour is not congenial to my temperament, nor do I propose to encourage their production in the home. As far as food to accompany cocktails or aperitifs is concerned, it seems to me that the only dividing line between this food and the *hors-d'oeuvre* should lie in the amount served of each delicacy and the 'vehicle' on or in which it is conveyed to the mouth. If you are going to serve smoked salmon as a first course at a meal, you will probably settle for fish pâté on *croûtons* with the drinks. If serving a pâté as a first course, then small pieces of smoked salmon will be in order with the cocktails.

My own solution to the 'bits and pieces with drinks' problem lies in the frequent use of savoury butters, especially those made with herring or bloater roe and those made with prawn, shrimp, crayfish or crabmeat (see pages 77–81). These butters can be spread on *croûtons* or small pieces of bread; alternatively, they can be incorporated into the yolks of hard-boiled eggs. This mixture is then returned to the halved whites of egg and garnished with a teaspoon of mayonnaise or any of the sauces derived from it (see pages 69–70). *Patum Peperium* can also be used in these ways, and is a bait always greedily taken.

THE CRAB.

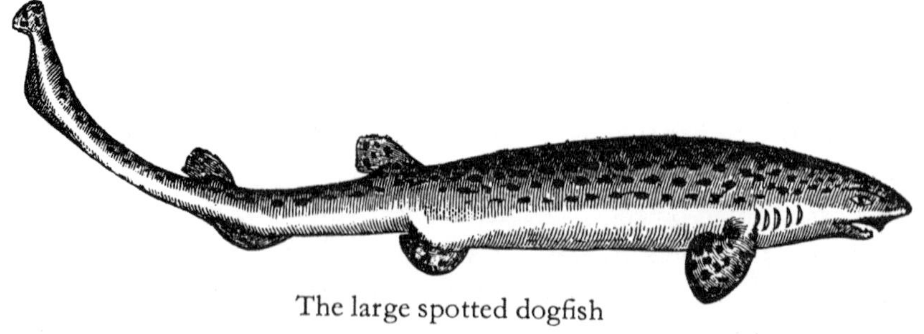

The large spotted dogfish

# Fish soups

It is sad to note that among a large number of traditional recipes collected by Florence White for her lively book *Good Things in England*, there is not one recipe for a genuine mixed fish soup; stewed eels and one oyster soup are all she can give us.

I find it extraordinary that in these 'sea-girt isles' so little attention has been given in the past to the fish soup. This can be as simple or as complex, as strong (in a wide variety of flavours) or as bland (even to sick-room standards) as desired. It is in soups that the versatility and compatibility of fishes can be seen at their best. This is one important advantage fish has over meat. You cannot mix beef, pork, mutton and poultry together without inducing an upsurge of nausea (though no doubt such unholy multiple marriages are not unknown in the modern pie factory). With fish, on the other hand, the individual flavours of several different varieties can be blended in soup to create a distinctive, new and delicious flavour.

The fish best suited to soups include all firm white fish, the crustacea, shellfish and cephalopods. The oilier varieties of fish, such as the herring, mackerel, sprat and sardine, do not perform well in soups, as the oil they exude can smell and taste of staleness under the chemical changes which occur during cooking.

As to garnish, these soups can be greatly enhanced by one – or more – of the savoury butters (see pages 77–81), but my own practice has often been just to sprinkle them with a dessertspoon of finely chopped parsley and chives in equal proportions, after stirring in a few drops of lemon juice.

*Cooking note:* For the successful and trouble-free making of these soups, the asparagus kettle (described on page 26) is invaluable. The fish for destruction can be put in first, spread out evenly over the bottom of the pan; the fish to be poached, cut up and served in the soup can then rest on the retractable perforated tray and be easily withdrawn when cooked.

Of the following recipes, the first one is what I would call a *basic* fish soup; simple to make, inexpensive, but nevertheless providing a most comforting first course for any dinner. It also demonstrates, in easy form, some essential procedures involved in making fish soup of any kind.

**Fish Soup** (basic recipe)
*ingredients for four* 3-*dl* (½-*pint*) *portions:*
450 gr (1 lb) white fish (see below)
1·5 litres (2½ pints) water
1 medium onion
½ stick celery
1 carrot
*bouquet garni* (thyme, rosemary, fennel)
1 large glass white wine
salt and pepper
1 heaped tablespoon parsley, finely chopped
50 gr (2 oz) butter

For the fish, 1 suggest 100 gr (4 oz) coley, a small whiting, 2 knobs skate, a 100-gr (4-oz) cutlet conger eel. If you are on good terms with your fishmonger, ask him to throw in some sole or plaice bones (nowadays a cod's head is too much to hope for).

Into a large, wide saucepan, put the water, the finely chopped onion, celery and carrot, the *bouquet garni*, white wine and seasoning. Now put in all the fish, place the pan on the fire and bring the contents briskly to simmering point. Reduce heat and let the fish poach gently for 5–6 minutes. By this time the coley and whiting will be near to being cooked. Remove first the conger, then the skate, from the pan. Remove their bones and return these to the pan. Now raise heat and boil fast to reduce the amount of liquid by about one-fifth. As the boiling proceeds, the whiting and the coley will disintegrate.

With a wooden spoon, pound the debris of fish in the pan, then strain through a sieve or work through a tamis into a bowl. Return the liquid to the pan. With a sharp knife, cut the skate and conger into small pieces and return them to the pan. Turn up the heat and let the skate and conger pieces simmer for 6 minutes, but do not boil. Adjust seasoning with salt and pepper and ladle into small soup bowls. Add a small nut of Parsley Butter (see page 78) to each, and serve.

*Cooking notes:* This recipe will produce a fish broth with only the very fine debris of the pounded fish in suspension (apart, of course, from the pieces of skate and conger). If a thicker, opaque soup is required, then small nuts of *beurre manié* (see page 56) in the proportion of 75 gr (3 oz) butter to 50 gr (2 oz) flour should be dropped into the liquid and boiled briskly until the desired consistency is reached (about 10 minutes). This should be done before the skate and conger are returned to the pan after being cut up.

The poaching time will vary with the rate at which the liquid has been brought up to simmering point – I myself favour a fairly brisk rate, especially in this and other soup recipes where the portions of fish are small.

I summarize here the procedures to be followed in the preparation of this basic type of soup.

**1** In the selection of fish which is to be disintegrated in the flavoured stock, your choice will determine the essential flavour of your end product.

**2** The fish which you choose to appear in the final soup must be poached only to the point at which it is just cooked, and then put to one side until the final stage of cooking, when it is returned to the pan to heat through.

**3** The stock must be reduced, and the fish left in it must disintegrate.

**4** The fragments of fish and the vegetables and seasonings must be pounded in the stock, and the whole passed through a sieve; your stock has now become your soup.

## Combinations of Fish

In varying the recipe described above, I have used the following combinations of fish:

| *To be poached, cut up and served in soup* | *For disintegration into stock* |
|---|---|
| Skate and conger | Whiting and coley (or smelt) |
| Gurnard | Cod and smelt |
| Haddock, codling | Gurnard |
| Monkfish | Small red mullet |
| Rock salmon (dogfish) | Garfish |
| Eel | Small squid* and dab |
| Lemon sole | Small octopus* and dab |
| Small red mullet | Squid* and plaice |
| Small bream | Plaice |
| Garfish | Dab and small red mullet |

*Where squid and octopus are used in the stock, they are not, of course, boiled to destruction or sieved, but are put aside, later cooked until tender, and used for other purposes.

In each case, the soup may be slightly thickened by the *beurre manié* method (see page 56).

It may appear to be vandalism to condemn red mullet, however small, to destruction in the stock pot, but this fish supplies a unique flavour to a stock, and we are all entitled to be Genghis Khans in our own kitchens.

## *The enrichment of soups*

In thickening or binding our basic fish soup with kneaded butter, we took a first step towards the rich *bisques* and *velouté* soups which are so seldom made at home. Suppose we go further and incorporate into our thickened basic soup the yolks of 2 eggs (in the manner described on page 55), and thereafter blend in, on a low heat, 50 gr (2 oz) butter. Our simple soup begins to look rich indeed. To increase its flavour, let us now add 1·5 dl ($\frac{1}{4}$ pint) of concentrated fish *fumet*, made from trimmings of Dover sole, and 2 tablespoons purée of celery heart, parsley and chives, loosened with 1·5 dl ($\frac{1}{4}$ pint) rich cream. For good measure, toss in a tablespoon of brandy and mix all together, and lo! – in one paragraph we have stumbled, perhaps irreverently, a long way from our basic, homespun recipe, and fallen head first into an expense-account *velouté* soup!

The point I wish to make is that, at any stage in the enrichment of our basic soup, we are at liberty to stop and go no further. At each stage we shall have an excellent and viable soup, but the temptation to go the whole hog must not, in a free society, be removed and so we move on to the *velouté* and the *bisque*.

## *Velouté soups*

The fish *velouté* is a smooth, velvety soup which relies for its texture on the generous use of eggs, cream and butter in its finishing stages. Attractive and savoury garnishes complete the picture. For me, such a soup makes a complete meal and anything that comes after is an anticlimax. Though restaurants seem to reserve the process for only the most expensive ingredients, such as lobster, sole, crayfish and prawns, we should learn to adapt it to humbler or underrated kinds of fish, which will be found to answer very well.

We can approach the making of *velouté* soups in two ways:

**1** We can start with a fish *velouté* sauce, made with a good stock, and thin it down to soup consistency with the reduced cooking liquor of the fish to feature in the soup, *or*

**2** We can make a special fish stock to suit the occasion, poach our fish in it and, after removal of the fish, thicken our stock to soup consistency by the *beurre manié* method.

**Basic recipe 1**

225 gr (8 oz) white fish
9 dl (1½ pints) good fish stock
6 dl (1 pint) fish *velouté* sauce (see page 59)
2 egg yolks
1·5 dl (¼ pint) cream
50 gr (2 oz) butter
1 tablespoon white wine *or* 1 dessertspoon sherry or Marsala *and/or* 1 dessertspoon lemon juice
salt and pepper
*for garnish:* any selected savoury butter

Poach the cleaned and gutted white fish in the stock for 3–4 minutes until just cooked. Remove fish; skin and fillet. Return skin, bones and head to stock, and boil up for 15 minutes. Meanwhile, pound your white fish to a purée and put aside. Strain the stock and add the *velouté*. Raise heat, and allow to simmer while stirring for 5–6 minutes. Remove from fire and stir in the pounded fish meat. Then pass through a fine sieve. Return to the pan and bring to simmering point. Remove from fire. Add the egg yolks, beaten up with the cream. Stir well together. Now work in the butter. Heat the soup up to simmering point and allow to simmer very gently for a few moments only. Add the wine *and/or* lemon juice, and test for seasoning with salt and pepper. Garnish and serve.

**Basic recipe 2**

225 gr (8 oz) white fish
1·5 litres ($2\frac{1}{2}$ pints) *court-bouillon* 2 (see page 58)
50 gr (2 oz) butter
50 gr (2 oz) flour
2 egg yolks
1·5 dl ($\frac{1}{4}$ pint) cream
50 gr (2 oz) butter
1 tablespoon white wine *or* 1 dessertspoon Marsala or sherry *and/or* 1 dessertspoon lemon juice
salt and pepper
*for garnish:* 1 tablespoon feathery-grated carrot and 1 tablespoon finely chopped parsley

Follow the preceding recipe, but after boiling the stock with the head, bones and trimmings of your fish, and straining it, thicken it with the kneaded butter and flour (*beurre manié*). Bind with egg, cream and butter as above.

## *A selection of velouté soup recipes*

### Potage Bagration

This is a *velouté* made with sole. Using 225 gr (8 oz) fillet of sole, which you have first lightly sautéed in butter, proceed by either of the two basic methods given above. Reserve a few small pieces of the sole to serve as a garnish for the completed soup. Garnish further with Caviare (lumpfish roe), Red Crab or Crayfish Butter.

### Velouté of Mussels

This splendid soup can be made by adding 6 dl (1 pint) of the liquid in which mussels have been cooked to the same quantity of *velouté* sauce which has been made from a fish stock strongly flavoured with leeks; complete the process of thickening with egg yolks, cream and butter. Serve 4 or 5 poached mussels as garnish to each plate of soup.

A stronger-flavoured version of this soup is obtained by adding a purée of mussels themselves to the *velouté*. Serve with Celery, Mild Fennel, or Parsley Butter.

**Velouté of Red Mullet**
The red mullet makes an outstanding *velouté* soup. Use the small fish and garnish with Parsley or Watercress Butter. After cleaning, the mullet should be well sautéed in butter before you fillet and pound the flesh, including the liver.

**Velouté of Monkfish**
This beautiful fish, the flavour of which 'equivocates' between the crayfish and the octopus, is at its best in a *velouté* soup. It should be served garnished with very small *goujons* of its own poached fillets and deserves a good Crayfish as well as a Parsley Butter.

**Velouté of Whiting or Smelts**
These are both well-known menu soups. For garnish, use a little of both a Black Pepper and a Parsley Butter.

Following the methods shown here, *velouté* soups can also be made with any of the following fish: gurnard, garfish, cod, hake, halibut, brill, dogfish (rock salmon), grey mullet.

**Velouté de Homard**
1 small lobster
50 gr (2 oz) butter
50 gr (2 oz) mushrooms, chopped
1 stalk celery, chopped
2 tablespoons parsley, finely chopped
1 small shallot, finely sliced
2 tablespoons brandy
1 glass white wine
6 dl (1 pint) fish stock (see page 58–9)
6 dl (1 pint) *velouté* sauce (see page 98)

Kill (see page 145) and chop the lobster – shell and all – into small pieces. Heat the butter in a frying pan, make a *mirepoix* by adding the mushrooms, celery, parsley and shallot and fry lightly. Add the pieces of lobster and let them take on a good colour. Then warm the brandy, set it alight and pour it over the lobster. Next, throw in the wine and pour over the fish stock. Simmer for 5–10 minutes and then strain off the cooking liquid. Now, pound the lobster, shell as well, with the *mirepoix* ingredients; sieve and add the purée to the *velouté* sauce. Stir in the strained cooking liquid and simmer for a few minutes. Bind with egg yolk, cream and butter, as in the basic recipes. Garnish with a few thin slices of lobster reserved for the purpose and with pats of Parsley Butter.

*Veloutés* of crawfish, crayfish and prawns are all made in the same way as *Velouté de Homard.*

## *The Bisque*

Great soups, these *bisques*! And popular with the restaurateurs – for whom the idea that a soup which is by tradition highly priced can be made partly of waste products (i.e. shell) must be irresistible. Irresistible, that is, to those restaurateurs who make their own *bisques*. But how many still do? The canning industry has really gone to town on the *bisques*, and the pretty tins that contain them can be seen everywhere. For me, their relationship to the real *bisque* is purely titular.

A proper consistency is obtained by using a larger quantity of fish than in the *velouté* to increase the bulk of purée in the *bisque*. Also the *bisque* should be thickened with 75 gr (3 oz) rice, cooked to a cream in a good stock. Before serving, 1½ tablespoons brandy and at least 2 tablespoons cream are added.

**Bisque de Homard** (Lobster *Bisque*)
For this menu favourite, the initial processes are the same as those given above for *Velouté de Homard:* i.e. the lobster is cut up, then cooked with *mirepoix*, then ignited with brandy and moistened with wine. But after the mixture of pounded lobster flesh, shell and *mirepoix* has been sieved, the resulting purée should be loosened with a good 9 dl (1½ pints) stock. To obtain a proper consistency, use a slightly larger lobster than you would for the *velouté*, and combine the lobster meat with 75 gr (3 oz) rice which has been cooked to a cream in a good stock. Before serving, 1½ tablespoons brandy and 1·5 dl (¼ pint) cream are stirred in. Garnish with Red Lobster or Red Crab Butter.

For *bisques* of crawfish, crayfish and prawns, the same processes are used as for *Bisque de Homard.*

## Crab Bisque

Crab makes a number of marvellous soups and (as it is easily available and not yet extravagantly priced) I have spent much time making them in different ways. Practice has suggested to me that the normal form of a crab soup should be a duet in which distinct parts are played by the white meat on one hand and the brown meat on the other. When this duet becomes a trio (only possible during the summer months when the red coral of the female is available), then we touch on perfection.

2 small cooked crabs – 1 male, 1 female
2 tablespoons *mirepoix* of chopped parsley, celery, shallot
50 gr (2 oz) butter
1 tablespoon brandy
1·2 litres (2 pints) good fish stock
50 gr (2 oz) rice
1 teaspoon horseradish cream
1·5 dl (¼ pint) white wine
juice ½ small lemon
salt, cayenne and black pepper

Open the crabs, extract the brown meat from the large shell and put it into a mixing bowl. Keep the red coral from the female on one side. Break up the body and the large claws, extract all the white meat and set aside. Discard all the shell except 4 of the thin legs. Chop these into small pieces (excluding the small claws at the ends).

Sauter the *mirepoix* in the butter for 1 minute. Throw in the chopped-up crab legs and add the lighted brandy; now pour in 9 dl (1½ pints) of the stock, and leave to simmer for 15 minutes.

Meanwhile, cook the rice to a cream in the remaining stock and set aside. With a wooden spoon, mash the brown crabmeat to a homogeneous paste with the horseradish cream. Now, strain from the pan the legs and the *mirepoix*, and pound. Sieve and return to the stock. Loosen the brown meat with 3 dl (½ pint) of the stock, and return to the fire. Stir well, but do not allow to boil. Now add the creamed rice, the wine and the lemon juice. Allow to simmer gently for 1–2 minutes. Add the flaked white meat of the crab and, at the last, the finely chopped red coral (when available). Test for seasoning with salt, red and black pepper. An alternative use for the red coral is to pound it with butter, parsley and chives and serve a generous pat of it with each bowl of soup.

*Cooking note:* The use of creamed rice as a thickening agent in a *bisque* is not mandatory, though I prefer it; vermicelli or even the despicable cornflour (which I never use) can be substituted in dire emergency. (If you are a cornflour devotee, you might as well conserve your energy and buy the tinned '*bisques*' referred to earlier.)

## *Soups with a béchamel base*

The following soups depend for their character as much on the stock used to loosen the *béchamel* to the consistency of soup and on the final garnish as on the particular fish used, whether white fish or shellfish. However, the flavour of the fish is never 'drowned' out.

### Crab and Leek Soup

the whites of 4 leeks, chopped fine
parsley stalks
1·5 dl (¼ pint) white wine
black and red pepper
salt
7·5 dl (1¼ pints) water
1 medium cooked crab
6 dl (1 pint) *Sauce Béchamel* (see page 64)
crabmeat croquettes (see method)
salt and pepper
50 gr (2 oz) Parsley Butter
1 dessertspoon chives, chopped
1 lemon, quartered
brown bread and butter

Make a vegetable and herb stock with the leeks, parsley stalks, wine, black and red pepper, salt and water; reduce it by boiling to 6 dl (1 pint). Mash the brown crabmeat with a wooden spoon until smooth, and amalgamate half of it with the *béchamel* over a low heat. Loosen the mixture with the strained prepared stock and allow to simmer gently, while stirring, for 5 minutes. Remove from heat and set aside.

Use the remainder of the brown crabmeat to make Crabmeat Croquettes (see page 131).

Now, season your soup with salt and pepper and, while stirring, bring it up to simmering point. Fold in the flaked white crabmeat. Ladle into hot soup bowls. Add a pat of Parsley Butter, some chives and 2 or 3 of the croquettes to each bowl. Serve with quarters of lemon and brown bread and butter.

### Crab and Sweet Pepper Soup

This is a variation of the soup described above. Substitute for the leeks in the stock 3 seeded red sweet peppers, 1 large onion, and 1 clove garlic, all finely chopped. Add 1 crushed clove garlic to the brown meat used in the croquettes. Use Paprika Butter as garnish.

### Salmon Head Soup

1 salmon head
9 dl (1½ pints) fish *or* vegetable stock
6 dl (1 pint) *Sauce Béchamel* (see page 64)
salt and black pepper
50 gr (2 oz) Parsley Butter

Poach the salmon head in the stock for 10 minutes. Take the head out, remove the flesh, flake and set aside. Return the head to the stock and boil until the stock is reduced by one-third. Loosen the *béchamel* sauce with the strained stock, add the flaked salmon flesh and allow to simmer for a few moments. Season and serve in hot bowls with Parsley Butter – or with another butter of your choice.

### Dover Sole Soup

1 small whiting
150 gr (6 oz) fillet of Dover sole
9 dl (1½ pints) fish or vegetable stock
6 dl (1 pint) *Sauce Béchamel* (see page 64)
salt and black pepper
50 gr (2 oz) Watercress Butter

Poach the whiting and the sole in the stock for about 7 minutes. Remove the sole and the whiting. Cut the flesh of the sole into small pieces and set aside. Fillet the whiting, pound the flesh and set aside. Return the whiting bones to the stock and boil until stock is reduced by one-third. Strain. Now loosen the *béchamel* with the stock. Add the pounded whiting and allow to simmer for 5 minutes.

Season with salt and pepper. Add your small pieces of sole and serve in hot bowls, garnished with Watercress Butter – or with another butter of your choice.

Sole is too expensive to use in quantity in soups. However, the above soup does enable you to enjoy a full-bodied soup, based on the pounded whiting, while also appreciating the flavour and *al dente* texture of the modest quantity of Dover sole.

Quite small quantities of fresh haddock, cod, codling, hake or coley, as an alternative to whiting, can supply sufficient body to the *béchamel*-based soups; used in the same quantities as in the foregoing recipe, they enable us to make inexpensive but excellent soups of the following fish which are now in the 'luxury' price range: turbot, John Dory, brill, halibut, scallops, prawns.

Using the *béchamel* base, all white fish and shellfish can be conscripted for service in soups. By adapting the simple process described above, it should be possible to produce a different soup of this kind for each week of the year.

## *Fishermen's soups*

There is another, and most important, range of soups to be considered. I refer to those splendid regional soups (though many of them could more fittingly be called stews) which spring from the tradition of the Italian, French and Spanish coasts (indeed, from the whole Mediterranean seaboard) and are associated in the minds of most people with the famous and over-exposed *Bouillabaisse*. Olive oil, tomato and garlic appear in most of these, and although they lack the smoothness and finesse that only eggs, butter and cream can supply, they are, dietetically speaking, far more wholesome than their 'Fauntleroy' cousins, the *veloutés*. The authority on these soups is undoubtedly Alan Davidson, who – in *Mediterranean Seafood** – gives detailed recipes which enable us to come very close to the real thing, even when all the ingredients stipulated are not available. Reading this book with its wealth of authentic recipes, varying from port to port, one is baffled to explain why no similar rich and varied tradition of fish soups has survived in the British Isles.

*Penguin Handbooks, 1972.

## Bouillabaisse

The following is Alan Davidson's recipe for a *Bouillabaisse* which does not call for expensive ingredients such as lobster.

'Buy fish as follows:
(a) a rascasse or two, depending on size
(b) some other fish with firm flesh such as monkfish, gurnard, weever or star-gazer, eel or moray or conger
(c) some delicate fish such as whiting or flatfish
(d) a few small wrasse or the like
(e) an inexpensive crustacean which might be squille [mantis shrimp] or a petite cigale
'Have two kilos in all. Gut and scale the fish, cut them in pieces where necessary and wash them.

'Now heat a wineglassful of olive oil in a large cooking pot and brown in this a large onion, finely sliced, and 2 cloves of garlic. Add ½ kilo of peeled and chopped tomatoes (or a corresponding amount of tomato concentrate) followed by about 3 litres of water (preferably boiling) and the fish from groups (a) and (b) and (d) and (e). Those from group (d) are intended to disintegrate in the cooking, adding body to the soup. Season with salt and pepper. Add chopped parsley and a pinch of saffron. (Why not add also a piece of orange peel, a clove, a bay leaf and a sprig of thyme, thus appeasing four pressure groups who might otherwise complain?) Pour a wineglassful of olive oil over all. Bring to and keep at a vigorous boil for 15 to 20 minutes. Add the fish in group (c) towards the end of this period, allowing just enough time for them to cook.

'When all is ready lift out the crustaceans and the fish which are still whole and serve them on one platter. Pour the broth over pieces of garlic-rubbed toast in soup plates (straining it in the process if you wish). Serve rouille alongside.'

*Cooking note:* It would be possible to substitute red mullet or gurnard for rascasse. Wrasse are available in British waters. Shrimps could be used in place of *squille* or *petite cigale*.

The *Bouillabaisse* is a one-pot soup and not as difficult to make as it sounds. The basic method is as Italian or Spanish as it is French. In all these regional, fishing-port soups, the proceedings are initiated by the sautering, in olive oil, of onion and garlic and, generally, peeled tomatoes. Water is then added, and the fish available (originally those not considered suitable for the carriage trade) are put into the liquid, some to disintegrate and enrich the body of the soup, others, in sequence depending on the texture of their flesh, to be removed from the pot when they are just cooked and eaten off a separate plate.

This is a field in which every freelance cook can do his or her own thing, and the following recipe is a typical example of what one can achieve without pretending that one is making a great regional soup.

**Kettle of Fish Soup**

1·5 dl (¼ pint) olive oil
4 shallots
2 cloves garlic
450 gr (1 lb) tomatoes
1·8 litres (3 pints) boiling water
1 small dab *or* whiting
1 small squid
1 small monkfish tail
2 small red mullet
8 uncooked prawns
pinch of saffron *or* 1 teaspoon turmeric
salt, red and black pepper
1·5 dl (¼ pint) white wine

*for garnish:*
4 tablespoons *Aïoli* (see page 69)
1 tablespoon parsley, chopped
thick slices toasted French bread

An asparagus kettle with a draining tray is invaluable for the making of this soup.

Heat the oil, in the bottom of the kettle (from which the draining tray has been removed), and add the chopped garlic and shallots to soften in it. Add the tomatoes, skinned and chopped, and continue to cook, mashing with a wooden spoon, until they are almost a purée and have thoroughly combined with the oil. Now pour in the water (using boiling water saves time), and also put in your dab or whiting, cleaned, and the small squid, cut in pieces. Cook briskly for 15–20 minutes. Now replace the draining tray in the kettle, with your monkfish tail on it. Lower the heat and poach for 12 minutes. Add the red mullet (scaled and cleaned, but with their heads on) and the uncooked prawns and cook for a further 10 minutes. Remove the kettle from the fire and, with all the fish in it, let it stand for 1–2 minutes. Remove the draining tray and transfer the monkfish tail, the mullet and the prawns to a dish. Put the kettle back on the fire and boil vigorously. Add the saffron, the salt, the red and black pepper and the wine, and cook the soup until the dab or whiting has disintegrated. Meanwhile, fillet the monkfish tail, and cut the flesh into small pieces; shell the prawns and replace all, with the mullet, on the draining tray. Put the tray back into the kettle and let all the fish get really hot. Remove the tray and arrange the fish on a hot dish. Ladle your boiling soup into hot bowls through a fairly wide-meshed strainer, and add a dessertspoon of *aïoli* to each bowl. Sprinkle with finely chopped parsley. Serve with thick chunks of toasted French bread. At the point of serving this and similar soups, the soup and the fish should be piping hot.

I often serve the pieces of monkfish in the bowl, leaving the prawns and mullet to be eaten as an accompaniment to the soup. The small squid used in this soup is there to impart its unique flavour which is an important element in the finished product, but we are at liberty to promote it to the draining tray if it is small enough to be tender at the close of the cooking operation, which takes just about 1 hour to complete.

By varying the ingredients of this soup, many other delicious soups can be made. However, the mixture of fish used above is, for me, one of the most satisfying.

## Shellfish Soup

With oysters at their present price, shellfish soup today means mussels, scallops and clams. The following basic recipe is my favourite quick soup of this kind. It can be applied, with adjusted quantities, to each of these shellfish alone, to any two, or (as given here) to all three together. Its aroma alone while cooking is a potent stimulant to the digestive juices.

1·2 litres (2 pints) water
2 dl ($\frac{1}{3}$ pint) white wine
juice $\frac{1}{2}$ lemon

the white of 1 small leek, finely chopped
2 shallots, finely chopped
pinch of saffron
10 good large mussels
4 large clams
4 small scallops
1 tablespoon mixed parsley and chives, finely chopped
1·5 dl ($\frac{1}{4}$ pint) double cream
salt and black pepper
1 lemon, quartered
brown bread and butter

In a large pan put the water, wine, lemon juice, leek, shallots and saffron. Add the cleaned mussels and clams. As soon as the mussels and clams open, remove them to a covered dish to keep warm. Bring the liquid in the pan to the boil, and continue to cook briskly until reduced by about one-fifth. Remove the pan from the fire, strain the liquid and return to the pan. Now add the scallops to the liquid and replace on the fire until the scallops begin to poach – 3 minutes should be sufficient. Now take the scallops out of the liquid and slice them once horizontally through the main muscle, and then twice vertically (this gives you 6 small pieces per scallop). Leave the coral tongues intact. Now remove the mussels and clams from their shells (if large, the clams should be chopped) and distribute them, with the pieces of scallop, in heated soup bowls. Sprinkle with the chopped parsley and chives. Allocate the coral tongues to your favourite guests. Now thoroughly stir the double cream into the liquid, test for seasoning with salt and pepper, and pour into the bowls. Serve with lemon quarters and brown bread and butter.

**Consommé au Caviare**

My general aversion to tinned soups does not apply to Crosse & Blackwell's Consommé (which has deservedly held its place in the hostess charts for many years). This is in frequent use for aspic dishes in my kitchen. It makes an impressive first course, set in the refrigerator in sherry glasses, and garnished with a generous dollop of whipped cream topped by a lavish sprinkling of black lumpfish roe 'caviare' – the justification for its inclusion in a fish cookery book.

Tinned turtle soup is even better for use with fish, but is too expensive for everyday employment. Tinned clam juice, with the addition of gelatine, is also a time- and labour-saving product especially appropriate for shellfish aspics.

Out of perversity, and to emphasize the loss we have sustained by the upgrading of the oyster and the skate, I give here as tailpieces to this chapter two recipes for fish soups as you would have been served them in the City of London in the eighteenth century. They are from *The English Art of Cookery** by one Richard Briggs, successively cook at the Globe Tavern, Fleet Street, the White Hart Tavern, Holborn, and the Temple Coffee-House.

**Richard Briggs' Oyster Soup**

'Take two pounds of scaite, skin it, two large eels, and four flounders, cut small, well washed and gutted, put them into four quarts of water, and when the scum rises skim it well, and put in two or three blades of mace, an onion stuck with cloves, two heads of cellery, a few parsley roots, and a bundle of sweet herbs; cover it close, and stew it for two hours, season it with pepper and salt and half a nutmeg grated; in the mean time get two quarts of oysters, and boil them in their own liquor, strain them in a sieve, and throw them into cold water, wash them well out, and beard them, pour the oyster liquor from the settlings into the soup, pound the oysters and twelve yolks of hard eggs in a mortar very fine, and strain the soup to them; mix them well up, and rub it through a tammy or napkin, then put it into a soup-pot, and give it a boil till it is as thick as cream; then pour it into a tureen, with crispt French bread at the top.'

**'Scaite, or Thornback Soup**

'Take three pounds of scaite or thornback and skin it, wash it well, and boil it in six quarts of water till it is very tender; take it up and pick all the fish off the bones, put the bones in again, with about two pounds of any sort of fresh fish, a little lemon-peel, a bundle of sweet herbs, twelve corns of whole pepper, two or three blades of mace, a little horse radish, an onion stuck with cloves, and the top-

*G. G. J. and J. Robinson, London, 1788.

crust of a penny loaf, with a little parsley, cover it close, and stew it gently two hours; take a French roll, cut a little piece out of the top, pick out all the crumb, and put it in the soup; rub it through a sieve, and pound part of the scaite or thornback in a mortar, mix the soup with it, and rub it through a tammy or napkin; put it in a soup-pot and make it hot, season it with Cayan pepper and salt; in the mean time mince the rest of the fish small, and put it in a stew-pan, with two spoonsful of the soup, a little butter rolled in flower, and a little pepper and salt; give it a toss or two, then fill your French roll, pour your soup into a soup dish or tureen, and put the roll in to swim at the top. This is a very rich soup, and cod or hollybert soup is made the same way.'

OYSTER DREDGING.

# A short guide to fish

In the foregoing chapters of this book, I have tried to devise an easy and progressive way into fish cookery for the cook at home. In the following brief guide, individual fish are introduced in alphabetical order, together with recipes for dishes particularly associated with and appropriate to that fish.

My suggestions for garnishes are few and simple, in comparison to those given in some books. Garnishes are fine elements not only in enhancing the taste of a fish, but also – particularly when we are cooking small quantities of a very expensive fish – in making a dish go further. However, the proliferation of rich garnishes for the sake of richness, or simply for décor, is one of the least admirable features of the *haute cuisine*.

I have also tried to escape from the tradition which has hitherto deprived unfashionable but excellent fish of the many fine sauces which have become the prerogative of an élite – sole, turbot, salmon, lobster and so on. *Tope Mornay, Monkfish Thermidor, Velouté de Porbeagle* – such outlandish couplings may suggest total anarchy in the Mad Hatter's kitchen. They will nonetheless be found extremely good to eat.

I believe that despite its basic application to English conditions and locally available varieties of fish, this book can be of use to readers in other English-speaking countries, such as Canada, Australia, New Zealand and South Africa. I have evolved a way of enabling such readers to apply its recipes to their indigenous fish and to overcome the difficulties of nomenclature. For example, a number of the sea-bream common in North American waters are called porgies; red mullet becomes goatfish, garfish becomes needlefish or saury, and pike in some Canadian lakes go by the name of muskelunge (muskies for short) or tigerlunge (a striped variety). But the variations in nomenclature from region to region are many, and any attempt to include a complete glossary would, in my opinion, fog the issue and require some thirty pages of listing.

This problem is not as daunting as it sounds, if we use my common-sense solution, though zoologists may turn pale at its effrontery. From the cook's point of view the important thing is to distinguish between the textures and qualities of fish (such as oiliness, toughness or softness, and so on) so as to apply to each an appropriate recipe. In order to facilitate this process, I have divided the great world family of fish into six categories. Those readers who live in countries where different fish are available from those found in Britain have only to observe the texture and degree of oiliness of their local product in order to be able to find, in this book, a suitable range of recipes for cooking it. For instance, if you live in South Africa where snoek (a member of the barracuda family) is to be found, you will be able to cook it according to the recipes given for any of the firm, meaty, oily fish in Category 5. Or if, in Australia, you obtain the much-prized rock cod, you can cook it according to the recipes given for any of the soft white fish in Category 1. In this way you will be able to discover the full potential of fish which, through the accident of geography, were unknown to those who laid the foundations of fish *cuisine*.

*Category 1: soft white fish,* which in cooking falls easily into flakes, and on overcooking turns to cotton wool. To this category belongs the whole of the cod family, which includes the following: hake, haddock, whiting, ling, coley and smelts. I also include in this category the soft flat fish such as plaice, lemon sole and dabs. All these fish require a maximum of care and a minimum of cooking.

*Category 2: white fish with medium-firm flesh.* Sea-bass and the breams (or groupers) are typical of this category. Other members elected are the grey mullet and the garfish (needlefish, saury), the conger and the Moray eel.

*Category 3: firm white fish.* Rich in pectin, they do not readily flake or fall apart in the cooking. This category includes Dover sole, brill, turbot, halibut, angler-fish, John Dory and skate. Coopted as members are the red mullet and the eel.

*Category 4: soft white fish, rich in oil.* Herring, shad, sardines, pilchards, anchovies, sprats, whitebait. These, like the fish in Category 1, require maximum care and minimum cooking. Not for use in soups.

*Category 5: firm, meaty fish, rich in oil.* Most typical of this group are the tunny family, which includes many varieties of mackerel, the bonito and the albacore. Other fish included here for cooking purposes are the dolphin fish, swordfish, amberjack, pompano, pilot fish, barracuda and – of fresh-water fish – pike and carp, although these last are not strictly oily, being rather dry in texture.

*Category 6: very firm, unscaled, cartilaginous fish.* The texture of these fish approaches the firmness of lobster. All edible members of the shark family belong here. Monkfish leads the field in this category, which includes porbeagle, dogfish, huss and many others.

No categories are required for the fish of the salmon family, the crustacea (lobster, crawfish etc) or the cephalopods (octopus and squid) as the nomenclature of these is pretty well stabilized throughout the English-speaking world.

## Anchovy

The anchovy is one of the most valuable ingredients of fish cookery and is most familiar first pickled in brine and then packed in olive oil in the small tins of fillets. A larger variety, which is heavily salted, pressed and packed in large tins, requires soaking and filleting before use, but these latter have a finer flavour.

Few dishes are not improved by the use of anchovy either as a unique seasoning in lieu of salt, as a garnish, or incorporated into *quenelles*, fishcakes and fish pies. It is a vital ingredient in greater or lesser strength (or in the form of anchovy essence) in many fish pastes and pâtés (it is, of course, the basis of *Patum Peperium* or Gentleman's Relish) and is in its own right the main ingredient of a number of Provençal and Mediterranean regional dishes of the simplest kind (see *Salade Niçoise*, page 86 and *Pissaladière*, page 187). The anchovy figures prominently in many recipes in this book.

The fresh anchovy, after being cleaned like any other fish, is usually egged and breadcrumbed and fried in olive oil; or split, grilled under a hot grill and served with lemon and savoury butter.

### Anchoïade

This is a simple paste made of anchovy fillets pounded with olive oil and vinegar in a mortar, sprinkled with chopped onion, spread on a slice of bread which has been rubbed with garlic, and baked in the oven. For each person allow 4 anchovy fillets, 1 tablespoon olive oil, 1 dessertspoon vinegar and 1 tablespoon chopped onion.

## *Angler-fish*

Not to be confused with monkfish (French: *ange de mer*), it can be treated in all the ways given for turbot or sole. Here is a particularly good recipe:

### Angler-fish with Orange Sauce

1 kg ($2\frac{1}{4}$ lb) angler-fish, filleted
3 Seville oranges
1·5 dl ($\frac{1}{4}$ pint) double cream
3 egg yolks
1·5 dl ($\frac{1}{4}$ pint) white wine
100 gr (4 oz) butter
salt, black pepper and cayenne pepper
seasoned flour
2 tablespoons parsley, chopped

After the fish has been filleted, sprinkle over it the juice of 1 orange and set aside. In a large bowl, beat the cream, egg yolks, white wine and juice of the remaining 2 oranges. Put the bowl over a pan of simmering water and stir vigorously until the sauce thickens. Melt half the butter and pour it into the sauce. Season with salt and the peppers.

The pieces of fish should be dipped into the seasoned flour and lightly fried on both sides in the remaining butter. Place the fish on a heated serving dish, pour the sauce over it and garnish with the parsley.

## *Bass*

All the methods used for cooking sole and salmon can be applied to the bass, which is now in regular supply on English markets. Larger fish can be stuffed with a fish or vegetable-and-herb forcemeat (see under **Carp**, below) before being poached in a *court-bouillon* or braised in the oven accompanied by wine and a *mirepoix* of vegetables previously softened in butter.

Alternatively, big fish can be cut into steaks or fillets (bass is a bony fish, but good bone-free fillets can, with care, be cut from it), and grilled, cooked *à la meuniére*, poached, or braised in the oven.

For smaller fish of between 225 and 450 gr (8 oz and 1 lb), cooking *à la meunière* or grilling whole is the best method. Serve with this fish a *Sauce Bercy* (see page 60), a *Maître d'Hôtel* Butter (see page 78), or another butter or sauce of your choice.

*Grillade au Fenouil* (bass grilled on a bed of fennel stalks) is a highly esteemed and consequently expensive dish in the South of France.

The following recipe is simple and trouble-free; even if, by oversight, the fish is left a little too long in the oven, it will still make a brave showing.

**Baked Bass**

bass of 1 kg (2¼ lb), scaled and cleaned
1 large Spanish onion, cut into fine rings
225 gr (8 oz) skinned tomatoes, fresh or tinned
3 dl (½ pint) water
1·5 dl (¼ pint) white wine
juice ½ lemon
1 good sprig each dried fennel and fresh parsley
1 stick celery
1 bay leaf
salt and black pepper
50 gr (2 oz) fresh butter

Into a good, heavy, lidded oval casserole, of a size which just takes the whole bass, put the fine onion rings and the tomatoes, chopped. Moisten with the water, wine and lemon juice. Let these ingredients cook on the top of the stove while the oven is being brought up to moderate (180°C/350°F, gas 4). When the onions and tomatoes have begun to melt and the mixture starts to thicken, remove from fire and allow to cool. Lay the bass on top, and push it down so that the mixture comes up round the sides of the fish, which it need not completely cover. Now lay the fennel, parsley, celery and bay leaf in the liquid round the fish and season with salt and pepper. Add the butter, which should be very cold and distributed over the fish in small pieces. Cover closely, put in the middle of the oven, and cook for 20 minutes. Remove the lid, raise oven heat to 200°C/400°F, gas 6, and cook for a further 10 minutes. Lift the fish out carefully on to a hot dish, discarding the fennel, parsley, bay leaf and celery. Test the liquid for seasoning and either pass it quickly through a sieve or pour it as it is over the fish. Serve.

## *Bloater*

A Yarmouth bloater, one of our traditional delicacies, is an unsplit herring, slightly salted and very lightly smoked. In my young days, bloaters were as ubiquitous as kippers; they are now almost collectors' pieces. I am informed that this is due to the fact that there seems to be little demand for them. A likelier explanation is that demand is not encouraged, as the very mild curing process used does not give them the kipper's life at the point of sale.

A bloater comes to us three-parts-cooked and, after decapitation and cleaning, only requires to be heated through. 2 or 3 minutes in a moderate oven (180°C/350°F, gas 4) or under a grill (turning once at half-time) should be sufficient. Poaching is not recommended.

With bloaters, as with herrings, a mustard sauce is usually served, though I find a horseradish sauce sets off the flavour of the fish rather better. To make the sauce, add 1 heaped teaspoon made English mustard *or* grated horseradish *or* horseradish cream to 1·5 dl ($\frac{1}{4}$ pint) *Sauce Béchamel* (see page 64). Any of the quickly made relishes (see Chameleon Sauce, page 54) or savoury butters (see pages 77–81) can be used as a change from this sauce.

Bloater roes, particularly the hard ones which fill the ventral cavity of the fish, are a great delicacy from which exciting pâtés (see page 84) and a savoury butter (page 79) can be made.

## *Bonito*

This is a small relation of the tunnyfish which is beginning to find its way on to British fish markets. A firm and oily fish, it is best cut into steaks and marinated for 2 hours before cooking:

### Baked Bonito

*for the marinade*:
2 cloves garlic, crushed
juice 1 lemon

3 anchovy fillets, pounded
freshly ground black pepper
1·5 dl (¼ pint) water
1·5 dl (¼ pint) white wine vinegar

After marinating, sauter the bonito steaks lightly on both sides in olive oil with a finely sliced onion and a crushed clove of garlic. Remove the steaks to a heatproof dish, and add to the pan 3 dl (½ pint) Special Tomato Sauce (see page 72). Stir all together and pour over the steaks. Bake in a moderate oven (180°C/350°F, gas 4) for 20 minutes. (This recipe is also very suitable for tunnyfish cutlets.)

As a member of the same family as mackerel, grilled steaks of bonito can be accompanied by a Mustard Sauce, a savoury butter or a Gooseberry Sauce (see under **Mackerel**, below, page 149). However, these recommendations should not deter you from trying out other sauces which you feel might be interesting.

### Bonito Kebabs

Bonito is an excellent fish for kebabs. Brush small pieces of the fish with a mixture of 1 tablespoon each of oil and lemon juice in which a clove of garlic has been crushed. Season with pepper and salt, and run the pieces on to skewers, leaving a good space between each piece of fish. Cook under a hot grill, turning as required, and brush with oil to cook all round; 10 minutes should do the trick. Serve on a hot plate with a little purée of shallots, parsley, celery and red sweet pepper (see Glossary); let the pepper dominate in this purée.

## *Bream*

This is an excellent sea fish, now available on fish markets. Grill the small ones and serve with a compound savoury butter (pages 77–81) or with any sauce used with turbot, brill or halibut (*q.v.*). The larger fish, poached and served with a good wine sauce (like that on page 61) can stand comparison with far more expensive large fish.

### Fillets of Bream Tananarivo

4 good fillets bream
1·5 dl (¼ pint) brandy
1·5 dl (¼ pint) white wine
1 tablespoon chives *or* shallots, chopped
100 gr (4 oz) butter
3 dl (½ pint) double cream
1 tablespoon green peppercorns, crushed
salt

Pack the fillets into a fireproof dish only just big enough to enable the fillets to lie flat. Pour the brandy and the wine over. Sprinkle with the chives and put on one side to marinate for 1 hour. At the end of that time, divide the butter up into small nuts and spread evenly over the fish. Bake in the oven (200°C/400°F, gas 6) for 20 minutes. Remove the fillets, place them on a dish and keep hot. Now stir the double cream well into the cooking juices (in the dish in which the fish was cooked) and add the crushed green peppercorns; season with salt, pour the very hot sauce over the fillets and serve.

**Dorade Antillaise** (Caribbean Bream)
As a variation, substitute rum for the brandy and 1 teaspoon cayenne pepper for the crushed green peppercorns in the above recipe.

## *Brill*

Brill, although the smallest of the large flat fish (the others being turbot and halibut), still comes to the fish shop too large for us to be able to cook the fish whole. Steaks of brill cut from a fresh fish and poached for 7 or 8 minutes in a well-seasoned white-wine *court-bouillon* and served with *Sauce Hollandaise* or one of its variations (see pages 67–8) can hardly be bettered. In my opinion, as a quality fish brill comes well before halibut and is equal in rank to young (or chicken) turbot.

Try brill in the potato-topped Basic Fish Pie (see page 181), adding to the *velouté* a purée of shrimps and chopped and sautéed mushrooms.

Use brill also in *béchamel*-based soups (Dover Sole Soup, page 104).

The combination of brill with mussels, as in the following simple recipe – a favourite of mine – heightens the flavour of both delicious ingredients.

**Fillets of Brill with Mussels**

20 good mussels
3 dl ($\frac{1}{2}$ pint) water
1·5 dl ($\frac{1}{4}$ pint) dry white wine
2 tablespoons parsley, finely chopped
1 shallot, finely chopped
small sprig of fennel
freshly ground black pepper
1 kg ($2\frac{1}{4}$ lb) fillets of brill
1·5 dl ($\frac{1}{4}$ pint) thick cream
1 dessertspoon chives, finely chopped
salt

Open the mussels as for *Moules Marinière* (page 153) in the water and wine, to which have been added 1 tablespoon parsley, the shallot, fennel and pepper. Remove the mussels, place them on a warm dish and cover with a clean cloth. Strain the liquid into a shallow fire-proof dish which will comfortably hold your fillets of brill. Allow to cool. Now lay the fillets in the dish, bring back to simmering point and poach for 8–10 minutes. Remove the fillets and place in a hot dish. Into your liquid now stir the cream and chives, and bring to bubbling point. Season with salt. Add the shelled mussels for 10–15 seconds only. Pour all over the fillets in the dish. Sprinkle with the remaining tablespoon of parsley and serve.

This recipe can be used for most white fish: cod, hake, plaice and, of course, turbot and halibut.

## *Buckling*

These are unsplit herrings, cured and smoked over a hot fire. Eat them cold like smoked trout or smoked eel, or just heated through in the oven. Serve with a savoury butter (see pages 77–81).

Buckling can also be used for fish pâtés (see Foulkes' Smoked Trout Pâté, page 84).

## *Carp*

A fresh-water fish of mysterious origins (China?) which can grow to enormous size and (reputedly) live to great age. Firm of flesh, not as dry as the pike, it can taste muddy if taken from muddy lakes, broads or ponds. The best method of cooking it whole is to stuff it:

**Carp stuffed with Forcemeat**

1 carp (1 kg or 2¼ lb)
100 gr (4 oz) *panada* (see page 189)
1 tablespoon onion, grated
1 tablespoon watercress, finely chopped
1 tablespoon parsley, finely chopped
1 teaspoon fennel shoots
salt and pepper

Clean and gut the carp. The remaining ingredients should be thoroughly worked together. Fill the cavity in the carp with the mixture, lay it in a lightly buttered ovenproof dish, dot with butter and bake in a moderate oven (180°C/350°F, gas 4) for 25–30 minutes.

**Carp stuffed with Chestnuts**

1 carp (900 gr or 2 lb)
*for the stuffing:*
100 gr (4 oz) *panada* (see page 189)
100 gr (4 oz) chestnut purée
1 tablespoon parsley, chopped
½ leaf of sage, finely chopped
1 teaspoon thyme, chopped
1 tablespoon grated onion
salt
black pepper
1 egg
*court-bouillon* (see recipe)

Clean and gut the carp. Mix the stuffing ingredients well together. Fill the carp with the mixture and sew the stomach up. Now lay the carp in as close-fitting a dish as possible and cover with a prepared *court-bouillon* made with white wine, onions, parsley, celery and thyme. Cover and cook in a medium oven (180°C/350°F, gas 4) for 40 minutes. Serve with *Beurre Blanc* (see page 74).

The flesh of carp can be used in *quenelles*, fishcakes and fish pies. Alternatively, cook carp *en matelote* (see under **Eel**, below). Small carp can be cooked *au bleu* (see under **Trout**, below).

See Richard Briggs' 1788 recipe for a stew of carp (the eighteenth-century innkeeper's recipe for carp *au bleu* is too cruel to print):

**'To stew Carp or Tench**

'Take a brace of carp or three tench, scale, gut, and wash them clean, cut the fins off close, put them in a kettle just big enough to hold them; put four ounces of butter in a stew-pan, melt it, and put in a large spoonful of flour, stir it till it is smooth, pour in a pint of good gravy, a pint of red port or claret, six shallots chopped fine, a bundle of sweet herbs, a little cloves, mace and all-spice, one onion, a spoonful of ketchup, and a little anchovy liquor, season it with pepper, salt, and Cayan pepper pretty high; boil it up for twenty minutes, then strain it over the fish, put in half a pint of fresh mushrooms, an ounce of truffles and morels, washed well and cut in pieces, half a pint of oysters washed well, cover it close, and put it over a slow fire, with fire on the lid, stew it gently one hour, and give it a gentle shake now and then, to keep the fish from sticking to the pan: in the mean time boil the roes, and cut them in square pieces, dip them in batter, and fry them brown in a pan of fat, with sippets cut three corner-ways; take your fish carefully out, and put them in your dish; skim the fat off the sauce, and squeeze in the juice of a lemon, pour it over the fish, and garnish with the roes, fried sippets, and horse-radish, and stick some of the sippets in the fish. You may, if you like it, skin, gut, and wash two small eels, flour them and fry them brown with butter, and stew them with the carp or tench.

'Put one large carp, a brace of tench, and two eels in a dish, put the carp in the middle, a tench on each side, the eels round, and the garnish round them. This makes an elegant top-dish for a large or genteel company.'

Richard Briggs describes 'Another way to fry Carp or Tench' on pages 174–5.

## *Clams and Cockles*

Both these bivalves, although they cannot stand comparison with oysters, scallops and mussels, are useful elements in fish cookery. They can be eaten raw, like oysters, with a squeeze of lemon, and have an exquisite taste of the sea – coupled, more often than not, with an abrasive seasoning of sand. The cockle industry in this country is strictly controlled, and the bulk of the dredge is put through sterilization routines to eliminate any risk of infection from bacterial pollution of the estuarial sands from which they come. This is why they are difficult to find uncooked. Whatever the sterilization process, it makes them tough and pretty well tasteless and useless for our purposes. Live clams, however, are not difficult to find and are a valuable ingredient for soups and sauces (see, for instance, page 109). They can also be treated, dressed and served in any way applicable to mussels and oysters.

## *Cod, Codling, Ling*

I have had one perfect experience with cod when, having wandered down to the beach at Deal, in Kent, I watched the proprietor ot a waterside hotel bargaining for three large codling. (A large codling is a large fish; a large cod is an extremely large fish.) I followed him into his hotel – it was around 11a.m., not an hour at which one could expect to be able to order either breakfast or lunch – and went into the bar. After a drink or two had been exchanged, the proprietor's wife came in to relieve him at the bar and he went out, saying he was going to cook himself a cod steak for breakfast. I seized the opportunity and said that I also had not had breakfast and that I would be grateful if he would let me join him. He was delighted to have someone to watch him handle the inch-and-a-half-thick steaks, pass them through the batter his wife had prepared and ease them into a basket which was then lowered into a deep, square cooking-pan of really hot lard. Ten minutes later I was cutting through the batter (which I always discard in batter-fried fish) to the virgin-white flakes which only just consented to detach themselves from the bone, and which shone up at me out of creamy and succulent juices. Ah, the taste . . . oh, the aroma . . .!

In this book I have been putting some emphasis on the less conventional fish such as garfish, gurnard, dogfish and monkfish in order to draw the fish cook's attention to the ever-increasing choice now being presented by the fishmonger. This does not mean that I consider cod to be in any way an inferior fish. Far from it. The only disadvantage to cod is the fact that it is one of the fish that suffers most – both in texture and in reputation – from bad cooking.

Cod and codling can be prepared in any of the ways suitable for turbot, due regard being paid to the fact that turbot requires longer cooking than cod. Fillets, poached for perhaps only 5 minutes, then put into a dish, covered with *Sauce Mornay* (see page 62) and browned in the oven, illustrate just one of the many ways of treating cod. All good sauces can be served with cod, and it can be used for soups, pies and fishcakes, as well as cold in salads.

When fresh, cod has a unique flavour which, regrettably, vanishes with freezing. A good fresh fillet or steak of cod, seasoned, brushed with butter and put under a hot grill (4–6 minutes on each side, depending on thickness) can be a revelation if one has not eaten cod for some time. But while really fresh cod is fine grilled, if we buy it from the fishmonger's slab, it tends to have lost its firmness and, I think, requires a good stiff sauce to hold it together.

### Cod with Creamy Egg Sauce

4·5 dl ($\frac{3}{4}$ pint) thick *Sauce Béchamel* (see page 64)
1 bunch watercress, finely chopped
2 tablespoons parsley, finely chopped
1 tablespoon horseradish cream
3 hard-boiled eggs
50 gr (2 oz) butter
4 fillets cod, weighing in all 675 gr ($1\frac{1}{2}$ lb)
1·2 litres (2 pints) *court-bouillon*

Into the *béchamel*, blend the very finely chopped watercress and parsley. Mix in the horseradish cream and season well with salt. Add the eggs, coarsely chopped, and fold in the butter at the last moment. Keep this sauce very hot while you gently poach the cod fillets in the *court-bouillon* for 4–6 minutes. Remove the fillets to a hot dish and pour over them the thick and steaming hot sauce.

Remember that all the classic sauces can be served with cod and other members of the cod family, such as coley, hake, fresh haddock.

I will add here a recipe, supplied to me by a friend, for the Australian rock cod. It applies beautifully to any delicate white fish in the cod family.

### Baked Rock Cod

75 gr (3 oz) butter
25 gr (1oz) flour
1·5 dl ($\frac{1}{4}$ pint) white wine
4 cutlets rock cod, weighing 675 gr ($1\frac{1}{2}$ lb) in all
juice 2 lemons
1 tablespoon parsley, chopped
pepper and salt

Melt half the butter in a good fireproof dish, and stir in the flour. When smooth, loosen with the wine, and cook for 1 minute. Lay in the fish, squeeze the lemon juice over it, and spread it with the remaining butter, pounded together with the parsley. Sprinkle with plenty of salt and pepper. Bake in a moderate oven (180°C/350°F, gas 4) for 30 minutes, basting occasionally.

Great care must be taken in this recipe, as always when baking soft fish, not to cook the fish beyond the point of no return.

With this recipe, my informant recommends a simple sweet and sour sauce, made as follows:

**Sweet and Sour Sauce**

1 dessertspoon onion juice (see page 65)
1 tablespoon tomato purée
1 tablespoon soya sauce
1 tablespoon honey *or* sugar
1 tablespoon wine vinegar
juice 1 orange
juice 1 lemon
1 dessertspoon olive oil
black pepper

Blend all these ingredients together in a small saucepan. Heat, and allow to bubble for 1–2 minutes only. Serve separately in a heated sauceboat.

**Cod roe** Fresh cod roes are excellent, egged and breadcrumbed and fried as cutlets, or made into fishcakes. They are also good for forcemeat stuffings for large fish, for instance replacing the whiting in the recipe on page 173.

**Smoked Cod Roe** This is one of our greatest delicacies and it is most adaptable for many purposes (see the dip on page 87). On its own, sliced, served with lemon quarters and brown bread, it rivals smoked salmon as an *hors-d'oeuvre*. For *canapés* to serve with drinks, pound it with an equal quantity of fresh butter and a generous sprinkling of freshly ground black pepper. In this form, it also makes an admirable savoury butter and garnish for fine white fish – the pinkish colour lending its own cachet to the dish.

## *Dried salt cod*

As a means of survival, something may be said on behalf of this form of cod. To me, it is not worth the time and trouble it takes to prepare, and it is often more expensive than the fresh fish. However, it is an important element in the diet of Mediterranean countries, where it is *de rigueur* as lenten fare, and cookery writers seem to be intellectually drawn to it. One way of preparing it is as follows:

**1** Soak the withered-looking cod carcase in plenty of water for 12 hours at the very least, changing the water twice during that time.

**2** Sweat 2 chopped cloves of garlic and 3 chopped onions in 1·5 dl (¼ pint) olive oil. Add 6 skinned and chopped tomatoes and 3 chopped red sweet peppers. Cook together for 20 minutes and set aside.
**3** Pour off the water from the cod, cover with fresh water, bring to the boil and cook for a minute or two. Drain; skin, fillet and trim your cod and cut it up into pieces. Put the cod into the pan with the other ingredients, adding a *bouquet garni* of 2 bay leaves, a sprig of rosemary, a sprig of thyme and a leaf of sage. Cook well together gently for about half an hour. Remove the herbs before serving.

Another famous recipe for salt cod is:

**Brandade à la Parisienne**

675 gr (1½ lb) salt cod
150 gr (6 oz) potatoes, mashed
2 tablespoons olive oil
2 cloves garlic, crushed
3 dl (½ pint) *Sauce Béchamel* (see page 64)
a little hot milk
salt and pepper
1 small white loaf
3 tablespoons cooking oil

The cod should be soaked in water for at least 12 hours, covered with fresh water and then poached until tender. Drain and flake it. Put the cod and the mashed potatoes into a saucepan and add half the garlic, which should have been lightly fried in the olive oil in another smaller saucepan first. Beat in the olive oil and gradually add the *béchamel* and the hot milk; season with salt and pepper. Beat thoroughly: the mixture should resemble a potato *mousseline*.

Cut off the top of the loaf and scoop out the breadcrumbs. (These should be put aside for use in *panadas* etc.) Mix the cooking oil with the remaining garlic and ½ teaspoon salt. Brush the inside and outside shell of the loaf with this mixture, put the loaf in a tin and bake in a moderate oven (180°C/350°F, gas 4) until golden-brown. Fill with the *brandade*, replace the top of the loaf and heat through well. It can be garnished with slices of tomato.

## *Coley (Saithe)*

This is a good, reliable fish, the flesh of which loses its off-putting yellowish colour when cooked. It is in the lower price range, and can be treated in all the ways applicable to other white fish. Perhaps it is best employed in pies, fishcakes and soups, though fillets poached and masked with any *béchamel*-based or *velouté* sauce make splendid eating. While this fish is looked down on by many, I feel it is certainly not to be despised.

Smoked saithe is a good substitute for smoked salmon in a pâté.

## *Conger Eel*

A firm and juicy-fleshed fish with a fairly strong flavour of its own, the conger eel should not be confused with the eel. The conger is a salt-water fish which grows to enormous length and size, whereas the eel proper is a fresh-water fish which only grows to a length of, say, 60 cm (24 in). Familiarity with it breeds anything but contempt, and I have come to like it more and more over the years. Even a very small quantity of conger will surprisingly enrich a soup, stew, or fish pie. Steaks of conger eel are also exceedingly good baked in the Special Tomato Sauce given on page 72 and cooked in a moderate oven (180°C/350°F, gas 4) for 25 minutes. The casserole for this dish should be small enough to make a tight fit of the ingredients. I recommend using conger in Highbury Pie (page 182) and in Soho Pie (page 183). For its use in stews, see the basic recipes on page 107. When poached conger goes well with *Sauce Soubise* (see page 66) or *Sauce Béarnaise* (see page 68).

Cut into small pieces, conger is excellent for fish kebabs (see under **Bonito**, above).

A disadvantage which should be pointed out lies in the separate, longitudinally placed sharp bones running through the conger. These are difficult to pull out of the raw fish, though it is an easy matter to locate them in the cooked fish and remove them with tweezers.

Here is a conger recipe for, perhaps, a special occasion:

### Conger Eel Portobello

100 gr (4 oz) butter
2 tablespoons onion, finely chopped
1 stick celery, sliced

450 gr (1 lb) conger, skinned and cut into small fillets 10 × 5 cm (4 × 2 in)
2 tablespoons brandy
1·5 dl (¼ pint) white wine
juice ½ lemon
salt and pepper
1 tablespoon parsley, finely chopped
3 dl (½ pint) Portobello Sauce (see page 74)

In a good wide, heavy pan with a lid, toss around in the butter the onion and the celery. As soon as they begin to take colour, put in the conger fillets and keep turning them over and around on a brisk flame for 5 or 6 minutes until they begin to brown; ignite the brandy and pour over the fillets, which should be kept moving around in the pan. As the flames die out, pour in the wine and then the lemon juice. Season with salt and pepper. Cover the pan and allow to cook on slow heat for another 6 or 7 minutes, shaking the pan thoroughly from time to time. Spoon the contents of the pan with the juices on to a hot dish, sprinkle with parsley and serve with Portobello Sauce.

## *Crab*

On crab in general, several things must be said. Apart from being one of the most delicious of the crustacea, crab is as safe to eat as any other kind of fish, provided you buy it alive – or ready-cooked from a reputable fishmonger (and provided it has not been opened, cracked or holed since it came steaming out of the boiler). Shop early for crab – they are popular and sell fast – and you will find them still steaming into the cool air; you will also have a wider choice of size and sex. For white meat, the male (with larger claws) is best; for body meat, buy the female at the proper season (in the summer months) when she is lined with a thick layer of pink coral. This is delicious either plain as a fine garnish, pounded with savoury butter, or used as an enrichment to an accompanying sauce. Judge a crab not by its size, but by its weight. Many a large, scarlet good-looker can prove to be thin and watery of flesh within. For notes on the cleaning and preparation of crab, see page 35. If you buy a large 1-kg (2¼-lb) live crab to take home, cook it by dropping it into a large pan of boiling salted water. Boil hard for 3 or 4 minutes, then reduce the heat and simmer for a further 20 minutes.

In all the recipes given below, frozen crabmeat can be used. It has the obvious advantage of being in season all the year round and is useful for increasing the proportion of white to brown meat in certain dishes, but it is expensive and sold in packages either too small or too big for most cooks' purposes. Then, too, the problems of thawing out can upset a cook's timetable; and finally, it has not the true sea flavour of the fresh seafood – and is not really good enough for the home kitchen when better can be bought for less money.

My first recipe is an eighteenth-century one from Richard Briggs. This is, I believe, the true traditional English dressed crab.

'**To dress a Crab.** Boil the crab well in salt and water, and when cold break it up, mix the meat in the inside of the shell well together, break the large claws, take out the meat, and cut it fine, lay it over the shell-meat as handsome as you can in the shell, put it in the dish, split the chine in two, and put at each end, crack the small claws and put them round; mix some oil and vinegar, a little mustard, pepper, and salt, and put it over the meat in the shell; garnish with parsley.'

Nothing could be simpler. Note that there is no bulking of the body meat, and the customer is left to extract the white meat from the chine for himself – and a surprising amount of meat there is in this bony, compartmented structure.

But if crab is to become a regular item of food in the home, it must be liberated from the straitjacket of this old English formula which inhibits its marvellous versatility. Experimenting in this field is exciting, and many inhibitions disappear with the tasting. Here are eight simple variations on the dressed crab theme, each of which has a distinct character of its own. Quantities given are for a small- to medium-sized crab, weighing 450 to 675 gr (1 to 1½ lb), and will serve four people as an *hors-d'oeuvre*, or two as a main course.

*To the pounded body meat of the crab, add, mixing all well together:*

**1** 1 teaspoon chopped chives; 1 teaspoon horseradish cream; a few drops of lemon juice; salt and freshly ground black pepper

**2** 2 small anchovy fillets, pounded; 1 teaspoon Worcester sauce

**3** 2 teaspoons finely chopped capers; the white of 1 spring onion, finely chopped; salt and freshly ground black pepper

**4** 3 large, soft black olives, stoned and pounded; 1 small clove of

garlic, crushed; salt and freshly ground black pepper
**5** 25 gr (1 oz) cream cheese; 1 teaspoon chopped chives; 1 chopped leaf of fresh basil
**6** 1 teaspoon each of red and green sweet pepper, finely chopped; 1 large black olive, stoned and pounded; lemon juice; salt and freshly ground black pepper
**7** 50 gr (2 oz) fresh button mushrooms, puréed in the blender; 1 teaspoon chopped chives; salt and freshly ground black pepper
**8** 1 small stick from the core of a celery head, finely chopped; the white of 1 spring onion, finely chopped; 1 teaspoon grated raw carrot; lemon juice; salt and freshly ground black pepper.

In each case, pack the mixture back into the shell of the crab and sprinkle it generously with chopped parsley; lay on it the white meat from the claws and chine; season with black pepper, adorn with sprigs of parsley and serve with a segment of lemon and with brown bread and butter. Crab dressed in this way should be prepared an hour before eating, covered and kept in a cool place so that the various seasonings have time to permeate the whole mass of the body meat.

**Crabmeat Croquettes**

brown meat from 1 small crab
1 teaspoon mustard *or* horseradish cream
few drops of anchovy essence
50 gr (2 oz) freshly made white breadcrumbs
2 egg yolks, beaten
4 tablespoons plain flour
3 tablespoons olive oil

Mash the brown crabmeat with a wooden spoon until smooth. Combine the mustard or horseradish and a few drops of anchovy essence with the crabmeat. Add sufficient breadcrumbs to stiffen the mixture. Mould the mixture into about 8 or 12 small cylinders 7·5 cm (3 in) long, and coat them with the beaten egg yolks on a plate. Then roll them in the flour. Allow them to stand in the air for about 10 minutes, then repeat the egging and flouring process. Fry the croquettes in hot oil, turning to cook evenly.

Use these croquettes in Crab and Leek Soup (see page 103), or serve them as an *hors-d'oeuvre* with the sauce of your choice.

For another soup based on crab, see *Crab Bisque* (page 102).

## *Crawfish*

This is a large crustacean, a match for lobster any day, but lacking the large claws of the lobster. All recipes applicable to lobster can be used for crawfish (see under **Lobster**, below). They are not easy to obtain and should be ordered when in season. In the spring of last year, not having come across any in my local fish shop for a year, I was impressed and excited to see two beautiful large, saffron-red crawfish crowning the white fish slab. So eager was I to acquire these beauties that I forgot to ask the usual questions, bought them for a prohibitive price and hurried home proudly, intent on cooking them in the *Homard Thermidor* manner. To my disappointment, on opening them, I found that they had been treated by some freeze-drying and chemical process and had been 'reconstituted' by thawing out and soaking in water. The flesh had no taste and was difficult to chew. It was an infuriating tragedy. I have been taken in before in this way, but only in a pretentious restaurant in a provincial city, where I was at least able to vent my rage immediately.

## *Crayfish*

You won't find these delicate little fresh-water crustaceans in the ordinary fishmongers' shops. Cooked and pounded with butter, they make perhaps the best of the savoury butters which can be used to enrich a *béchamel* (see *Sauce Nantua*, page 66) or to garnish soups, grilled or poached fillets of fine white fish, or other shellfish. They make a splendid *bisque* (see basic recipe for *Crab Bisque*, page 102).

## *Cuttlefish*

See under **Squid**, below.

## *Dab*

These small flat fish are usually fried whole in egg and breadcrumbs. They are useful for enriching the body of fish soups and stocks, but are otherwise of no particular interest.

## *Dogfish (Rock Salmon)*

This is a member of the shark family whose face fishmongers never let us see. It is surprising that the fine qualities of this first-class seafood are still not sufficiently recognized. It rises beautifully to the challenge of the finest sauce and makes a marvellous *velouté* soup. It is full of pectin and therefore is useful for making *fumets* which will set when cold. It also makes good fish kebabs (see under **Bonito**, above). The general public eats a good deal of dogfish fried in batter in fish-and-chip shops; I have myself often bought dogfish in them, but the execrable batters used have finally driven me away.

Dogfish is one of the perfect fish for curry dishes (see pages 195–8), and for cooking *en matelote* (see under **Eel**, below). It can also be used in Highbury Pie (see page 182).

## *Dublin Bay Prawns (Scampi)*

See under **Prawns**, below.

## *Eel and Elvers*

When I used to fish for codling on the beach at Sandgate near Folkestone, I more often got eel or dabs on our bait of razorfish. Though we would eat dabs, nothing at that time would persuade us to consider eel as edible, let alone a delicacy, and we discarded the eels with disgust at the effort it took to get them off the hook. Thus one of the silliest of taboos resulting from a silly upbringing has prevented me from enjoying a great gastronomic experience until the last few years.

Here is a good recipe for a *matelote* of eel in which this fish appears at its best. The recipe is a basic one, and can be applied to many other kinds of fish, such as monkfish, dogfish or conger, provided allowance is made for the texture of the fish used when allotting the time needed to simmer it in the sauce.

**Matelote d'Anguilles** (eels with red wine)

900 gr (2 lb) eels
50 gr (2 oz) butter
1 large onion, chopped
2 tablespoons flour
6 dl (1 pint) red wine
salt and freshly ground black pepper
*bouquet garni*
1 clove garlic, crushed
4 mushrooms, roughly chopped

Skin the eels (see page 34 for instructions as to how to do this). Then chop the eels into 2·5-cm (1-in) pieces and set aside. Melt the butter in a good, heavy pan, put in the onion and cook until transparent. Now stir in the flour to make a white *roux*. Loosen the *roux* with the red wine and stir until it reaches simmering point. Season with salt and pepper and add the remaining ingredients except the eel. Allow to simmer for 12 minutes. Now put into this sauce the pieces of eel and simmer gently for 20 minutes. Remove the pan from the fire, extract the eel, and arrange the pieces in some sort of mound in the centre of a hot dish. Set aside and keep warm. Return the pan to the fire and simmer, while stirring, until fairly thick. Pour sauce over the mound of eel pieces and serve with thick *croûtons* of bread fried in butter.

**Jellied Eels**

These are good only if the jelly used is the product of a rich fish stock (in which you will have simmered the skinned eels for 20 minutes), reduced to a pectin-rich *fumet* which does not require the aid of gelatine leaves or powder to set. Clarification of the *fumet* (as described on page 63 under Chaudfroid Sauce) is not necessary, but the liberal working-in of finely chopped parsley and chives is. Skate or conger bones used in the stock will produce the effect required. Add your pieces of eel to the *fumet* when it is cold and just on the point of setting. Cover and put in the refrigerator. Serve the eels with quarters of lemon and brown bread and butter.

**Fried Eel**

Before passing the pieces of skinned eel through egg and bread-crumbs, they should be poached in a good stock for 20 minutes, taken out and allowed to cool. Browning in really hot deep oil should take only a few minutes. Serve with *Sauce Tartare* (page 70), **Sauce Verte** (page 70) or *Sauce Gribiche* (page 72).

See also the recipe for Eel Pie on page 184.

**Smoked Eel** is a good runner-up to smoked salmon, and Smoked Eel Pâté (see page 85) makes an expensive luxury go a long way. Used in fish salad with other cold fish such as tunny, smoked eel lends distinction to what may have become a routine dish. Boned, the flesh pounded with seasonings and blended with a Panada Frangipane (page 189), smoked eel makes the most delicate of *quenelles*.

**Elvers** In Gloucestershire, these infant eels (which arrive in their billions from their breeding grounds in the Sargasso Sea some time in the early spring) are very popular fried in hot bacon fat after a thorough washing to remove slime. Before being fried, they are shaken in a bag with fine flour. English country-dwellers sprinkle them with vinegar, but I prefer to substitute lemon juice.

An alternative method, and perhaps the best way of ridding them of slime, is to bring them to the boil in seasoned water, then drain them and allow them to cool. Now fry them in butter in which chopped onion has softened, but not browned (use garlic instead – or as well – if you like). Remove from pan, drain, sprinkle with plenty of finely chopped parsley and serve with real bread and butter.

## *Garfish*

My first encounter with garfish was way back in the early 1930s, night-fishing off Aghios Nikolaos. As the bright light in the stern of the boat passed over the absolutely still surface of the water, there would be a sudden breaking of the surface and a long thin shape would pass swiftly by, skittering over the water as it inspected the acetylene lamp and then disappearing – unless the alert fisherman with the long rusty iron sword sticking out sideways from the boat stunned it in flight and hauled it in.

This is a very exciting fish and one that I never expected to see in English fish shops, where it is now plentiful and not expensive. The garfish is an extremely elegant fish, from its 'woodcock' beak to its hydrodynamic fins and tail. That such an elegance of form should be structured on a framework of bright green bones is almost too much to bear. That such a marvel in nature should also be exceedingly good to eat makes it simply one of the wonders of the world.

### Garfish Spectacular

When you buy garfish, ask the fishmonger to clean it, leaving on the head and tail. I find it best to buy larger ones – say 60 cm (24 in) long, excluding beak, so as to be able to get thick, long fillets from it.

1 kg (2¼ lb) garfish
6 dl (1 pint) *court-bouillon*
3 dl (½ pint) white wine
225 gr (8 oz) rice, boiled

Cut off the head and the tail, and divide the body of the fish into three equal parts. Poach the pieces in the *court-bouillon*, to which you will have added the white wine, for 8–10 minutes, depending on the thickness of the fish. Remove and put on a plate to cool. When cool, skin the fish with a sharp knife. Cut the fish into 5 cm (2 in) segments, opening them down the back so as to expose the beautiful green bones. Place them on a generous bed of rice. For special effect, the head and tail can be poached too and served projecting from the ends of the dish.

Any of the recipes customary with sole, turbot and brill can be adapted for fillets of garfish. When the fish has been poached (see above) it should be left to cool and skinned with a sharp knife. Cut each piece down the back to the green central bone with the smaller bones radiating from it and work away the four fillets, from which you will have to detach a thin edging of very small bones.

Truly, a great fish. Cook also *en matelote* (see under **Eel**, above); use in fish pies and soups; fry in egg and breadcrumbs, or grill after coating with a *Sauce Caroline* (see page 73).

## *Grayling*

This fresh-water fish is not easy to find unless you have friends with fishing rights or with stretches of unpolluted river running through their grounds. It is every bit as good as trout, but has not been thought worth while breeding, like trout, in fish farms. Cook by any method applicable to trout.

## *Gurnard*

The gurnard is a delightful rosy red in colour, with a large head shaped rather like a bulldozer, and its face wears a taciturn and

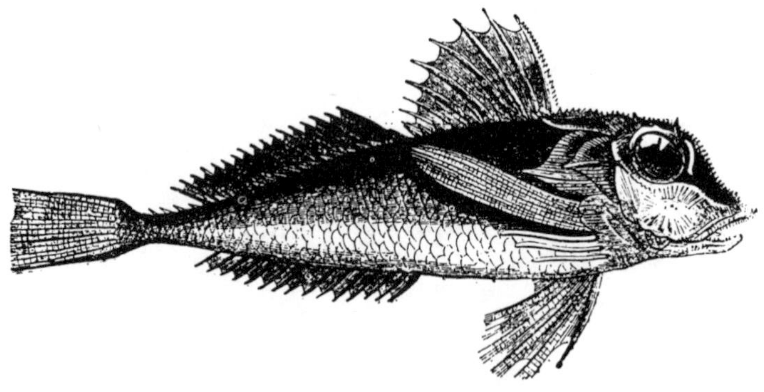

sceptical expression. It is excellent for use in soups, but can also be grilled, fried or poached. The proportion of the head to the tail and body meat makes it quite expensive to buy. Keep the head on, and clean the fish through the gills: the effect of the whole fish, so bright in hue and so glum in expression, adds a touch of surrealistic charm to any table. Fairly firm of flesh, the gurnard can be cooked in any of the ways applicable to the red mullet (see under **Mullet**, below), and it should definitely be included in any attempt at a *Bouillabaisse*. The head can be used in making stock.

## *Haddock*

Fresh haddock can be cooked in all the ways suitable for its cousins, the cod and codling. There is little to choose between cod and haddock fresh, but when they are smoked an enormous gap opens up between them. Smoked cod fillets (I don't mean the heavily salted and dried kind) are quite pleasant poached or baked and served with a butter sauce and chopped-up hard-boiled eggs, or put into a curry sauce; but smoked Finnan haddock ranks in the highest class of delicacy. The fact that we have it so often has blunted the edge of our appreciation of it.

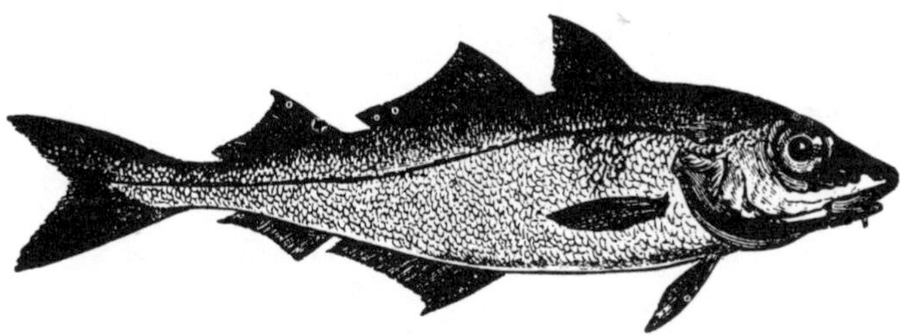

Its true worth is demonstrated by the simplicity of treatment which shows it at its best.

Lay the smoked haddock in milk or water, or a mixture of both, to cover. Bring to the boil slowly. The moment the liquid boils, turn down the heat and let the fish simmer for 1 minute. Then turn off the heat and leave the fish to coddle for up to 5 minutes (test with a fork under the main bone). Put the fish on a hot dish and pour over it melted butter seasoned with freshly ground black pepper. Also serve with it pats of savoury butter. *Maître d'Hôtel* (see page 78) is the best.

Although the above method of cooking cannot be surpassed, smoked haddock makes other excellent dishes, of which the following are a selection: Kedgeree (see page 194), Smoked Haddock Mousse (see basic recipe on page 89), *velouté* soup (page 98), soufflé (page 203) and Smoked Haddock Pâté (see basic recipe for Foulkes' Pâté on page 84).

**Aberdeen or Arbroath Smokies** Almost as good as smoked salmon are these small haddock which have been cooked, unopened, by smoking over a hot fire. They can be eaten as they are, warmed through, or creamed into a paste to be eaten with toast and butter.

## *Hake*

Hake is a kind of elongated cod with a marginally tighter texture. Like the rest of the family, it is good cut into steaks and fried in batter or egg and breadcrumbs. As a fish to which this country is accustomed (like cod, it conducts its own publicity throughout the year on the fishmonger's slab), it is in big demand and consequently expensive. Personally, I find that it lacks the flavour of cod, but cutlets of hake in the round are easy to handle in the kitchen. It is excellent in fish pies and makes good fishcakes. It is at its best stuffed and cooked in the oven in foil.

**Merluche en papillote** (Stuffed Hake)
1 good thick middle cut of hake, weighing 1 kg ($2\frac{1}{4}$ lb)
*For the stuffing:*
100 gr (4 oz) breadcrumbs soaked in milk and then squeezed to remove surplus liquid
4 anchovy fillets
1 sage leaf, chopped
1 dessertspoon parsley, chopped
1 dessertspoon chives *or* shallot, chopped
1 dessertspoon capers, chopped
liberal sprinkling black pepper
salt
3 dl ($\frac{1}{2}$ pint) Rich Tomato Sauce (see page 66)

Pound all the ingredients of the stuffing together and pack lightly into the fish. Now lay it on a sheet of foil in a fireproof dish. Pour on the Rich Tomato Sauce. Fold and firmly close the foil over it. Bake for 35 minutes in a moderate oven (180°C/350°F, gas 4). Serve from the dish in which it has been cooked, spooning some of the sauce on to each stuffed portion of fish.

## *Halibut*

This is the largest of the flat fish and definitely one of the aristocrats of the white fish world, though, for me, the slight tendency to dryness in the flesh puts it well below turbot, sole and brill. It has the highest nutritional value, and halibut liver oil is a rich source of Vitamin D.

Cuts from smaller fish are the best to buy; if possible, avoid the tail end, in which the dryness of the flesh is more pronounced. Halibut can be cooked in all the ways applicable to **Sole** and **Turbot**, below.

Here is a good recipe for halibut which will help to counteract its dryness.

### Halibut with Leeks and Black Olives

2 tablespoons olive oil
50 gr (2 oz) butter
the white and green of 4 leeks, thinly sliced into rounds
8 large black olives, stoned and chopped
2 tablespoons white wine
6 dl (1 pint) water
salt and black pepper
four 150 gr (6 oz) halibut steaks
2 tablespoons parsley, chopped

In a shallow, heavy pan which will accommodate your steaks comfortably, heat the olive oil and the butter. Throw in the leeks and chopped olives, and cook briskly until the leeks are thoroughly soft; a considerable amount of liquid will come from the leeks. Add the wine and the water, season with salt and pepper and stir well. Now put in your fish (the steaks will not be completely covered) and bring all to simmering point. Simmer very gently for 10 minutes, basting the unsubmerged parts of the fish continuously. Then turn the steaks and repeat the operation for a further 10 minutes.

Remove the steaks to a hot dish. Boil up the contents of the pan for half a minute. Pour over the steaks, sprinkle with parsley and serve.

A purée of spinach into which a handful of chopped watercress leaves has been stirred goes beautifully with this dish.

## *Herring*

The fresh herring, weight for weight, supplies more nourishment than any other fish. (Hence the healthy though impoverished Scots student who used to set off to university with food for a term – a barrel of herrings and a sack of oatmeal.)

After being cleaned, herrings can be cooked in a number of ways. When really fresh, they are best brushed with melted butter, seasoned with salt and pepper and grilled under a hot fire; if whole, make incisions in the flesh before grilling – alternatively, open out the herrings by pressing face down on to a board and then remove the main bones. The herrings can be sprinkled with oatmeal before grilling.

Fry herrings in the pan for about 6 minutes on each side. Brush with melted butter, wrap in foil and bake in a hot oven (220°C/425°F, gas 7) for roughly 15 minutes. When cold, poached, grilled or baked herrings make a splendid pâté to serve as an *hors-d'oeuvre* (see page 84). For eating as a cold dish, cook them very slowly in a marinade, when they are called Soused Herrings (see below). Pickle them and call them Bismarck Herrings; smoke them and call them kippers (see **Kippers**, below), bloaters (see **Bloaters**, above) or buckling (see **Buckling**, above). Herrings are all things to all men.

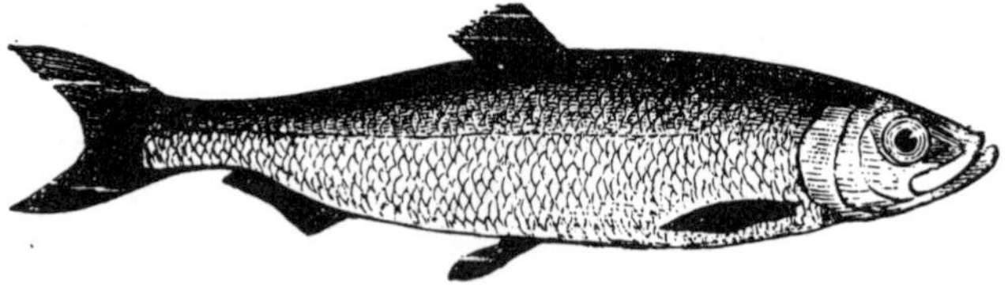

The herring is too rich in oil (10 per cent) to use in soups or to serve with rich sauces made with butter, cream and so on; serve, rather, condiments such as mustard or horseradish, or relishes (see Chameleon Sauce, page 54).

Sauter roes (hard or soft) in butter for about 2 minutes on each side and then lay them on *canapés* or toast; pound them with anchovy fillets as a variation.

These two recipes are taken from *The Herring Book*, issued many years ago by the Herring Industry Board.

**Baked Herrings with Mushroom Stuffing**

4 herrings
50 gr (2 oz) mushrooms
1 tablespoon breadcrumbs
1 tablespoon parsley, chopped
juice ½ lemon
1 large soft roe *or* 2 hard roes
salt and black pepper
½ teaspoon butter

Prepare the herrings as follows: cut off the heads and tails, clean and bone the fish. Chop the mushrooms finely, mixing with the breadcrumbs, parsley, lemon juice, salt and pepper, and bind with the roe. Butter a pie dish or casserole, lay in it the fish filled with the stuffing, cover and bake in a moderately hot oven (190°C/375°F, gas 5) for 10 minutes. Remove covering and brown for another 5 minutes.

**Soused Herrings**

6 or 8 herrings
1 tablespoon mixed pickling spice
1 breakfast cup vinegar
1 breakfast cup water
1 level teaspoon salt
1 large onion, finely sliced

Cut off the heads and tails, clean and bone the fish. Roll up with a slice of onion inside each fish. Pack in a baking dish (not a baking tin). Scatter pickling spice between the rolls, add the remainder of the sliced onion. Sprinkle with salt and pour in the vinegar and water mixed together. Bay leaves may be added if liked.

Bake in a slow oven (140°C/275°F, gas 1) for 1½ hours. If preferred, do not bone fish but lay flat in a dish, alternately thick end to thin end.

Different districts have their own traditional methods of preparing soused herrings and a small piece of bruised root ginger, half a dozen stalks (stems only) of parsley, fresh shallots and even chunks of cucumber can be added to the baking dish.

**Rollmops**

These are raw herrings filleted and marinated in spiced vinegar. They are delicious and easy to contrive. The following quantities are for 6 servings.

6 herrings
3 pickled gherkins, sliced
3 shallots, sliced
1 dessertspoon capers, chopped
6 dl (1 pint) wine vinegar
1 tablespoon spirit vinegar
2 shallots, finely sliced
2 tablespoons salt
2 whole cloves
6 black peppercorns, crushed
1 large bay leaf
pinch of cayenne pepper *or* few drops Tabasco sauce
1 teaspoon sugar

Clean and fillet the herrings and flatten them, skin down, on a board. Cover each fillet with a mixture of the chopped gherkins, shallots and capers. Roll up the fillets from the tail; skewer them with short cocktail sticks to prevent them from unrolling. Place them in a terrine (or a glass jar) so that they make a tight fit. Pour over them a marinade made from the remaining ingredients, cover closely and leave in the refrigerator for 4 days.

The addition of the spirit vinegar sharpens the marinade and accelerates the pickling process.

## *Inkfish*

See under **Squid**, below

## *John Dory*

This very delicious fish, to be classed with the brill, turbot, sole élite, is another large-headed, sullen-faced, wide-jawed creature whose visage is not often displayed by the fishmonger. Treat it in the kitchen as you would treat the aristocrats just mentioned, if only for the reason that, weight for weight, he will cost you as much – the head and innards being two-thirds of the weight of the entire fish.

Small John Dorys can be used as substitutes for the rascasse in regional soups and stews such as *Bouillabaisse* (see page 106) and *Bourride* (see page 200).

## *Kippers*

These are herrings, decapitated, split open, laid in brine and smoked. The best, reputedly, come from Loch Fyne in Scotland, though kippers do not carry identity cards and I have had many disappointments in buying them.

For really sweet kippers in the peak of condition, you have just got to rely on your fishmonger. Chance buying is risky, but choose the small ones. A disturbing modern factor is the increasing size of kippers; some are so big that the kippering does not go right through the flesh as it does with the small ones. However, let us say that you are having a run of luck and have bought some really fine kippers. Here are some of the ways in which you can deal with them.

**1** Put them under the grill until the large bone buckles up and starts to burn. Brush over with butter.

**2** Put them into a pan of boiling water, turn off the heat, and leave for 6 minutes. Drain and brush with butter.

**3** Fillet; pound the flesh of cooked or raw kipper with seasonings and mix with a simple *panada* (see page 189) to make *quenelles*.

**4** Fillet the cooked kipper, whether grilled, fried, baked or poached, and pound the flesh to make a fish pâté (see pages 84–5).

**5** Mix the flesh with creamed potatoes and seasoning to make fishcakes (see page 188).

See also page 90 for Marinated Kipper Fillets.

During World War II, no one on overseas service could understand why kippers could not have been included in the rations. (The fact is that they are quite difficult to keep.) However, the kipper ranked with Lili Marlene in a soldier's fantasies. On returning from the Middle East after six kipperless years, I managed to eat eight kippers at one sitting without any effort.

## *Ling*

This is another member of the cod or hake family. (See under **Cod**, above.)

## *Lobster*

Prince-cardinal of the crustaceans – though the crawfish (*langouste*) can claim equal rank. This is one kind of seafood which no one in their senses should ever dream of eating in restaurants at their own expense.

The proliferation of new luxury-hotel seafood restaurants and the influx of tourists able to afford to eat lobster has brought a very real threat to the lobster population of the United Kingdom. As already mentioned, an eager market exists for the small, 675-gr (1½-lb) lobster which divides conveniently into two expensive portions; and as these are over-fished, the species must be in serious danger of becoming extinct.

Something is being done to adjust the balance in the development of fish farming on a considerable scale, mainly in Scotland; every encouragement is being given to these enterprises by the Ministry of Agriculture and Fisheries, whose research stations are at the service of any farming enterprise which cares to consult them.

In my opinion the large 2–3 kg (4½–6 lb) lobster has a much better flavour than the small one, and it is much more serviceable (and also less expensive) when it comes to making hot lobster dishes with sauces at home.

Eating it at home is still expensive, although when everything is taken into account, lobster once a week probably only amounts to the price of one – or possibly two – of the blood-dripping porterhouse steaks eaten daily by those bowler-hatted carnivores who chomp their way through a whole herd of Aberdeen Angus in a year.

If you are using live lobster, throw the lobster in boiling salted water and boil it for 15 minutes for the first 450 gr (1 lb) of weight, plus 10 minutes for each subsequent 450 gr (1 lb). Probably the most delicious way of serving a lobster is to boil it in the manner just described before splitting it in half, removing the sac from the head and the intestinal thread from the tail and then brushing it with melted butter and lemon juice seasoned with black pepper; now put it under the grill for 10 – 15 minutes (basting all the time) and serve it with more butter and lemon.

I should also note here that in the original recipes for *Lobster Newburg* and *Homard à l'Américaine*, live lobsters have to be cut up, claws and all, and sautéed in butter until they turn bright red. When cutting up a live lobster, everyone would like to be certain that the first stroke of the knife brings instant death to the wretched victim. To accomplish this, a fairly heavy, broad, sharp knife is useful; this should be brought very firmly down to cut through the joint at the base of the head, thus separating the head from the tail shell in one swift stroke.

I feel that many people are deterred from serving lobster at home by having to kill the lobster themselves by either of these methods. Accordingly, for all the recipes given below, cooked lobster meat is used. If you buy your lobster ready-cooked from a really reliable fishmonger, the results of the finished dishes will be little different – and, if you are at all squeamish, you will be saved a lot of *angst*. All you have to do with the cooked lobster is cut it in half and remove the sac from the head and the intestinal thread from the tail.

Recipes for lobster soups will be found on page 101 (*bisque*) and on page 100 (*velouté*).

The following recipes for lobster apply equally to crawfish and (*mutatis mutandis*) the smaller crustacea, and to all firm fish of the shark family (for instance, dogfish, monkfish, porbeagle and tope). When using these other fish (and also when you wish to serve smaller quantities of lobster), scallop shells, instead of lobster shells, can be recruited for serving.

## *Hot lobster dishes*

All the lobsters appearing in fishmongers' shops nowadays seem to be of the same commercially viable size. The following recipes are for '*tête-à-tête*' dinners for two; by discarding the lobster shells and dividing the lobster pieces and the sauce between four scallop shells, the quantities will be sufficient for a first course for four people. For a main course for four people, the quantities given in the recipes below must be doubled. A small lobster weighing roughly 675 gr (1½ lb) will serve two people as a main course.

**Lobster Newburg** (lobster with cream, wine and *béchamel*)
Cut the flesh of a cooked lobster in pieces and sauter them briskly in 25 gr (1 oz) butter for 1 minute. Pour over them 1·5 dl (¼ pint) sherry *or* Madeira. Cook briskly, stirring your lobster pieces around for a minute. Reduce the heat and pour into the pan enough cream to sauce all the pieces well. Now fold in 3 dl (½ pint) *Sauce Béchamel*

(see page 64), and then bind with 2 egg yolks, first beaten up with 1 tablespoon cream. Fill the lobster half-shells with the mixture. Garnish with chopped and sautéed mushrooms.

**Lobster with Sauce Nantua**

Cut the flesh of a cooked lobster in pieces and sauter them in 25 gr (1 oz) butter for 1–2 minutes. Pour over them 1 tablespoon lighted brandy. Next add 3 dl ($\frac{1}{2}$ pint) *Sauce Nantua* (page 66). Cook, reducing a little. With the mixture, fill the lobster half-shells and garnish with Red Crab Butter (page 78), Crayfish Butter (page 79) or any other savoury butter of your choice.

**Lobster with Sauce Mornay**

Chop up the cooked lobster and sauter it in 25 gr (1 oz) butter for 1–2 minutes. Add 3 dl ($\frac{1}{2}$ pint) *Sauce Mornay* (page 62) and sprinkle with a mixture of finely grated Parmesan and Gruyère cheese. Place mixture in half-shells and put under a fierce grill to brown nicely.

**Homard à l'Américaine**

50 gr (2 oz) butter

*a mirepoix of the following:*
1 tablespoon carrot, grated
1 tablespoon onion, chopped
1 tablespoon celery, chopped
1 tablespoon parsley, chopped
1 tablespoon chervil, chopped

the cooked and chopped meat of 1 small lobster, 450–675 gr (1–1$\frac{1}{2}$ lb)
1 tablespoon brandy
1 glass white wine
3 dl ($\frac{1}{2}$ pint) *velouté* sauce (see page 59)

Make the *mirepoix* by stewing in the butter the carrot and the herbs; lay the lobster pieces in it. Ignite the brandy and pour it flaming over the lobster. Stir well and add the white wine. Cook briskly for 5 or 6 minutes to reduce a little. Then add the *velouté* sauce. Serve with plain boiled long-grain rice.

**Homard à l'Armoricaine**

Proceed as in the preceding recipe (*Homard à l'Américaine*), but enrich at the end with 2 tablespoons cream and the yolks of 2 eggs.

**Homard Thermidor** (lobster with white wine sauce)
Chop up the cooked lobster and sauter it in 25 gr (1 oz) butter with 50 gr (2 oz) diced mushrooms for 1–2 minutes. Pour on 3 dl ($\frac{1}{2}$ pint) *Sauce Bercy* (page 60) into which 1 teaspoon made English mustard *or* horseradish cream has been thoroughly stirred. Fill the half-shells with the mixture and garnish with chopped parsley.

Lobster sautéed in butter can be served with a variety of sauces. Try the following: *Cardinal* (page 61), *Marinière* (page 60), *Aurore* (page 59), *Normande* (page 61), *Poulette* (page 60) and *Régence* (page 61).

The quantities of sauce given in the above recipes relate to the lobster weighing 450–675 gr (1–1$\frac{1}{2}$ lb). If, however, you can find a really big lobster, the amount will have to be doubled or even tripled.

## *Cold lobster dishes*

Cut the cooked lobster in half, from head to tail. Remove the sac from the head and extract the intestinal thread from the tail. Loosen the flesh in the shell, leaving it whole, or remove the flesh and cut into slices or dice. It can then be served separately with an accompanying sauce, or coated in a sauce and returned to the shell.

Eat cold lobster with any of the following sauces: Vinaigrette (page 71); Mayonnaise and all its variations (pages 69–70); *Hollandaise* and its variations (pages 67–69); Special Tomato Sauce (page 72). If you are feeling particularly daring, try lobster with Portobello Sauce (page 74).

A Lobster Cocktail can be made by the method given for Prawn Cocktail on page 90.

## *Mackerel*

For these small cousins of the tunnyfish (several times removed, as far as texture is concerned), I have ambivalent feelings. As a boy on the Island of Achill, I was taken out in a coracle to fish for them with lines and crude paternosters carrying six hooks each. A shoal had been sighted close in to shore and there was a choppy sea. My fears that I would be seasick and draw shame on myself were only equalled by anxiety lest I should put a clumsy foot through the frail skin of the coracle. Perish the shoal, I thought. But then we were into it and in all the excitement that followed, my resentment and fear of being seasick vanished. Every hook of every line that came up had a gleaming fish on it. Re-baiting was a feverish activity, occupying more time than the fishing, and getting the fish off the hooks was a bloody business. Gradually, as we grew tired and the coracle became dangerously low in the water with the weight of mackerel we had taken, we gave up the effort of baiting and slung the tackle over the side unbaited – and still they came, simply for the taste of what was on the hooks. We gave up eventually and pulled in to the shore, and I staggered up to my small room in the local hotel and fell on my bed and to sleep. I awoke a few hours later and looked out of the window to see the beach, half pebble, half sand, covered with glistening fish, thrown up probably on the last wave of the tide before it ebbed swiftly. We had mackerel that evening, and for breakfast the next day, and the next, and the next – they were delicious, but . . . Many years later, I stood on the waterfront at Khalkis, looking down at hundreds of the same fish jostling each other and fighting at the mouth of a sewage outfall. I never ate mackerel in Greece.

I now sing the praises of this beautiful, many-coloured and delicious fish, which I eat at least once a week when it is in the fish shops – usually heavily scored, grilled and served with a lot of lemon and a Horseradish Butter (see page 80). In this country, they are as safe to buy as any other form of fresh food. What is more, they are probably the cheapest fish on the market today. They can be grilled (opened up), just brushed with lemon and butter and sprinkled with pepper and salt; or they can be baked in the oven with Special Tomato Sauce (see page 72). You can souse them by slowly cooking them in a marinade in the oven at 140°C/275°F, gas 1 (see page 141). Poach them gently – 6–8 minutes for any fish weighing up to 450 gr (1 lb) – and serve them with quarters of lemon and a simple *Beurre Blanc* sauce (see page 74), with one of the relish-type sauces (Chameleon Sauce, page 54 or Pickled Walnut Relish, page 76), or with Portobello Sauce (page 74).

On more serious occasions grilled, poached or baked mackerel can be served with a *Béarnaise* made with butter (page 68), a *Bercy* (page 60) into which 1 teaspoon made English mustard has been thoroughly stirred or, best of all, a gooseberry sauce, which is the traditional sauce to be served with this fish. As apple sauce is to pork so gooseberry sauce is to mackerel.

**Grilled Mackerel with Gooseberry Sauce**

Use good fresh fish weighing 450 gr (1 lb) or just under for this recipe. A fish of this size makes a full meal for one; as a first course, however, one fish of this size can serve two people. In either case, the fish must be prepared and grilled whole as follows.

Decapitate, gut and clean the mackerel in the normal way, and wipe dry. With a sharp knife, deeply score the outside of the fish with 3 diagonal cuts down to the bone. Make 100 gr (4 oz) *Maître d'Hôtel* Butter (see page 78); melt half of this and brush it over the fish and its wounds. Have the grill really hot to start with and put the fish under this fierce heat for 1 minute. Brush the fish again with the butter, reduce grill heat to medium and continue to cook the fish, basting frequently, for about 7 minutes. Now turn the fish over and score it deeply with 3 diagonal cuts to the bone at a wide angle to, and between, the cuts on the side already cooked. Brush with the savoury butter and repeat the cooking process for the second side. Basting should ensure that the mackerel has interesting burns scattered over its skin and at the edges of the diagonal cuts.

Meanwhile, make the sauce by boiling 450 gr (1 lb) carefully topped and tailed *unripe* gooseberries in 3 dl ($\frac{1}{2}$ pint) water until soft and fairly thick. Pass through a blender or sieve to obtain a smooth purée.

Serve on a hot plate, with pats of the remaining *Maître d'Hôtel* Butter dressing the wounds of the mackerel. Serve the Gooseberry Sauce separately.

**Smoked mackerel** Serve this as you would smoked eel.

## *Monkfish*

In French, *ange de mer*, this is not to be confused with **Angler-fish** (above).

Monkfish is the finest of a group of hitherto rather despised fish, all belonging to the shark family, which deserve the best culinary treatment. This group includes porbeagle, dogfish and tope; all methods described here for cooking monkfish may confidently be applied to its three relatives.

The monkfish has the face of a friendly demon designed by Hieronymus Bosch, and a tail that is food fit for angels. Fishmongers carefully protect the public from its gaze, but twice recently I have slipped through the security net and met the fish face to face, once in Soho and once in the Portobello Road. Looked at steadily, it returns a wide, saturnine grin which displays awesome teeth but no animosity, and it is more pathetic than frightening in its ugliness. The flesh of the monkfish tail is firm and delicious, with something of the flavour and texture of lobster. At the present time it is at the lower end of the price range. My only dread is that its increasing use and the discovery of its qualities may make it fashionable for restaurant dishes and consequently remove it from regular supply to the shopping public. There are ominous reports that it is being used to supplement lobster and scampi dishes in forward-looking restaurants.

Monkfish stands up well to all the accepted famous sauces. I find that it is best presented as small fillets or steaks. In even smaller portions it makes an excellent fish pie (see Highbury Pie, page 182) and is also better than conger eel in fish soups.

Treat it like lobster, crawfish or prawns and scampi. Think of *Ange de Mer Newburg*, *Ange de Mer Cardinal*, *Ange de Mer Mornay*, *Ange de Mer Thermidor*, *Ange de Mer Américaine* – each of which you will serve in scallop shells as *Coquilles Ange de Mer Newburg* . . . and so on.

Begin dinner parties with a flourish, with *Velouté d'Ange de Mer* or *Bisque d'Ange de Mer*.

Gather in a warm kitchen in winter round *Ange de Mer en Matelote* (see under **Eel**, above) and in summer make kebabs with it (see under **Bonito**, above).

Try it out with every sauce you can think of, and it will be a revelation to you.

There is not, as far as I know, a Monkfish Board in existence, and I have positively no interest to declare in the marketing of monkfish. It is simply by using it frequently, that I have come to regard it as one of the best fish in the stud book.

## *Mullet, Grey*

The grey mullet is a very old friend of mine, and I used to enjoy it cleaned, brined in sea water and smoked over pine needles, thyme and chips of pinewood, as well as in its usual guise of a fresh fish. I have not come across smoked grey mullet since, but I have no doubt that one day I shall be wandering through Soho and will see it hanging in a shop, well beyond my budget. I cannot believe that in those far-off days when my palate was far more sensitive than it is now, I can have been mistaken in finding it delicious. It must certainly have been better than the smoked cod that is being sold today, and was caviare compared with the dried cod which hangs like withered bats from the ceiling and which, on Aghios Nikolaos, I had to try to revive for the workmen's meals.

Why do people refer to the grey mullet in such patronizing terms, as if it were some kind of desperate social climber? It did not choose its name in order to cash in on the reputation of its undoubted superior, the red mullet. And what has happened to its roe which, dried, pressed and smoked, is the basis of the one and only true *Taramasalata*? Fine slivers of this roe were an expensive *mezé* in 1934, when I used to sit, sipping *ouzo*, outside Orphanides' Bar in Athens. (All other *mezé*, except clams, were free in those days.) I have bought very large grey mullet during the last year, choosing the fat ones which had every appearance of being *enceintes*, but I have not yet succeeded in finding one filled with roe.

Small grey mullet are best grilled, deeply scored with the gashes filled with a rather strong savoury butter (grated horseradish, finely chopped celery and onion, a teaspoon of salt and a teaspoon of pepper, pounded together with 50 gr [2 oz] butter). If your grey mullet weighs over 1 kg (2¼ lb), it is better to stuff it with a savoury fish forcemeat and bake as in the following recipe:

### Baked Grey Mullet

1 grey mullet weighing 1 kg (2¼ lb)
300 gr (12 oz) fish forcemeat (see page 173)
100 gr (4 oz) butter
2 onions, chopped
4 small tomatoes, skinned and chopped
1 tablespoon parsley, chopped
1 stick celery, chopped
1·5 dl (¼ pint) white wine

Scale and clean the mullet and stuff it with the fish forcemeat. Melt 50 gr (2 oz) of the butter in a frying pan and throw in the other ingredients to cook briskly for 10 minutes, stirring frequently. Transfer to a dish just large enough to take the grey mullet, which should then be laid on this bed of vegetables; sprinkle the wine over the fish and dot with the remaining butter cut into very small pieces.

Baste the fish while it cooks in a moderate oven (180°C/350°F, gas 4) for 30 minutes.

Serve with Butter Sauce (page 55) or *Sauce Béarnaise* (page 68).

Fillets of grey mullet can be fried in egg and breadcrumbs, or cooked *à la meunière*, and served with any of the *béchamel-* or *velouté*-based sauces (see pages 59—66). Poached and served cold, grey mullet should be accompanied by *Sauce Rémoulade* (page 70).

## *Mullet, Red*

This is the fish which has put the grey mullet (no relation) into the shade. It is easy to see why. Grilling is the ideal method of cooking this fish with the unique flavour. Very small ones can be passed through a thin batter and cooked whole and uncleaned. Larger ones should, I feel, be gutted, taking care not to remove the liver which is the source of much of this fish's special taste. Whether fried, grilled or baked *en papillote* (see page 41) with herbs and butter, red mullet should be served with lemon, pepper and salt, and *Maître d'Hôtel* Butter (page 78).

Baked (sprinkled with wine) and served cold, garnished with slices of lemon or orange and a few black olives, whole red mullet can be accompanied (but not masked) by a variety of sauces. See the variations on mayonnaise (pages 69–70) or try a *Béarnaise* with an oil base (page 68).

The sacrifice of a small red mullet to a stock for a soup (see page 97) or a sauce (see page 59) is well worth while. It makes an outstanding *velouté* soup (see page 100).

Although the bones are troublesome, it is rewarding to fillet a good-sized red mullet, and to flake and pound its flesh and liver in order to make an exceptional fish pâté, following the recipe on page 84.

As a rock fish, this is one of the stock ingredients of *Bouillabaisse* (see page 106) and other regional soups and stews.

I have never had a smoked red mullet, but I suspect that, if treated in the same way as bloaters or Arbroath smokies, mullet might prove to be an outstanding delicacy.

## *Mussels*

My favourite meal is two dozen oysters, followed by *Moules Marinière* (the recipe for which will be given in a moment) – taken, naturally, with champagne. If I have to choose between the two shellfish, I find it an agony to decide, but in the long run I come down on the side of the mussels. (As between God and the mussel, well, there you *have* got a tussle.) I have already indicated my strong attachment to these bivalves, so before I grow dithyrambic I shall deal with the practical side of cooking and serving them.

When buying mussels, get about 20 per cent more than the recipe requires in order to be sure of having enough after the damaged ones have been rejected.

**Moules Marinière**

3 quarts mussels
½ bottle Entre-deux-Mers white wine
5 black peppercorns, crushed
the white of 1 leek, finely chopped
3 sprigs fennel
1 shallot, finely chopped
4 stalks and heads parsley, finely chopped
4 tablespoons parsley, finely chopped

Clean and prepare your mussels (see page 35).

Into a wide, two-handled gallon pan with a heavy lid, put the wine with the pepper, leek, shallot and the herbs (reserving the chopped parsley). Check over your mussels once more and load them, as gently as possible, into the pan. Shake them down so as to make them comfortable. Put on the lid. Now let the fire roar under the pan. The moment you sense that steam has been raised, curb your desire to remove the lid, but give one or two good shakes to the pan; after 30 seconds, slide it off the fire and give it one more shake. After a further 15 seconds lift the lid and give one last shake. Let the mussels sit for a minute, while their juices drain into the pan. Now remove your mussels to a colander (sitting on a bowl to collect any juices which may drain from them). Meanwhile, cover the mussels with a cloth and keep them warm. Now, strain the juices from the big pan into a smaller, more convenient one. Add the strained mussel juices from the bowl under the colander. Set on the heat and bring to the boil. Distribute your mussels in large, heated soup plates or bowls. Put the finely chopped parsley into the liquid just off the boil and pour over the mussels in the plates.

For another version of *Moules Marinière*: after removing the mussels from the pan, simply thicken the cooking liquid with kneaded butter and flour (*beurre manié*, see page 56).

**Moules Poulette**

Proceed as for *Moules Marinière*, but add the cooking liquid (reduced by a half by boiling) to 3 dl (½ pint) *Sauce Poulette* (see page 60). Pour over mussels in the half-shell and sprinkle with finely chopped parsley.

One of the joys of mussels is that they can be served stuffed in a very wide variety of ways, each in the half-shell covered with a teaspoonful of a delicious sauce; for suggestions, see Stuffed Mussels, page 88.

The mussel is a very important element in many seafood dishes: fish pies, soups, rice dishes (see *Seafood Aurore*, page 193 and Pote's *Paella*, page 191).

## *Octopus*

To the Japanese, the octopus carries no sinister connotations, and the affairs of fisher-girls with their octopus lovers are enshrined in some of their most exquisite *netsuke*, which depict these strange embraces. However, for those brought up on Jules Verne and Victor Hugo, this denizen of all temperate waters still stirs up deep residues of fear.

Before the war, these eight-legged creatures were only to be found in a few specialist shops in Soho and the East End of London, in dried form. They used to hang like shrivelled wreaths, not immediately identifiable as anything possibly edible. These withered objects were exciting to cook. (They can still be bought at Chinese emporiums.) They should be thrown on to a very hot griddle, when the performance will begin. For a short time, nothing seems likely to happen; then, suddenly, movement will be detected and the beast will start to come alive, gently writhing and stretching its eight tentacles in an attempt to disentangle itself. Marvellous juices will begin to bubble and sing as they touch the hot plate. When one side is cooked almost to singeing and has turned a blackish purple, it should be turned over, and again cooked to singeing. The thin ends of the tentacles will then be found to be deliciously crisp and make a splendid accompaniment to drinks before a meal. The thicker portions are delicious to chew – but only for strong teeth and tireless jaws.

Apart from this wasteful method of cooking dried octopus, long soaking (at least 48 hours) and slow cooking thereafter with onion, rosemary, garlic and bay leaf will produce a good octopus stew, comparable with the recipe for fresh octopus given below.

**Kyria Eftychia's Octopus Stew**

(I may say that Kyria Eftychia's original recipe omitted the sieving of the contents of the pan in the final stages.)

675 gr (1½ lb) octopus tentacles
3 dl (½pint) olive oil
4 cloves garlic
4 anchovy fillets
6 tomatoes, skinned and chopped
1 bottle red wine
3 carrots, sliced
1 bay leaf
a sprig of thyme
a sprig of marjoram
2 sticks celery
8 shallots
6 black peppercorns, crushed

Prepare the octopus as described on page 36. Heat the olive oil in a good, heavy stewpan and when just hot, put in the octopus. Cover and cook briskly for 10 minutes. Reduce heat and put in 2 cloves garlic, the anchovies and the tomatoes. Cook gently for 15 minutes. Now put in half the bottle of red wine, and add the carrots, the bay leaf, thyme, marjoram and celery. Cover and cook very slowly for 1 hour. At the end of that time, loosen the mixture with the rest of the red wine, and allow the whole to simmer for 3 long hours.

Remove the octopus on to a dish and set on one side to cool down. Meanwhile, pass the contents of your pan through a sieve and return the juices to the pan.

Cut up the octopus into 5-cm (2-in) pieces and put them back into the mixture, together with the shallots, peeled but whole, and the 2 remaining cloves of garlic, chopped. Cook slowly for 1 hour.

Just before serving, crush the 6 black peppercorns and stir them well in. Serve in bowls with thick pieces of real bread.

Octopus, as I have mentioned elsewhere, adds a good deal to any stock for making soups with firm, strong-tasting fish. Really small 'baby' octopus can be fried whole in a batter and served with lemon and a good savoury butter.

## *Oysters*

For me, there is only one way to eat oysters: live, in the deep shell, with the juice of the fresh lemon. In addition, my jaded palate demands a little red pepper or a teaspoon of Green Peppercorn Relish (see page 76). I will also accept oysters served in cocktails, provided the sauce is right. Choose a sauce from those I have suggested on page 90. See also Angels on Horseback (page 91).

However, for those who insist on gilding the lily, I here include Richard Briggs' Oyster Stew. If you *must* cook oysters, it would be hard to find a better way.

**'To stew Oysters.** Take a quart of large oysters, put them in a saucepan and set them*, strain the liquor from them through a sieve, wash them well and take off the beards; put them in a stew-pan, and drain the liquor from the settlings, put to the oysters a quarter of a pound of butter mixed with flour, a gill of white wine, and grate in a little nutmeg, with a gill of cream, keep them stirring till they are thick and smooth, put sippets at the bottom of the dish, pour the oysters in, and put sippets all round.'

## *Perch*

These fresh-water fish should be handled with gloves on, as the spines of the fin which runs down the back can sting like a bee. They are excellent fish, but require careful cleaning. They are best cooked

*Cook very lightly until oysters turn from being a gelatinous colour to white

for 10–12 minutes in a well-salted *court-bouillon* containing a little vinegar, skinned and then served with melted butter.

For interest's sake, or for the adventurous, here is Richard Briggs' rugged approach.

**'To fry Perch.** Scale, gut, and wash them clean, wipe them dry with a cloth, make a batter with flour, ale, and the yolk of an egg, and dip the fish in on both sides; have a pan of hogs-lard or beef-dripping boiling hot, fry them on both sides of a fine brown, put them on a coarse cloth before the fire to drain; fry a handful of parsley crisp, put the fish in a hot dish, and garnish with the crispt parsley, with anchovy sauce in a boat. You may dress roach, dace, and gudgeons in the same way.'

## *Pike*

Pike is not a fish I cook very often, but when one comes my way, I poach it in a strongly flavoured *bouillon*, made with two-thirds water to one-third white wine, and containing bay leaf, thyme, onions and grated horseradish. When it is cooked, I put it, whole, on a large dish, sprinkle it with chopped parsley and the leaves of watercress, and then pour hot melted butter over it. I also have a small tureen or boat of *Beurre Blanc* sauce (see page 74) on the table.

It should be noted that Richard Briggs' basic cooking method in the following recipe is *not* boiling, but poaching in a fish kettle.

**'To boil a Pike.** Scale, gill and gut the fish, and wash it well; make a stuffing in the following manner: Chop a dozen oysters small, the crumb of a penny loaf soaked in cream, a quarter of a pound of butter, two anchovies chopped fine, a little grated nutmeg, some sweet herbs and parsley, with a little lemon-peel shred fine, season it with pepper and salt, mix it up well together, put it into the belly and sew it up; then tie a string round the nose, and with a large needle or skewer put it through the middle, and make it in the form of an S, by tying the string to the tail, and put it on a drainer; have a fish kettle of spring water boiling, with a handful of salt, put it in and boil it gently according to its size; (a pike of eight pounds will take a full hour boiling, bigger or less in proportion) take it up and set it across the kettle to drain; put it in your dish, and garnish with fish patties, or fried oysters and horse radish, with strong anchovy sauce and plain butter in boats. You may if you please boil it without the stuffing.'

It would be possible to substitute mussels for oysters in the above recipe.

The flesh of the pike, minced fine and well seasoned, makes very fine *quenelles*. Here is a recipe for the famous *Quenelles de Brochet:*

**Quenelles de Brochet**

450 gr (1 lb) pike meat
2 teaspoons salt
½ teaspoon freshly ground black pepper
pinch of ground mace
225 gr (8 oz) butter
300 gr (12 oz) *panada* (see page 189)
2 eggs
4 egg yolks

Pound the pike flesh to a paste with the seasonings. Beat in the butter and the *panada* until all is smooth. Now put in the eggs and egg yolks, and beat until the whole mixture is homogeneous. Form the mixture into small balls, sausages or any other shape required, and poach in boiling salted water for at least 10 minutes.

These *quenelles* can be served as garnishes with other dishes, or on their own with a *Beurre Blanc* sauce (see page 74), Special Tomato Sauce (page 72), *Sauce Mornay* (page 62) or *Sauce Béarnaise* (page 68).

## *Pilchards*

Fresh pilchards (which are grown-up sardines) are delicious, though perhaps not quite in the class of their offspring. However, they can be treated in all the ways applicable to the sardine (see under **Sardine**, below).

Tinned pilchards are cheap, and can be used to make fish pâtés and fishcakes, though the fresh fish is always preferable. When

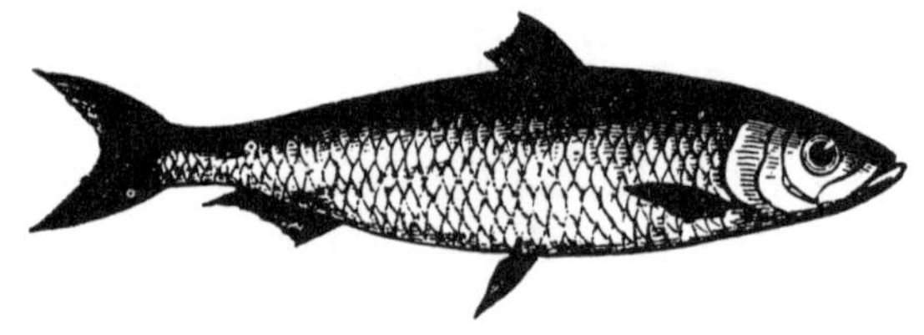

buying tinned pilchards, look out for the dreaded words 'in tomato sauce'. I fell into this trap with a tin of sardines the other day. I am always on my guard with pilchards, but I was not aware that the poor sardine is now often denied her natural element of olive oil and forced into a bed of clotted gore.

## *Plaice*

Why do people sigh or remain wholly impassive at the mention of plaice? This fish, especially when large, deserves a much better reputation than has been accorded it. It has been condemned almost exclusively to the deep-frying basket and has been greatly degraded by the dreadful commercial batters to which it has been subjected.

Fillets of plaice can be treated in any of the ways applicable to sole, but, as with cod, a very great nicety of timing is required to prevent overcooking. Plaice are particularly good cooked *à la meunière* and also – it must be admitted – deep-fried in a *good* home-made batter (which, to some degree, protects them from overcooking). Serve with *Sauce Hollandaise* (page 67), *Sauce Tartare* (page 70) or one of the savoury butters (pages 77–81).

**Batter for Fish**

50 gr (2 oz) plain flour
pinch salt
1 egg
1·5 dl ($\frac{1}{4}$ pint) milk

Beat the flour, salt and egg until smooth and blend in the liquid. This batter should be enough to cover sufficient fish for four people.

The flesh of plaice is excellent for making fishcakes and fish pies, and, when pounded, for enriching soups.

## *Porbeagle (Tope)*

Another member of the shark family which is beginning to be taken seriously. Cook porbeagle in any of the ways given for **Monkfish**, above.

## *Prawns, Dublin Bay Prawns (Scampi)*

These delicious crustaceans can be cooked in most of the ways applicable to lobster (see under **Lobster**, above). You should, however, be completely on your guard against scampi in pretentious pubs where they tend to be tasteless, coated in a repellent batter and served, for some inexplicable reason, in a basket.

To cook fresh prawns or scampi, throw the shellfish into a boiling *court-bouillon* for 10 minutes, when they will be perfectly cooked. If, however, you wish to make – for instance – a Prawn Newburg or *Crevettes à l'Américaine* (see pages 145 and 146), they should be boiled for only 2 minutes, taken from the water and allowed to cool before the shell is removed. Proceed, using the whole shelled prawns instead of lobster pieces, but reducing the cooking time so that the prawns are not overcooked in the final dish.

Prawns and scampi can be served hot in any of the following sauces: *Aurore* (page 59); *Bercy* or *Poulette* (page 60); *Normande* (page 61); *Gratin* (page 62); Rich Tomato (page 66); *Hollandaise* (page 67); *Béarnaise* (page 68), as well as in many others. Try substituting them for eels *en matelote* in the recipe on page 133.

For serving with cold prawns and scampi, there are all the mayonnaise-based sauces to call on (see pages 67–70), as well as *Sauce Gribiche* (page 72) and Aspic (page 206). The shellfish can be served whole or sliced, with any green salad or in a mixed fish salad (see page 204).

They are extremely popular in fish cocktails (page 90), make wonderful soups – *bisque* (page 101), *velouté* (page 100), or *béchamel*-based (page 103).

They add savour to, and are very ornamental garnishes for, rice dishes such as *Paella* (page 191). They are good subjects for a curry, whether unorthodox (page 196) or traditional (page 197).

## *Rascasse*

This is a small rock fish, found in the Mediterranean, which is particularly good used in any attempts at making a *Bouillabaisse*.

## *Rock Salmon*

See under **Dogfish**, above.

## *Saithe*

See under **Coley**, above.

## *Salmon*

The survival of the salmon is a matter in which we should all take a very serious interest as, at the present rate of competitive over-fishing and of river pollution, its days would appear to be numbered. My own 'affair' with salmon has been life-long. The only advantage of being in the choir at school, which meant long hours of practice while others played games or daydreamed, was that every summer term there would come the fine day of the choir treat. In a horse-drawn brake, our heads crammed to bursting with the polyphonies of Byrd, Tye, Tallis and Taverner, we would be driven out to Burnham Beeches where, a trestle table being laid, we would watch the choir master, who was a great angler, practise surgery on what appeared at the time to be a very leviathan of a salmon. We ate it with mayonnaise and salad, and it was followed by rare delights such as trifle and jelly, swimming in cream.

Other salmon haunt me, such as the one I was promised by the owner of a small pub in Ross-on-Wye. The river was flooding at the time, and after a night's dreaming of the salmon which on the morrow would be mine, I set out in the morning around opening time to collect my prize. Alas, the floods had risen so swiftly in the night that they had cut off all possible access to the pub.

### Poached salmon

The salmon has one danger; its flesh has a slight tendency to dryness; people particularly value the middle cut which is more succulent. The salmon is one fish which, in my opinion, is better poached than grilled. Use a *court-bouillon* cooked for 45 minutes, made with wine, carrots, onions, thyme, parsley and celery, half a level teaspoon salt and 3 black peppercorns to every 6 dl (1 pint) of water. Put your salmon, or portion thereof, into the cool *court-bouillon* and bring slowly to simmering point; simmer gently for the required time (see page 41). Lift out your salmon, drain, place on a hot dish and remove the skin with great care. Whether masked with sauce or simply sprinkled with melted butter, a whole salmon should be brought to table with at least the traditional garnish of finely sliced rounds of cucumber, lemon wedges and sprigs of parsley.

Eating salmon hot is such an intense experience that it is not usual to serve elaborate vegetables with it. A simple dish of new potatoes, boiled with mint, is the austere but ideal accompaniment.

Sauces which go particularly well with hot poached salmon are the *Hollandaise* and its derivatives (see pages 67–68), *Beurre Blanc* (page 74) and *Nantua* (page 66). But it is difficult to think of a sauce (with the possible exception of *Aïoli*) which would be out of context with poached salmon.

No fish could be more delicious when cold than the salmon, served with a *Hollandaise* or mayonnaise (see pages 67 and 69), and accompanied by the cucumber with which this fish has a special affinity.

Left-overs of cooked salmon can be made up into delicious fillings for *coquilles* (scallop shells) with any of the *béchamel-* or *velouté*-based sauces (see pages 64 and 59) or as in the following recipe.

**Coquilles de Saumon Mornay** (salmon in scallop shells)

50 gr (2 oz) butter
4 tablespoons *duxelles* of mushrooms, onion and parsley (see Glossary)
225 gr (8 oz) remnants of cooked salmon
675 gr ($1\frac{1}{2}$ lb) potato, cooked and creamed with milk and butter and well seasoned with salt and pepper
6 dl (1 pint) *Sauce Mornay* (see page 62)

Melt the butter in a saucepan, add the *duxelles* and the flaked salmon to heat through. Heat 4 scallop shells in the oven. Arrange a 2·5-cm (1-in) thick edging of mashed potato round each shell. Put 2 table-spoons *Sauce Mornay* into the bottom of each shell; then distribute the salmon mixture and coat with the remaining *Sauce Mornay*.

Put the *coquilles* at the top of a hot oven (200°C/400°F, gas 6) for 10 minutes or until nicely browned.

Salmon has a texture particularly suitable for mousses (see page 89) and soufflés (page 203). It also makes excellent fishcakes (page 188), pâtés (page 84) and *quenelles* (page 189). Salmon kedgeree (page 194) is justly renowned.

**Quiche de Saumon** (salmon tart)

This is a good way of using up the left-over fragments from a poached salmon or portion thereof – or from any other left-over cooked fish. The tart to contain the filling can be made from short-crust (see page 186) or flaky pastry.

150 gr (6 oz) pastry
150 gr (6 oz) cooked salmon, flaked
1 tablespoon parsley, finely chopped
4 eggs
1 egg yolk
1·5 dl ($\frac{1}{4}$ pint) thick cream
1 tablespoon grated Parmesan or Gruyère cheese
salt and black pepper

Roll out the pastry thinly and line a 25-cm (10-in) flan case with it. Bake blind in the oven at 180°C/350°F, gas 4 for 12 minutes. Spread the flakes of salmon evenly over the bottom of the tart; sprinkle with the parsley. Now beat up the eggs and the extra egg yolk and fold in the cream and the cheese. Season with a pinch or two of salt and a sprinkle of black pepper. Cover the salmon with the mixture and bake in a moderate oven (180°C/350°F, gas 4) for 15 minutes.

Left-over salmon can, alternatively, be used to make Salmon Pizza – see basic recipe on page 187.

Cooking *en papillote* (see page 41) is a splendid way of dealing with whole smaller salmon (of say, up to 2 kg – 4½ lb), or with salmon steaks, but however much seasoning is sealed in with the salmon (which admittedly emerges from the oven with all its juices intact), these do not seem to be absorbed into the flesh as thoroughly as when the fish is cooked slowly in a really well-made *court-bouillon*. (After cooking *en papillote*, the juices in the bag or foil should be strained and used to reinforce whatever sauce is to be served with the fish.)

**Smoked Salmon** is, of course, the king of the smoked fishes, and it is hard to imagine a more delicious meal than as much smoked salmon as one wants with lemon, black pepper and thin slices of brown bread and butter. The sandwich, usually a pedestrian form of nourishment, seems to be lifted on to a more rarefied plane when it contains smoked salmon. Small cuttings of smoked salmon pounded up make an excellent smoked fish pâté, following the basic recipe on page 84.

See also Solomon's Rolls (page 83).

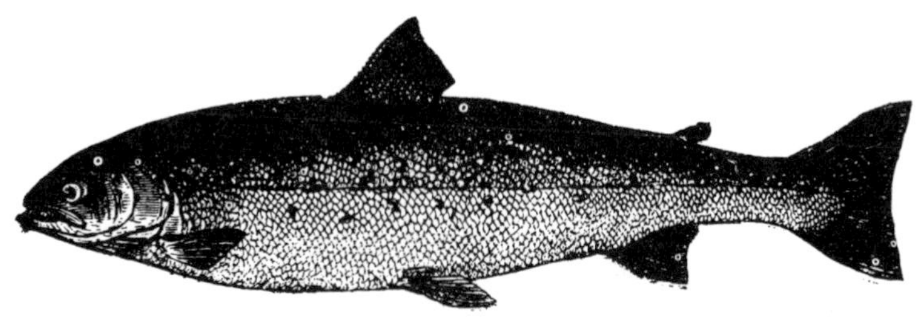

## *Salmon Trout*

It is possible endlessly to debate the respective merits of the salmon and the salmon trout, that fish which marries the taste of salmon with the texture of trout. It is its texture which, for me, just slightly tilts the balance in its favour. Salmon trout (also known as sea trout) can be cooked in all the ways suitable to **Salmon**, above.

## *Sardines*

These juvenile pilchards are delicious fresh. After cleaning, grill, fry or bake them, and serve them with any of the savoury butters, and with quarters of lemon. They are also good with Special Tomato Sauce (page 72), and Chameleon Sauce (page 54).

Tinned sardines in olive oil are possibly the most successful achievement of the metal-box men. Eat them just as they are, cold, or with a relish (see pages 76–77), or grilled and served on toast. Pound them, drained of their oil, with seasonings for pâté (page 85), fishcakes (page 188), or for cocktail or after-dinner savouries (see page 91). The tinned sardine is a fish with which anyone can do their own thing and come up with something new to serve with drinks or as an *hors-d'oeuvre*.

The filleting of tinned sardines is to my mind comparable with the genteel practice of allowing the nail of the little finger to grow three inches long, in order to prove unfamiliarity with manual labour.

Sardines canned in other oils or in tomato sauce are greatly inferior to those in pure olive oil.

Fresh (or frozen) sardines are not cheap when they appear on the market. As I can personally account for five or six at a sitting (plain grilled and seasoned only with lemon juice, salt and pepper), indulgence is for me only an occasional pleasure. However, Alan Davidson gives an economical Spanish recipe to serve four people:

**'Tortilla de Sardinas Frescas**

'A Spanish omelette with fresh sardines

'This is a Balearic recipe, for which you will need 4 fresh (or frozen) sardines and 6 eggs.

'Clean, scale and debone the sardines, discarding the heads but leaving the tails intact. Separate the yolks from the whites of the eggs. Beat the yolks with a little salt and some chopped parsley. Beat the whites with a little salt, separately.

'Heat olive oil in a large pan. Lightly fry a chopped clove of garlic in it. Combine the yolk and the white mixtures and add half of it to the pan, over a low heat. As this starts to cook, quickly lay out the sardines over it, opened out, and sprinkle over them some paprika and lemon juice. Then pour the rest of the egg mixture on top. Run a thread of olive oil round the edge of the pan, to prevent sticking.

'Cook the tortilla very gently, and turn it over once so that both sides are browned. (Turning it over is tricky, and I prefer to finish off the top side under the grill – but this needs a large grill.) The sardines will be cooked satisfactorily inside the tortilla, and the dish is both unusual and good.'

**Sardines en Papillote** (baked sardines)

When you buy sardines from the fishmonger, resign yourself to paying for ice as well as for fish. This means that you only get five or six fish to the 450 gr (1 lb). For four people you will therefore require 1·5 kg (3 lb).

1·5 kg (3 lb) sardines
2 onions, finely sliced
1 tablespoon parsley, finely chopped
900 gr (2 lb) tomatoes
1 tablespoon wine vinegar
2 tablespoons olive oil
1 tablespoon chives, finely chopped
salt and black pepper

Let the sardines thaw out in the refrigerator (6 hours) if necessary. Behead and gut them; wash away all blood and dry well.

Into a good, wide earthenware dish put the sliced onion and the parsley. Lay the sardines on this fragrant bed. Skin and slice the tomatoes and lay them on the sardines so as to conceal the fish altogether. Sprinkle on first the vinegar, then the olive oil and, finally, the chives, salt and pepper.

Cover with foil and cook in a moderate oven (180°C/350°F, gas 4) for 35 minutes. This makes an absolutely delicious dish to be eaten hot or cold.

See also Alan Davidson's *Pasta con le Sarde* (Sicilian Macaroni and Sardine Pie (on page 202.)

## *Scallops*

No praise is too high for this meaty bivalve of subtle flavour, which, with the opening of each new hotel or restaurant, becomes more difficult for the ordinary shopper to find.

When buying scallops, insist on getting both shells – not just the flat one, but also the beautiful (and most useful) conch in which Botticelli's *Venus* rises from the sea.

After cleaning (see page 34), sauter them in butter in which a little grated onion and parsley have been sweated, turning them after 2 minutes' very gentle cooking. (Turn them once if small; twice, at the same interval, if large.) Spoon the butter over them as they cook. Season them with pepper, and serve with *Maître d'Hôtel* Butter (page 78).

### Coquilles St Jacques

8 small to medium scallops, cleaned and trimmed (see page 34)
6 dl (1 pint) *court-bouillon*
6 dl (1 pint) thick *Sauce Béchamel* (page 64) into which 1 dl ($\frac{1}{4}$ pint) of double cream has been thoroughly stirred
2 tablespoons fine breadcrumbs
2 tablespoons parsley and chives, finely chopped

Put the scallops into as small and shallow a pan as will enable you just to cover them with the *court-bouillon*. Heat up to simmering point and allow to poach for 4 minutes. Remove the scallops to a dish and cut them up into 3 or 4 pieces each, keeping the orange 'tongues' intact. Reduce the cooking liquid rapidly by half; add the residue to the enriched *béchamel* sauce and cook for 5 minutes.

Now put 2 tablespoons of this sauce into the bottom of each of 4 deep scallop shells. Distribute the scallop pieces equally among the shells and cover with the remaining *béchamel*. Sprinkle with the breadcrumbs and brown under the grill or in a hot oven (200°C/400°F, gas 6) for 5–10 minutes. Before serving, sprinkle with the parsley and chives.

This is a basic recipe. Scallops can be served in the shell with any of the *béchamel-* or *velouté-*based sauces.

Alternatively, poach scallops in a good stock for 4 minutes. Take them out, cut them up into 6 or 8 pieces, keeping the coral 'tongues' intact, and give them the company of a few cooked shrimps or prawns, poached mussels, or small pieces of cooked firm fish (such as sole, monkfish, turbot, white crab meat, tender pieces of small squid). Place in the deep scallop shell and pour over them any of the *béchamel-* or *velouté-*based sauces. Serve garnished with parsley, or sprinkle with breadcrumbs and butter (or with Parmesan cheese) and brown under the grill. Or you can use rather less sauce, cover with buttered mashed potato and brown in the oven or under the grill. There are endless variations to this kind of treatment of scallops.

Many people like scallops with bacon. The poached scallops are alternated with thin slices of bacon (or wrapped in them) and grilled on skewers.

Scallops make marvellous fish soups – *bisque* (page 101), *velouté* (page 99), and mixed shellfish soup (see page 108). See also the *béchamel-*based soups.

## *Scampi (Dublin Bay Prawns)*

See under **Prawns**, above.

## *Shad*

These oily fish are members of the herring family and can be treated in similar ways. They are estuarial and now rarely found in English river mouths. The Loire and the Garonne rivers in France have the shad in plentiful supplies. Here is a recipe:

**Shad stuffed with Spinach and Sorrel**

3 small onions, finely sliced
50 gr (2 oz) butter
225 gr (8 oz) spinach, shredded
225 gr (8 oz) sorrel, shredded
2 tablespoons double cream
2 hard-boiled eggs, shelled and chopped
salt and black pepper
1 kg ($2\frac{1}{4}$ lb) shad, cleaned and scaled

Melt the butter in a medium-size saucepan and add the onions; cook them until softened and then add the spinach and sorrel. Leave over a gentle heat until a thick purée evolves. Blend in the cream and hard-boiled eggs, season with salt and pepper, and fill the cavity of the fish. Sew it up if necessary. Lay the fish in a large ovenproof dish, dot with butter and bake in a moderately hot oven (190°C/375°F, gas 5) for about 25–30 minutes. Serve with pats of Parsley Butter.

## *Shrimps*

These, the smallest of the crustaceans, are ideal in size for universal use in fish cookery – though on their own, boiled for 5 minutes, they should not be eschewed as a first course. Put 225 gr (8 oz) cooked unshelled shrimps before each guest, and let them get on with it. The results will be: i) that inane conversation will cease, ii) that the consumption of your good wine will diminish, iii) that you will be able to study human nature at its best or worst, and iv) that it will put a stop to smoking until you come to the real fish dish of the meal. However, it is more customary to serve potted shrimps – which it is far more economical to prepare yourself than to buy ready-potted.

### Potted Shrimps

Throw 450 gr (1 lb) shrimps into 6 dl (1 pint) *court-bouillon* containing chopped onion, thyme, fennel and a bay leaf, seasoned with salt and black pepper. Boil fast for 5 minutes. Drain and allow to cool. Then peel the shrimps and press them into small terrines standing in very hot water. Melt 75 gr (3 oz) butter in a pan until hot but not quite boiling; season it with a little grated nutmeg and some black pepper. Pour slowly on to your shrimps to cover. Allow to cool, then cover the terrines and put them into the cool part of the refrigerator. (I hate the butter to be frozen rock-hard.) Serve each person with an individual terrine and with toast, butter and lemon quarters.

For the use of shrimps in soups, made dishes etc, follow the instructions under **Prawns**, above.

Shrimp Butter (page 80) is a perfect accompaniment to sole, turbot, brill and so on (whether grilled, poached or cooked *à la meunière*), and also to plain boiled lobster or crawfish.

## *Skate*

The spreading of light by cookery writers has brought this stimulating fish up from its former British role below stairs, to take its rightful place in fish cookery. While, deep-fried, it is still one of the mainstays of take-away fried-fish shops (where it is battered to death daily), perhaps the guise in which we most often order it in restaurants is with black butter (*Raie au Beurre Noir*). I give Elizabeth David's recipe for this (from *French Provincial Cooking*).

**'Raie au Beurre Noir.** Supposing that you have a piece of wing of skate, weighing $1\frac{1}{4}$ to $1\frac{1}{2}$ lb, the other ingredients are an onion, a couple of sprigs of parsley, a little salt and 2 tablespoons of vinegar... Bring gently to the boil, with the pan uncovered. Thereafter let it gently simmer for 15 to 20 minutes. Lift it out and put it on a dish or board so that you can remove the skin and the large cartilaginous pieces of bone and divide the fish into 2 or 3 portions. This has to be done with some care, or the appearance of the fish will be spoiled. Transfer it to a fireproof serving dish, sprinkle it with chopped parsley, and keep it hot over a low flame while the black butter is prepared.

'For this you put 2 oz of fresh butter into a small frying-pan and heat it over a fast flame until it foams and begins to turn brown. At this precise moment, not sooner nor later, take the pan from the fire, for in a split second the butter will take on the deep hazel-nut colour which is *beurre noir*. (It should be only a little darker than *beurre noisette*, which is light hazel-nut colour.) Pour it instantly over the fish. Into the pan in which the butter has cooked, and which you have replaced on the fire, pour 2 tablespoons of wine vinegar, which will almost instantly boil and bubble. Pour this, too, over the

fish, and bring at once to table; for, like all dishes in which *beurre noir* figures, the ideal is only attained when the dish is set before those who are to eat it with the sauce absolutely sizzling.'

While this is the classic recipe, there are many people who would be deeply disappointed if their *raie* were not lavishly scattered with small capers and chopped parsley.

With grilled, fried or poached skate try the Pickled Walnut Relish on page 76, or one of the Chameleon Sauces (pages 53–55). It can also occasionally be served with *béchamel*- or *velouté*-based sauces; try it with *Sauce Soubise*, (page 66) and with *Sauce Béarnaise* (page 68). Poached Skate is good coated with *Sauce Caroline* (page 73). Skate makes excellent soups, both on its own (page 110) and with other fish (see the basic recipe on page 95). The amount of pectin it contains makes it ideal for concentrated stocks and aspics.

## *Smelts*

These small and powerful-tasting fish are best eaten deep-fried. They need no batter, but should be rolled in flour, egg and breadcrumbs and cooked until crisp in very hot oil. To grill them, split them down the back, brush with butter and season with salt and pepper; grill for a few minutes on each side, and serve with a savoury butter. The flesh of smelts can be used to give bulk to savoury forcemeats for stuffings or *quenelles*, and to add flavour and richness to stocks, soups and sauces.

## *Snappers*

Snappers, pinkish greyish fish, are now in fishmongers' shops in many areas. They are extremely good to eat even though they are a deep-frozen import.

I personally treat them like small mackerel, though they are nothing like mackerel in colour or design, and are usually available at a standardized weight of about 225 gr (8 oz) each. After scaling and cleaning, score them and grill them like mackerel and serve with Pimento Butter (see page 80); or cover them with Special Tomato Sauce (page 72) to which 1 teaspoon cayenne pepper and 1 large red sweet pepper (chopped) has been added, and bake for 20 minutes in a hot oven (200°C/400°F, gas 6).

## *Dover Sole*

The Dover sole is a fish 'custom-built' for the fish cook and fulfils his, or her, every requirement. The meat is firm and white and the flavour delicious. In spite of its firm flesh, it is succulent and full of juice. It is easy to fillet and can be made to perform in spectacular dishes. It takes an almost perverse cook to overcook it, and even if it has to be kept waiting on a hot plate for some time, it shows it less than almost any other fish. Apart from its excellence, this is no doubt why it is the perfect food for the restaurateur.

There are so many 'name' dishes for various ways of dressing sole that we have to be selective, giving those recipes which are basic and which best suit the fish itself, and omitting those which depend on over-elaboration and fussy garnishes for their renown.

A whole grilled sole, with *Maître d'Hôtel* Butter and wedges of lemon, is justly admired. When waiters ask me if I would like it off the bone, I always indignantly refuse, as I much enjoy carrying out the surgery myself. However, much as I appreciate a grilled sole, if given the choice, I usually plump for *meunière*.

**Sole Meunière** (for whole sole or fillets)

Clean and skin the sole and fillet if desired. Dip the sole in seasoned flour. Fry it in clarified butter (see Glossary) and place it on a hot dish. Add to the frying pan 50 gr (2 oz) fresh butter and the juice of 1 lemon. Cook briskly for a moment or two, pour over your sole, and serve garnished with quarters of lemon and sprigs of parsley.

This dish needs no sauce to go with it, but it can be served with *Sauce Tartare* or *Rémoulade* (page 70).

Undoubtedly, *à la meunière* is the best way of frying sole, but here is a deep-frying recipe:

**Sole Colbert**

Open the sole down the middle of the skinned side, along the spine; carefully lift the fillets a couple of centimetres (an inch or two) on each side. Cut the spine in several places with sharp scissors. Egg and breadcrumb the sole and fry it in deep fat. Carefully remove the main bones and fill the opening in the sole with *Maître d'Hôtel* Butter (page 78).

In the following recipes, where a sauce with which to cover the sole is given, the cooking juices of the sole should be added to the sauce.

### Sole Maître d'Hôtel

Poach your fillets of sole in a good *court-bouillon*. Serve with *Maître d'Hôtel* Butter and garnish with parsley. Vary this simplest of dishes by serving it with any other savoury butter.

### Sole au vin blanc

Poach your fillets of sole in white wine seasoned with pepper and salt. Serve covered with White Wine Sauce (page 61) or with a Cream and Butter Sauce (page 73).

### Sole Bercy

Serve the poached sole covered with *Sauce Bercy* (page 60).

### Sole Bonne Femme

As above, covering with *Sauce Bercy* (page 60), to which finely chopped and sautéed mushrooms have been added.

### Sole Mornay

As above, covering with *Sauce Mornay* (page 62). Sprinkle with grated cheese, and brown quickly under the grill.

### Sole Nantua

As above, using *Sauce Nantua* (page 66). Garnish with crayfish tails, prawns or shrimps.

### Sole Normande

Poach your sole in the liquor in which mussels have been cooked. Serve covered with *Sauce Normande* (page 61), and garnish with poached mussels.

### Sole Véronique

Grapes do not figure much in the tradition of fish cookery; indeed *Véronique* is the only recipe I know which makes use of them. It is well worth cooking, but only if you have the right kind of strong-scented muscat grape. Even with these grapes it is necessary – in order to allow their essentially delicate flavour to come through – to use a rather mild stock and to exercise restraint in seasoning.

Spread 1 dessertspoon grated onion over the bottom of a large, buttered fireproof dish; on this, lay the skinned and trimmed fillets of sole. Cover them with wine; season, and poach the fillets for 12–15 minutes.

Meanwhile, make a *velouté* sauce (see page 59), and put the peeled grapes to warm in a pan standing in very hot water.

Remove the fillets and lay them in a covered serving dish to keep warm. Add the strained juices from the dish to the *velouté* and stir well in. Now put three or four grapes (sliced) into the sauce to cook gently for 45 seconds. Finally, pour the sauce – which should be not too thick to flow, but thick enough to adhere – over the fillets. Garnish with grapes cut in half (with the cut side down) and serve.

**Paupiettes de Soles**

Fillets of sole can be stuffed in two ways. Either lay the forcemeat on one side of the fillet and fold the other half over it; or cover the whole fillet more thinly with your chosen forcemeat, roll the fillet up, and tie it together (or pin it together with a cocktail stick).

Here is a recipe for a good forcemeat for sole:

*Fish forcemeat*

100 gr (4 oz) white breadcrumbs (fresh ones are essential)
enough milk to soak them
50 gr (2 oz) mushrooms, finely sliced
25 gr (1 oz) butter
50 gr (2 oz) cooked whiting, flaked
Salt and black pepper

Soak the breadcrumbs in the milk for 5 minutes and squeeze them dry. In a small saucepan gently fry the mushrooms in the butter until just tender. Pound the whiting with the squeezed breadcrumbs and the mushrooms until the mixture is smooth; season with salt and pepper.

*Paupiettes* should be covered with a chosen sauce and baked in a moderate oven (180°C/350°F, gas 4) for about 25 minutes.

The flesh of smelts or shrimps (or crabmeat) can be substituted for the whiting in the forcemeat.

## *Lemon Sole*

Excellent eating, but a much softer fish than Dover sole; it can, however, be treated in the same ways as Dover sole.

## *Sprats*

These delicious small fish look like small herrings – but are quite different. If you have a large, heavy iron frying pan, scatter salt over the surface, heat the pan up until it is really hot, throw in your sprats (few enough at a time to ensure that each fish is touching the pan) and keep shaking the pan. When scorching begins, turn the sprats over to cook on the other side. Turn them out on to a really hot dish. Sprinkle with lemon juice and black pepper, and eat them with your fingers. (To me this is quite as happy a communal eating experience as the much-touted *fondue* ritual.)

## *Squid (Inkfish), Cuttlefish*

The very young specimens of these cephalopods can be floured or battered and fried in deep oil, and are delicious eaten with no other accompaniment than a squeeze of lemon.

The larger specimens require to be cut up and very slowly stewed in a generous *mirepoix* of onions, garlic, parsley, celery and tomato which has been softened in olive oil and loosened with half a bottle of red wine and twice that amount of water. Cooking time depends on the size of the cephalopod, but slow cooking for 2 to 3 hours is sufficient for medium-sized specimens. Serve in bowls, with chunks of real bread. If you like, put a dessertspoon of *Aïoli* (see page 69) into each bowl. This dish is excellent eaten cold.

## *Sturgeon*

For most of us, the sturgeon's chief claim to affection is the knowledge that it is the source of the roe from which caviare is made.

## *Tench*

This river fish is hard to scale, but of good quality. It is at its best cooked *en matelote* (see under *Eel*), or baked in the oven in a *Sauce Gratin* (page 62).

Richard Briggs, who always approaches river fish with enthusiasm, gives the following recipe:

**'Another Way to fry Carp or Tench*** Take three carp or tench,

*See also Richard Briggs' recipe 'To Stew Carp or Tench' on page 122.

scale them, and pull the guts out by the gills but do not open the bellies, wash them clean, and with the point of a knife slit them down the backs on each side of the bone, from the head to the tail, raise the flesh up a little, and take out the bone; take another carp or tench, cut all the fish off and mince it small, with a few mushrooms, chives, sweet herbs, and parsley shred fine, season them with beaten cloves, mace, nutmeg, pepper and salt, beat them in a mortar very fine, and put in the crumb of a roll soaked in cream, two ounces of butter, with the yolks of three raw eggs; stuff your carp or tench, and sew the back up with a needle and thread, wipe them with a cloth, flour them, fry them in butter to a fine brown, and lay them on a coarse cloth before the fire to drain; pour all the fat out of the pan, put in a quarter of a pound of butter, shake in some flour, keep it stirring till the butter is a little brown, then put in half a pint of white wine, half a pint of ale, an onion stuck with cloves, a bundle of sweet herbs, and two blades of mace, cover them close, and stew them gently fifteen minutes; then strain it off and put it in a stew-pan again, add two spoonfuls of ketchup, an ounce of truffles and morels cut small and boiled in half a pint of water, put the water in, with half a pint of oysters blanched, liquor and all, (when your sauce is hot season it with Cayan pepper and salt) put in the fish and stew it twenty minutes, squeeze in the juice of half a lemon, put the fish in the dish with the sauce all over them; garnish with fried sippets and lemon.'

As in Briggs' recipe for pike, mussels can be substituted for oysters.

## *Tope*

See under **Porbeagle**, above.

## *Trout*

Small trout are best grilled and served with *Maître d'Hôtel* Butter or Chivry Butter (page 78), or cooked *à la meunière* (page 40) and served with melted butter and lemon juice.

### Truite au bleu

This recipe can only be carried out with trout freshly taken from the water – which, nowadays, implies the possession of a fish tank. The live trout should be stunned by a sharp blow on the back of the head; it should be swiftly gutted and the gills removed, but it should not be scaled, beheaded or washed. Put it into a pan and sprinkle with 2 tablespoons boiling vinegar. Boiling *court-bouillon* to cover is then added and the fish is poached for the time indicated in the table on page 41.

The trout – which, under the stimulus of the boiling vinegar followed by the boiling stock, will have curled up on itself and turned blue (well, wouldn't you?) – is best served with a *Beurre Blanc* Sauce (page 74) or a Cream and Butter Sauce (page 73).

**Trout with Almonds**
Children in their early teens seem to regard this dish as the height of bliss and sophistication. Allow 1 trout per person. The trout are dipped in seasoned flour and fried in butter for about 4–5 minutes on either side. They are then removed from the pan and kept warm. Allow 50 gr (2 oz) unblanched almonds for 4 people. Cover them with boiling water and leave for a few minutes, by which time the almonds should pop out of their skins when squeezed. Halve them and brown them in the butter. Pour over the trout as a garnish and serve.

**Truite en Gelée**
Cold trout is delicious served in a natural jelly. The trout are poached in a strong *court-bouillon* of one-third white wine, and then filleted. Skin, head and bones are added to the stock, which is boiled to reduce by at least a third. The strained liquid is poured over the trout and left to cool. Refrigerate for several hours before serving, during which time the liquid will form a light jelly.

**Smoked trout** is an expensive delicacy, and should be eaten just as it is, with lemon juice and perhaps a sprinkling of red pepper. However, it makes an excellent and quite economical pâté for use as a first course or on cocktail savouries (see Foulkes' Pâté, page 84).

## *Tunny (tuna)*

Fresh tunny, a fish for which the Italian nation has a profound passion, is rarely available at fishmongers' shops in Britain. If you find some, steaks can be braised in the following manner:

**Braised Tunny**

Put your tunny steaks in hot olive oil to brown lightly on each side. Remove, and put aside to keep warm. Now put into your olive oil 2 shallots, chopped; 2 carrots, sliced; a stick of celery, finely chopped, and 4 tomatoes, skinned and chopped. Add a sprig of thyme and cook for 15 minutes. Now put your tunny steaks back into the braising pot, and add wine to cover them. Put the lid on your pan, and cook for 1 hour in a slow oven (170°C/325°F, gas 3).

Tinned tunnyfish is extremely useful for *hors-d'oeuvres*, salads (see *Salade Niçoise*, page 86), a sauce for spaghetti (page 201), and also makes an excellent pâté (see page 85). See also *Baked Bonito* (page 118).

## *Turbot*

Turbot probably ranks second only to sole in the white-fish hierarchy. It is best when poached or grilled, with the simplest of accompaniments, such as a savoury herb or shrimp butter. Lobster Sauce, if made sincerely, sets it off extremely well, and *Béarnaise*, *Bercy*, *Tartare* and *Hollandaise* are all acceptable.

All the methods of cooking used for sole can be applied to fillets of turbot and to small chicken turbot; every kind of garnish used with sole will go with turbot.

## *Whelks and Winkles*

Whelks are shellfish of good flavour, but they are rather tough. They can be of service in flavouring a stock for a sauce to go with a shellfish pie or a rice dish.

Winkles, if you have the patience and are good with a pin, are useful last-minute additions to shellfish soups, sauces and so on.

## *Whitebait*

The delicious small fry of the herring and the sprat seem to be growing larger every day, so that imperceptibly we may find ourselves accepting sprats as whitebait. In a net bag of chilled whitebait I bought recently, about a third were the size of small sprats. In my young days, whitebait were extremely small fish and appeared to be all of one size.

Whole whitebait should be shaken up in a bag with flour and deep fried in hot oil until crisp. Salt, pepper and lemon juice are all that is needed to accompany them.

## *Whiting*

This is a member of the cod family with very white flesh which is flaky and full of flavour. It can be treated in all the ways suitable for fairly soft white fish (for instance, sole and plaice). It is probably best split down the back and grilled, after the main bone has been removed. Opened flat, it can be fried or poached, and served with butter and lemon or any sauce used with white fish. The flesh of whiting is excellent for making forcemeats for stuffings and *quenelles* (see page 189). In my youth, for some unknown reason, every whiting served had to be biting its own tail.

Small whiting are best deep-fried in a batter; egged and breadcrumbed and fried in a shallow frying pan; or lightly scored, brushed with butter and quickly grilled. With all these methods, one or two savoury butters (such as *Maître d'Hôtel* and Chive Butter) are the best accompaniment. With larger whiting, we can expand this repertoire.

### Savoury Baked Whiting

1 whiting, 675–800 gr ($1\frac{1}{2}$–$1\frac{3}{4}$ lb)
100 gr (4 oz) *mirepoix* made from peeled tomatoes, onions and mushrooms, chopped fine and sautéed in butter until fairly dry
125 gr (5 oz) butter
salt and black pepper
25 gr (1 oz) Parmesan cheese, grated

A good size makes whiting easy to fillet by cutting straight down the back, keeping the knife blade pressed close to the main bone. Lever up and remove this bone and the other bones attached to it. Do not divide the fish in two, but lay it flat in a well-buttered fireproof dish. Cover with the *mirepoix*. Dot with butter, season with salt and pepper and place in the middle of a moderate oven (180°C/350°F, gas 4) for 20 minutes. Now raise the oven heat to high (200°C/400°F, gas 6), sprinkle the Parmesan over the fish and put the dish at the top of the oven for 5 minutes. This dish needs no sauce.

**Poached Whiting**

A very simple way with larger whiting is to split them down the back (like smoked haddock) and poach them gently for about 6 minutes in milk seasoned with finely chopped onion, parsley, pepper and salt. When only just cooked, dish up with several good lumps of savoury butter. Try Anchovy and Watercress Butters. (The milk left over from the poaching can be used in the making of a fish soup or sauce.)

THE CARP.

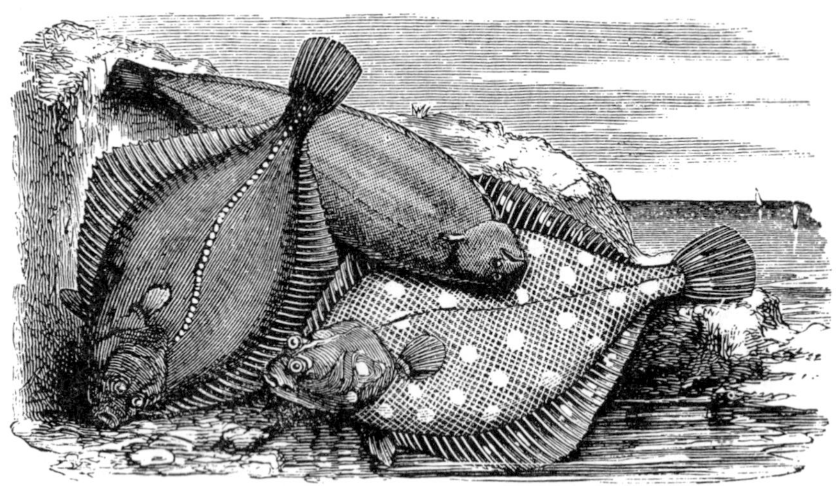

The flounder, the sole and the plaice

# Miscellaneous fish dishes

## *Fish pies*

Memories of school fish pies almost inhibit me from writing on the subject. Every Friday when the dinner gong sounded, we would assemble, a brave band of twenty-four small, high-minded boys, and with heads covered by raincoats, walk through the rain, two by two, the few hundred yards to the dining room and our weekly ordeal, to bear which only the tortures of the Christian martyrs, in which we were extremely well versed, gave us the necessary fortitude. A mish-mash of cods' heads, tails, bones and eyes, covered with a viscous sticky paste tinted faintly pink, the whole surmounted by broken-up watery potatoes in which sinister dark patches shone like black eyes on the mend – the vision is hard to exorcise.

It was not until the late 1930s that I was converted to fish pie. When all the world, and even Wheeler's, was in its infancy, I used to visit that excellent seafood bar mainly to eat oysters (and often to cash cheques with its affable and friendly owner). In addition to serving oysters, lobster and crab salads, Wheeler's produced an excellent fish pie which became a regular part of my diet. What made it exciting was that none was ever quite like the last one, the ingredients changing from day to day. I hope this tradition still lives on.

**Basic recipe**

For a good fish pie, we need first a good, well-flavoured stock, in which our fish can be poached and which can then be reduced by fast cooking to perhaps half its original volume for use in the making of a thick fish *velouté* sauce.

The following pie serves five or six people.

*for the stock:*
1·2 litres (2 pints) water
1 stick celery
1 small leek
2 medium onions
1 large carrot
*bouquet garni* (thyme, bay leaf, parsley stalks)
a cod's head *or* the bones of filleted fish from your kindly fishmonger
2 glasses white wine
salt and black pepper
1 kg (2¼ lb) white fish (to include cod, hake or coley)
3 hard-boiled eggs
63 gr (2½ oz) butter
75 gr (3 oz) flour
1 heaped teaspoon parsley and capers, chopped
675 gr (1½ lb) buttered mashed potato

When you have prepared your stock (see page 58), poach the fish in it for 5–6 minutes. Remove with a perforated fish slice and put it in a pie dish. Remove all bones and skin from the fish and break it up so that it is spread out evenly in the dish. Add the eggs, shelled and finely chopped.

Make a thick *velouté* (see page 59) with the flour, butter and reduced stock. Season, and stir in the parsley and capers. Pour the *velouté* over the fish. Cover with the well-buttered mashed potato, and cook at the top of a medium-hot oven (190°C/375°F, gas 5) for 25 minutes. For the last few minutes, raise the heat to 200°C/400°F, gas 6, to ensure browning of the potatoes. Alternatively, brown under the grill.

*Cooking note:* For pies of this kind where a soft covering (in this case, potato) is used, it is important to use a large pie dish, so that there is ample room for covering the fish in the sauce; otherwise, the sauce will tend to bubble out over the edges of the dish.

**Variations** Parsley and capers give this pie its individual character, which can be varied by substituting other ingredients. For example, try chopped celery leaves and thinly sliced small pickled gherkins, or finely chopped fresh fennel sprigs and fresh basil leaves.

Of course, if the budget can stand it, sole, turbot or brill can be substituted for the less expensive fish mentioned above.

**Highbury Pie** (scallop and mussel pie with mushrooms and sweetbreads)

100 gr (4 oz) lambs' sweetbreads, prepared (see method)
4 good large scallops
9 dl (1½ pints) *court-bouillon*
1 glass white wine
12 mussels
100 gr (4 oz) fresh button mushrooms
1 sprig fennel, finely chopped
1 heaped tablespoon chives and parsley, finely chopped
6 dl (1 pint) *Sauce Béchamel* (see page 64)
675 gr (1½ lb) mashed potato
25 gr (1 oz) butter

Prepare the sweetbreads in advance, as follows: steep them in a bowl of water for several hours, changing the water 2 or 3 times during that period. Put them in a pan of water with a bay leaf, salt, pepper and 1 tablespoon wine vinegar. Bring to the boil, skimming off all scum as it forms, and boil for 2 minutes. Remove from pan and detach all skin and membrane. Press between 2 plates with a good weight on top for a couple of hours. The sweetbreads will now be ready to use.

Clean and trim the scallops and poach them in the *court-bouillon* to which the white wine has been added. Poach for 5 minutes, remove from pan and set aside. Now throw the cleaned mussels into the *court-bouillon*, bring to the boil and, as soon as they are open, remove them from the pan and set aside. Strain and reduce the liquid to a *fumet* by boiling, and add to the thick *béchamel*.

Chop the mushrooms up finely and purée them in the liquidizer with a little water. (For this dish the mushrooms must be very fresh.)

Chop the scallops as described for Shellfish Soup (page 108) and dice the sweetbreads. Lay these in the bottom of a hot pie dish, mixed, and distribute the mussels evenly over them. Spread the mushroom purée over all. Stir the fennel, chives and parsley into the *béchamel* and then pour carefully over the pie. Cover thickly with well creamed and buttered mashed potatoes. Pattern the potato with a fork, dot with butter and cook in a hot oven (200°C/400°F, gas 6) for 25 minutes or until nicely browned.

**Variations** Highbury Pie is versatile. As it stands, it is a shellfish pie, the sweetbreads giving it its special character. Any really firm white fish can be used instead of mussels and scallops, for instance small monkfish, dogfish or conger fillets. For a very special occasion, use lobster.

### Soho Pie

I usually make this with conger eel, but it is a good recipe for all strong-textured and flavoured fish, including skate, dogfish, squid and octopus.

2 cloves garlic, chopped
3 shallots, finely sliced
3 tablespoons olive oil
450 gr (1 lb) tomatoes, skinned and chopped
3 anchovy fillets, pounded
675 gr (1½ lb) conger eel
*court-bouillon*
6 dl (1 pint) *Sauce Béchamel* (see page 64)
black pepper
675 gr (1½ lb) mashed potatoes

Sweat the garlic and shallots in olive oil for 3 or 4 minutes. Add the tomatoes and the anchovies. Allow to cook vigorously until you have a good thick purée. You will need to keep pounding and stirring with a wooden spoon until the tomato begins to break down.

Poach the conger eel in sufficient *court-bouillon* (in which carrot and leek predominate) to cover. Skin and fillet the fish and cut into small pieces, roughly 5 cm (2 in) square. Keep these aside in a hot pie dish.

Add the thick tomato mixture to the *béchamel* and season. Cook together for 10 minutes, and pour over the conger eel in the pie dish.

Cover with creamed potatoes, and brown in a hot oven (200°C/400°F, gas 6).

*Cooking notes:* If you use squid or octopus, extra time will be needed to cook them in the *court-bouillon* until tender. The potato and fennel root pie covering given below can equally well be used for this pie.

**Eel Pie (with Mussels)**
675 gr ($1\frac{1}{2}$ lb) eels
*court-bouillon*
20 mussels
6 dl (1 pint) thick *velouté* sauce
675 gr ($1\frac{1}{2}$ lb) mashed potatoes
1 tablespoon parsley, chopped
1 tablespoon chives, chopped

Skin the eel (see page 34) and cut it up into 5-cm (2-in) sections. Poach them for 12 minutes in a *court-bouillon* made with onion, fennel, parsley stalks, lemon juice, white wine, black pepper and salt. Take the eels out and keep warm in a covered pie dish. Allow the *court-bouillon* to cool down while you are thoroughly cleaning the mussels. Now put the mussels into the cool *court-bouillon* and bring to the boil so that the mussels open. Remove the mussels from their shells and put them in the pie dish with the pieces of eel.

Add the strained *court-bouillon* to the *velouté* sauce. Pour over the eel and mussels. Cover with creamed and buttered potato and bake at the top of a hot oven (220°C/425°F, gas 7) for 10 minutes. Sprinkle with the chopped chives and parsley before bringing to the table.

## *Coverings for fish pies*

In the recipes just given, the covering of the pies is buttered potato, and I believe this tradition is a sound one; however, it should not be allowed to become a straitjacket and prevent experimentation. Pastry coverings can also be used, and simple recipes for pastry are given on page 186. Other suggestions for coverings are *gnocchi* and omelette. Here, meanwhile, are two other coverings which can be used in the above recipes:

**Potato and Fennel Root**

3–4 potatoes
1 fennel root
salt and black pepper
1 dessertspoon chives, chopped
milk as required
50 gr (2 oz) butter

Peel the potatoes and slice them thinly. Trim the fennel root and slice it in the same way. Interleave the slices of potato with slices of fennel root, sprinkling on each slice a little salt, black pepper and chives. Place your interleaved ingredients in a small, tightly lidded pan that will enable them to fit closely standing up on edge. Pour in milk to cover, and dot with small pats of butter. Seal with foil so that the lid fits absolutely tightly. Allow to cook in a moderate oven (180°C/350°F, gas 4) for 35–40 minutes or until tender. When cooked, spread the potato and fennel slices as evenly as possible over the hot fish mixture. Cook in a hot oven (220°C/425°F, gas 7) for 10–15 minutes. (Potatoes cooked in this way, but without the fennel, are called *Pommes Anna*.)

**Spinach**

1 kg (2¼ lb) spinach
salt and black pepper
25 gr (1 oz) flour
75 gr (3 oz) butter
25 gr (1 oz) Parmesan cheese, grated
25 gr (1 oz) breadcrumbs

Wash and clean the spinach. Put it in a large saucepan with very little water and boil it for 5–6 minutes until cooked. Drain and pound the spinach. Season with salt and pepper. Make a *roux* with the flour and one-third of the butter (see page 56). Put in the spinach and cook together, stirring vigorously. If the mixture gets too thick and tends to burn, add a very little water – but the mixture must be of a fairly stiff texture to serve its purpose. Cover the hot fish pie with it, dot with butter, sprinkle with Parmesan and breadcrumbs, and bake in a hot oven (200°C/400°F, gas 6) for 10–12 minutes.

This covering goes especially well with pies made with carp, turbot and salmon.

### Shortcrust Pastry

225 gr (8 oz) self-raising flour
½ teaspoon salt
125 gr (5 oz) butter
3 tablespoons cold water

To the flour and salt in a bowl, add the butter cut into small pieces; work in with the fingers. Sprinkle in the water, a little at a time, and mix thoroughly. Form into a ball and allow to stand in a cool place for an hour before using.

The pastry should be rolled out on a floured board and cut to fit the pie dish. It should be no thicker than 3 mm (⅛ in). Paint the top of the pastry with a little milk mixed with the yolk of an egg and bake it in a hot oven (220°C/425°F, gas 7) for 15 minutes, then reduce to 180°C/350°F, gas 4 for a further 15 minutes.

*Cooking note:* The pie should be allowed to cool before the pastry covering is put on to prevent the fat in the pastry from melting.

### Puff Pastry

150 gr (6 oz) fine plain flour
¼ teaspoon salt
1·5 dl (¼ pint) cold water
150 gr (6 oz) butter, softened

Sieve the flour and salt into a bowl. Make a well in the centre of the flour, pour in the water and knead lightly into a good dough. Then roll out 1·25 cm (½ in) thick on a floured pastry board into a square. Put the butter in a block in the middle. Fold up like a packet and roll out. Fold into three and roll out again. Repeat this process four more times (six times in all). Allow to stand in a cool place for an hour before using; to cover a pie, follow the instructions given under Shortcrust Pastry, above.

### Shrimp Vol-au-vents with Sauce Aurore

Roll out thinly puff pastry made with 150 gr (6 oz) flour (see above). Shape the *vol-au-vent* cases and place them on a greased baking tray. Bake in a hot oven (230°C/475°F, gas 9) for about 15 minutes or until the pastry cases have risen. Meanwhile, cook 450 gr (1 lb) shrimps over a fast flame for 5 minutes in 6 dl (1 pint) well-flavoured *court-bouillon*. Leave the shrimps to cool, shell them and add to 6 dl (1 pint) *Sauce Aurore* (see page 59). Fill the *vol-au-vent* cases and sprinkle them with 1 tablespoon finely chopped parsley.

**Tunnyfish Pizza**

*pizza dough:*
225 gr (8 oz) plain flour
½ teaspoon salt
3 tablespoons water
1 tablespoon olive oil

*for the filling:*
1 large onion, chopped
1 clove garlic, crushed
6 large black olives, stoned
1·5 dl (¼ pint) olive oil
1 tablespoon tomato purée
100 gr (4 oz) tunnyfish
8 anchovy fillets
25 gr (1 oz) Parmesan cheese, grated

To the well-mixed flour and salt in a bowl, add the water; knead all together. Work in the olive oil thoroughly; shape into a ball and allow to stand for 2 hours before using. Line a greased 30-cm (12-in) shallow tin with the pizza dough.

Cook the onion, garlic and olives gently in the olive oil until the onion becomes soft and transparent. Add the tomato purée and cook briskly for 4–5 minutes, stirring all the while. Reduce heat and stir in the flaked tunnyfish.

Fill the pizza flan with the mixture and lay the anchovy fillets in a lattice pattern on top. Sprinkle with Parmesan cheese and bake for 12–15 minutes in a moderately hot oven (200°C/400°F, gas 6). This serves four or five people as an *hors-d'oeuvre* or two as a main course.

**Pissaladière**

This is the pizza of the South of France, sold from innumerable *guichets* in the old quarter of Nice on Sunday mornings.

2 large onions, sliced in rings
1·5 dl (¼ pint) olive oil
12 large black olives, stoned
black pepper
8 anchovy fillets
pizza dough (see previous recipe)

Cook the onion rings in the olive oil until they soften and become transparent, but do not allow them to become brown. Put the olives in to cook gently with the onions, towards the end of their cooking time. Season with pepper. Line a 30-cm (12-in) flan or pizza case with dough made as in the previous recipe and fill this with the onion mixture. Lay the anchovy fillets criss-cross over the top. Cook in a moderate oven (190°C/375°F, gas 5) for 12 minutes.

## *Fishcakes*

This is a basic recipe which can be used for virtually any fish except, perhaps, the cephalopods. All kinds of cooked or tinned fish can be called into service. This quantity makes about 10 to 12 fishcakes.

**Basic recipe**

225 gr (8 oz) filleted fish
1 tablespoon parsley, chopped
1 tablespoon chives, chopped
½ teaspoon grated horseradish *or* English mustard powder
450 gr (1 lb) potatoes, mashed without milk or cream but lightly buttered
1 teaspoon anchovy essence
1 teaspoon Worcester sauce *or* Green Peppercorn Relish (see page 76)
2 egg yolks, lightly beaten
50 gr (2 oz) seasoned breadcrumbs
oil and butter for frying

Pound or mince the fish (if it is tinned, all liquid should be drained off). Beat in the herbs and the horseradish or mustard powder. Combine in a large mixing bowl with the mashed potato, the anchovy essence and the Worcester or Green Peppercorn Relish. With a large wooden spoon, beat all together until the ingredients are evenly distributed throughout the mixture. Now mould into circular cakes, 2 cm (1 in) thick by 7·5 cm (3 in) in diameter. Pass through egg and breadcrumbs, and let them stand for an hour. Just before cooking, egg and breadcrumb again. Fry in a shallow pan in oil and butter, until brown on both sides. Serve with a generous helping of a savoury butter.

This is one of the best ways of making a hot dish out of tinned fish, such as salmon, sardines, pilchards or herrings. If potato is not used, your minced fish and seasonings may form a mixture too loose to handle. In this case, add breadcrumbs as required; or add a *panada:* the soft white crumb of a loaf, soaked in milk, squeezed dry and pounded.

## *Quenelles*

The *quenelle*, a kind of poached savoury fish dumpling, is seldom cooked in the home in Britain. In restaurants, we find them made with pike, the dryish meat of which is admirably suited to the processes involved. *Quenelles de Brochet* (*quenelles* of pike) is a classic dish of the French tradition (see page 158).

*Quenelles* are made of pounded or minced fish, well seasoned with herbs and spices, combined with special doughs, known as *panadas*, in the proportion of 2 parts fish meat to 1 part dough.

First, two recipes for these doughs:

### The Bread Panada

The simplest form of this dough is the soft crumb of white bread, soaked in milk, squeezed dry and then pounded into a smooth dough in a mortar. Note that I have already suggested the use of this dough in the fishcake recipe above, in place of potato.

The addition of egg yolk, minced fish, seasonings and beaten egg whites makes one kind of *quenelle* for poaching in boiling salted water. The following is a more complicated form of *panada*, based on flour instead of breadcrumbs.

### The Frangipane Panada

This *panada* is not named after the flower, but is attributed to Frangipani, an Italian who was in France during the reign of Louis XIII.

125 gr (5 oz) flour
4 egg yolks
100 gr (4 oz) melted butter
2 dl ($7\frac{1}{4}$ fl oz) boiling milk
pinch each of salt, pepper and nutmeg

With a wooden spoon, mix the flour and the egg yolks well in a bowl. Pour in the butter, add the seasonings and stir well. Then pour in the milk very slowly, stirring all the time. Cook gently for 6 minutes while beating with a whisk. Spread out on a flat, buttered dish, cover with buttered paper and leave until cold. This should make up to 300 gr (12 oz) dough.

## Mixed Fish Quenelles

The following basic recipe for *quenelles* can be applied to any white fish, crustacean or shellfish. The choice of seasonings for the fish forcemeat is a matter of personal choice for the cook, as is the choice of which sauce to serve with the *quenelles*.

150 gr (6 oz) dogfish (rock salmon) fillets
225 gr (8 oz) whiting fillets
150 gr (6 oz) cooked white and brown crab meat
3 anchovy fillets
1 clove garlic
1 shallot
white of 1 leek
1 tablespoon parsley and thyme, mixed
2 eggs
½ teaspoon cayenne pepper
juice ½ lemon
300 gr (12 oz) Frangipane *Panada*

Pound or put through the blender all the above ingredients, retaining only the *panada*.

Now pound the forcemeat mixture into the *panada* in a large mortar and work strongly until the mass is homogeneous. Scoop out from the mass 1 heaped dessertspoon of the mixture at a time (keeping the spoon shape). Lay these *quenelles* in a shallow pan containing enough boiling salted water to cover completely. Poach for 8–10 minutes. Remove, drain and set up in a sort of pyramid-shaped mound on a hot dish. Pour the sauce over this mound – the choice of sauces is almost unlimited. Three which I myself would suggest are the Special Tomato Sauce (see page 72), *Sauce Mornay* (page 62) or *Sauce Béarnaise* (page 68).

These dumplings are pretty solid fare. The quantities given here should produce 24 *quenelles* – enough to feed 4 ravenous people or 6 hungry ones, as a main dish. Three *quenelles* apiece should be sufficient for 8 people as a first course.

*Quenelles* may also be cooked 'dry', by laying them on a buttered sheet of foil in a baking tin and cooking them in a moderate oven (180°C/350°F, gas 4) for 10 minutes. When juices from the interior of the *quenelles* begin to show signs of bubbling out, they are cooked.

The remains of cooked fish can be used in making *quenelles*, though obviously these will not have quite the savour of those made with uncooked fish.

*Quenelles* open another door through which the free-range cook can wander and try his or her hand at many different variations of fish seasonings and accompanying sauces.

## *Fish with rice*

**Pote's Paella** (Paella Valenciana)

The making of *Paella* in its country of origin can, according to Dr Allan Pote, a polymath and enthusiastic *Paella*-cook, be a very dramatic affair. Three different kinds of firewood are required for the outdoor stove and a certain amount of fatalism or faith is required in the final stages when, after a feverish period of chopping and cutting up and frying and boiling and mixing all together, a final expert adjustment to the firing is made, and all concerned walk away from it for half-an-hour's prayer or liquid refreshment. This is a Sunday dish and (with the help of God) when they return, the fire has died down and the *Paella* is perfectly cooked.

'Paella is a rice dish found throughout Spain and is really a peasant dish flavoured with meat, fowl and shellfish, having a characteristic deep yellow colour which is imparted to the rice by the use of saffron. The cost of this last ingredient is now so prohibitively high that turmeric is almost universally used, although a small amount of saffron added at the end of cooking can enhance the final flavour, giving the dish its characteristic aroma.

'The name Paella comes from the large, flat, iron or steel pan in which the food is cooked. The best ones are hand beaten out of a single piece of sheet steel, but are hard to find, and vary in size from a foot to five feet in diameter.

'The classical Paella comes from the district of Valencia with its lagoons and paddy fields where most of Spain's rice is grown. Traditionally it must contain lean pork, chicken, lobster or large prawns, and mussels. Garnish is provided by green peas and strips of green and red sweet peppers. An enormous amount of garlic is employed, and I personally use fried onion in addition, although this is frowned upon by the traditionalists.

'*Paella* (sufficient for 6 very greedy people)
1 small chicken, cut into small pieces. The giblets can be included.
2 bay leaves
bouquet garni
2 teaspoons of turmeric
saffron if available
450 gr (1 quart) of fresh mussels
1 medium sized onion, finely chopped
salt and pepper
1 head of garlic, skinned and left as whole cloves
olive oil
225 gr (8 oz) lean pork (diced)
225 gr (8 oz) fresh squid or calamar in season (care being taken to remove the eyes and ink sac as this can ruin the meal and result in a dark purple mess)
1 medium sized langouste or lobster tail cut into chunks
1 dozen Dublin Bay prawns, or equivalent (whole)
1 cupful of green peas
1 each of green and red peppers (tinned red peppers will serve equally well)
225 gr (8 oz) pork fat or lard
round rice, Spanish or Italian, 2 handfuls per person, or $\frac{1}{2}$ litre by volume (dry)

'*Method*

**1** Boil the chicken pieces, with the bay leaves, bouquet garni and turmeric, in a saucepan until tender but not pliable. Drain and set aside in a warm place. Conserve the stock.
**2** Quickly boil the cleaned prepared mussels, shells and all, in a minimum of water. When they are open and have discharged their milky juice, drain and set aside. Conserve the juice.
**3** In a separate frying pan fry the onion and garlic cloves in olive oil until tender and slightly brown. Drain and conserve the oil.
**4** Fry the pork chunks in the oil until tender. Drain and set aside.
**5** Fry the squid pieces quickly (4 minutes) in the same oil.
**6** Cut the lobster tail into cubes, fry them for 6 minutes in hot oil and set aside.

**7** Pour off some of the oil. Salt the prawns and cook them on both sides in smoking oil for about 4 minutes. Set aside – they will be used to decorate the dish later.
**8** Cut the sweet pepper into strips and fry in oil until tender – set aside – they also provide the garnish. You now have all the meat, chicken and fish ingredients partly cooked in a warm (not hot) oven.
**9** Take the Paella (a very large frying pan does just as well). Place on the hotplate, or on an asbestos mat if you are using gas, and put in the lard and the oil (strained).

'Put in the rice and add more oil if necessary until all the rice is well soaked. Fry the rice gently for a few minutes, but *do not* let it get brown. Then add all the ingredients to the pan, except the prawns, sweet peppers and peas. Increase the heat and mix everything together until frying vigorously. While this is going on, combine the chicken and mussel stock (which should be yellow from the turmeric), bring quickly to the boil and pour onto the ingredients in the pan. It is important that the volume of stock is twice the *volume* of the rice, so for $\frac{1}{2}$ litre of dry rice we use one litre of stock. Continue at full heat until everything is bubbling merrily. At this stage stir everything about and add the peas.

'As soon as the rice begins to take up the stock the stirring must stop, and the dish is not touched again. Just before the stock is completely absorbed decorate the top of the pan with the prawns and sweet pepper strips, cover with foil to keep in the steam and the flavour, and turn the heat to the lowest possible, and leave for about 20 minutes.

'It is ready when the rice on top is tender. If you have made a good Paella the rice will be slightly "al dente" and not soggy, and every grain will be separate.

'For serving place the pan in the centre of the table – it is a splendid sight. Let your guests help themselves.'

**Seafood Aurore**

| | |
|---|---|
| 1 shallot, chopped | 8 large prawns |
| 4 parsley stalks | 4 scallops, cleaned and trimmed (see page 34) |
| 2 sprigs of fennel | 24 mussels, cleaned (see page 35) |
| 6 dl (1 pint) white wine | 6 dl (1 pint) *Sauce Aurore* (see page 59) |
| salt and black pepper | 150 gr (6 oz) rice |

Fill a 20-cm (8-in) shallow pan with water to a depth of 10 cm (4 in). Put in the shallot, the parsley stalks, fennel sprigs and the wine. Season. Bring to the boil and throw in your prawns; cook for 5 minutes, then reduce to simmering point and throw in the scallops. Simmer for 5 minutes. Remove the prawns and scallops from the liquid and set aside, covered, in a warm dish. Now pour the liquid into a pan big enough to take the mussels; put in the mussels and boil briskly, shaking the pan, until all the mussels open. Remove and drain the mussels (retaining the juices obtained), shell them and set them aside with the other fish. Add any juices drained from the mussels to the pan. Boil up and reduce the cooking liquid by half. Strain and add this liquor to the *Sauce Aurore* and cook, stirring, for 6 or 7 minutes.

Now throw your rice into a large saucepan of boiling salted water. It should take 15–20 minutes to cook. Meanwhile, shell the prawns and cut up the scallops into 6 or 8 pieces, leaving the coral tongues whole. Add prawns, scallops and mussels to the *Sauce Aurore*, and raise to simmering point.

Drain the rice and arrange it *en timbale*, around the edge of a circular dish. Pour your fish and sauce into the centre. Garnish the rice with alternate thick pats of *Maître d'Hôtel* Butter (see page 78) and Pimento Butter (see page 80), and sprinkle it with freshly ground black pepper. Have some smaller pats of the two savoury butters available on a separate dish.

Some people prefer a greater proportion of rice than is allowed for here.

**Kedgeree**

450 gr (1 lb) smoked Finnan haddock
milk to cover
100 gr (4 oz) butter
3 hard-boiled eggs, chopped finely
black pepper
1 dessertspoon chives, chopped
1 dessertspoon parsley, chopped
225 gr (8 oz) rice, boiled

Poach the haddock in sufficient milk just to cover for 6 minutes. Fillet and flake the haddock flesh; add the butter, just melted, and the finely chopped egg. Spread this mixture over the rice in a wide dish. Sprinkle with pepper, chives and parsley; fold the rice over the mixture, cover and make very hot in the oven before serving on very hot plates, with tomato chutney and segments of lemon to hand. A very fine hangover food!

A teaspoon of curry powder, loosened with 25 gr (1 oz) melted butter and poured over the flaked haddock as it lies on the rice before being folded in, makes another version of this dish pleasing to many, but not to me.

Most fresh white seafish may be treated in this way – including codling, coley, lemon sole and grey mullet. Flakes from the head and tail remaining from a salmon are particularly good in kedgeree – in this case, definitely without benefit of curry.

## *Fish curries*

It is a simple matter to make a curry-powder sauce and pour it over any poached or sautéed white fish, but to my mind this is a decadent way of using the fine traditions of Eastern cookery. Devotee as I still am of dear old Abdullah of the curry paste in a jar and the powder in a tin, and though Vencatachellum is still an emotive name for me, conjuring up as many undergraduate debauches as military brew-ups on the tented plains of rat-infested and mosquito-ridden Iraq, I feel I should call a halt and ask the question: at exactly what point does a mixture of Eastern spices and aromatics become a curry? Exactly when does transubstantiation take place? When, let me face it squarely, does the soul enter the curry embryo? These high metaphysical problems are today, I learn, being thrashed out in factories in the vicinity of Willesden Junction, and not, as I had always dreamed, in a model village some one hundred miles east and south of Ootacamund. Disillusioned, but still dry-eyed, I have decided that it is time to dismantle the standard, establishment curry powder. Of the eleven or twelve ingredients of the average curry powder, remove one at a time. First remove the cayenne pepper. Well, the taste is not quite the same, and the brow is not covered with beads of perspiration. Next remove the turmeric; at once not only the taste but also the colour changes radically, and perhaps for the better. Proceed without fear, and remove in turn the coriander, the cardamom, the clove, the cumin, the pimento, the cinnamon and the bay leaf, the mace and the nutmeg – and what are we left with?

Black pepper, ginger and garlic. By peeling away the leaves of the artichoke, we have got to the heart of the matter. Whether or no a mixture of these three elements can legitimately be called a curry, they form the basis of my next recipe.

### Black Pepper and Ginger Curry

3 dl (½ pint) *Sauce Caroline* (see page 73, and see recipe below)
12 large prawns
150 gr (6 oz) cooked crabmeat
juice 2 lemons
3 roots preserved ginger in syrup
4 large cloves garlic
1 heaped tablespoon freshly ground black pepper
4 anchovy fillets
1·5 dl (¼ pint) olive oil
1 tablespoon tomato purée
1 tablespoon white wine
150 gr (6 oz) rice

First, make the *Sauce Caroline*, substituting a dessertspoon of the syrup from the preserved ginger for the sugar in that recipe. Keep warm on the side of the stove for use later.

Put your prawns into a wide, shallow pan of boiling salted water (just enough to cover them), and boil hard for 10 minutes. Remove, and when they are cool enough, shell them and return the shells to the cooking liquor. Boil to reduce to 3 dl (½ pint) at the most. Strain, then add this liquor to the *Sauce Caroline*, and again boil up and reduce by half – to 1·5 dl (¼ pint).

Reserve the crabmeat, 1 root of ginger, 1 clove of garlic and the black pepper. Now chop up and pound to a paste the remaining ginger and garlic with the lemon juice and the anchovy fillets. Put the resulting purée in a saucepan with the olive oil, and simmer, while stirring, for 10 minutes. Add the tomato purée, and cook the thick mixture for another 4 or 5 minutes.

With a sharp knife, bisect the prawns from head to tail (removing the black thread of intestine). Put the 24 pieces into the syrupy *Sauce Caroline*, moving them round so that all the pieces are coated with the sauce.

Now, slice the reserved ginger and garlic very fine and put them in a pan with a little cold water. Bring to the boil, and cook for 3 minutes. Drain the slices and put them aside on a plate.

Plain boiled rice is the proper accompaniment to this dish and, while it is cooking, assemble the separate elements of your 'curry' as follows. Into a shallow earthenware dish with a cover, put the thick oil and tomato sauce. Over this, sprinkle half the freshly ground black pepper. Now spread the crabmeat evenly on top. Next, cover the crabmeat with the thin slices of blanched garlic and ginger. Arrange on the top the bisected and syrupy prawns, and scatter on the rest of the pepper. Loosen the remains of the syrup in the pan with the white wine, and sprinkle this over the dish. Cover and cook in a moderate oven (180°C/350°F, gas 4) for 15 minutes.

This is a hot dish in the peppery sense and, since it comes to the table in fairly solid form, is a considerable promoter of thirst. I take fairly large quantities of Tuscan wine with it, but lager may be preferred by some.

Scampi or crayfish and squid can be given the same treatment, as can the firmer kinds of white fish. Turbot, brill, halibut, sole and eel should be only very lightly poached before being cut up and coated with the *Sauce Caroline*, and in the final stages may require a few minutes longer in the oven. Monkfish, dogfish and porbeagle, cut into small fillets, are also excellent cooked in this way.

**Miriam Mohamed's Fish Curry**

Passing from the heretical and perhaps perverse recipe given above, I now go to the opposite extreme with a luxurious authentic curry in which every (well, nearly every) spice of the orient is deployed to splendid effect.

Mrs Miriam Mohamed, as she then was – to whom I am indebted for this recipe – became a specialist in fish curries when she was married to a professional fisherman in Cape Town. Every Sunday, enthusiastic guests would flock to her house to feast on the lavish hospitality of curries made from fresh snoek and also from the large crawfish (known in South Africa as crayfish) which her husband had caught in the waters around the Cape peninsula the night before.

As a substitute for snoek in the following recipe, its creator suggests cod, but I find that a firmer fish such as conger eel, dogfish or monkfish responds better – though a longer cooking period than the 10 minutes she allows for cod is needed. I would also like to note that when she refers to 'curry powder', she refers to a blend of spices freshly prepared at home, or bought, freshly made, from an Indian shop – and not to remnants of powder discovered in a tin at the back of the kitchen store cupboard.

3 dl (½ pint) boiling water
50 gr (2 oz) tamarind
1 large onion, sliced
50 gr (2 oz) butter
1 tablespoon vegetable oil
450 gr (1 lb) tomatoes, quartered
1½ heaped teaspoons garam masala
1½ heaped teaspoons curry powder
1½ heaped teaspoons ground cumin
1½ heaped teaspoons turmeric
1 green chilli, chopped
1 small piece stick cinnamon
3 cloves
4 whole black peppercorns
450 gr (1 lb) cod

**1** Pour the boiling water over the tamarind, cover and leave to infuse for 1 hour.
**2** Fry the onion in the butter and oil until brown.
**3** Add the tomatoes and cook for 10 minutes.
**4** Add all the dry ingredients, pour in the tamarind water and cook for 10 minutes.
**5** Add the fish, cut into small pieces, and cook for a further 10 minutes. Serve with boiled rice and chutney.
For a lobster or crawfish curry ( prawns could also be used), vary the above recipe as follows: omit stage 1, and, at stage 4, add 2 or 3 green coriander leaves to the other ingredients, and pour on 3 dl (½ pint) plain water.

**Fritto Misto**
oil and butter for frying
batter (see page 159)
4 scampi (Dublin Bay prawns), shelled

4 prawns, shelled
the bag and tentacles of 1 small squid, simmered until tender
150 gr (6 oz) firm white fish (monkfish, sole, turbot)
4 small scallops
8 mussels, cleaned and opened (see page 35)
8 small button mushrooms
1 tablespoon capers, chopped
1 tablespoon parsley, finely chopped
salt and black pepper
juice 1 lemon
2 tablespoons white wine

My recipe for this dish involves both deep and shallow pan frying. First, roll the scampi, prawns, squid (cut into small pieces), mussels and button mushrooms in the batter. These will be fried in the shallow pan, in a mixture of hot oil and butter.

Cut the firm white fish into small pieces and the scallops into 2 pieces each, and roll all in the batter. These will be deep-fried in oil.

Begin with the shallow frying, turning the ingredients occasionally until just golden-brown. Now set the basket of the fish for deep frying in the pan of hot oil.

Remove the cooked fish from the shallow frying pan; place on a hot dish and cover to keep warm.

While the deep frying proceeds, remove with a perforated slice any burnt fragments of batter from the shallow pan. Heat the fat up and pour in the lemon juice and the white wine, adding the chopped capers. Let all bubble for 1–2 minutes until the deep frying is complete. Then remove basket, drain and place the contents on the hot dish with the other cooked ingredients. Pour the contents of the shallow pan (seasoned with salt and pepper) over all. Sprinkle with parsley and serve.

## *Fish stews*

No better example of the fish stew can be found than the *Bourride*, which is one of the great dishes of Provence. I give the recipe for this which Mrs David provides in her *French Provincial Cooking*.

## La Bourride

'M. Bérot, once *chef des cuisines* on the *Île de France* – a liner celebrated for its good cooking – served us his own version of this dish at the Escale, a hospitable and charming restaurant at Carry-le-Rouet, a little seaside place west of Marseille.

'The ingredients you need for four people are 4 fine thick fillets of a rather fleshy white fish. M. Bérot uses *baudroie* or angler-fish, but at home I have made the dish with fillets of John Dory, of turbot, of brill (*barbue*).

'In any case, whatever fish you choose, be sure to get the head and the carcase with your fillets. Apart from these you need a couple of leeks, a lemon, a tablespoon of wine vinegar, at least 4 cloves of garlic, 2 or 3 egg yolks, about one-third of a pint of olive oil, a couple of tablespoons of cream, and seasonings. To accompany the *bourride* you need plain boiled new potatoes and slices of French bread fried in oil.

'First make your stock by putting the head and carcase of the fish into a saucepan with a sliced leek, a few parsley stalks, a teaspoon of salt, a slice of lemon, the wine vinegar and about 1¼ pints of water. Let all this simmer gently for 25 to 30 minutes. Then strain it . . .

'Now put a tablespoon of olive oil and the white of the second leek, finely sliced, into the largest shallow metal or other fireproof pan you have; let it heat, add the spare clove of garlic, crushed; put in the lightly seasoned fillets; cover with the stock; let them gently poach for 15 to 25 minutes, according to how thick they are.

'Have ready warming a big serving dish; take the fillets from the pan with a fish slice and lay them in the dish; cover them and put them in a low oven to keep warm.

'Reduce the stock in your pan by letting it boil as fast as possible until there is only about a third of the original quantity left. Now stir in the cream and let it bubble a few seconds.

'Have your *aïoli* ready in a big bowl or a jug over which you can fit a conical or other sauce sieve. Through this pour your hot sauce; quickly stir and amalgamate it with the *aïoli*. It should all turn out about the consistency of thick cream. Pour it over your fish fillets. On top strew a little chopped parsley and the dish is ready . . .'

A recipe for that other great Provençal dish – *Bouillabaisse* – is given on page 107.

## *Fish with pasta*

Let us escape from the dreaded omnipresent *bolognese* and recognize, with a welcoming cry, that most forms of pasta can be served with fish sauces. Pastas are particularly useful for creating substantial dishes with small quantities of fish or shellfish. Prawns or mussels can be added to Special Tomato Sauce (see page 72) and poured over a dish of well-buttered spaghetti. Flaked tunnyfish, added to the same sauce, makes a substantial meal. Vary these dishes by using a *Sauce Marinière* (page 60) or *Normande* (page 61). Here is a recipe for a popular Southern Italian dish:

**Spaghetti alle Vongole** (spaghetti with clams)
450 gr (1 lb) spaghetti
2 kg (4½ lb) clams
3 tablespoons olive oil
2 onions, finely sliced
2 cloves garlic, crushed
450 gr (1 lb) tomatoes, skinned and deseeded
salt and black pepper
2 tablespoons parsley, finely chopped

In a large pan of boiling, salted water, cook your spaghetti until just *al dente*. Meanwhile, wash the clams thoroughly in cold water and put them into a large saucepan over a moderate flame to open in the same way as mussels (see page 153). Remove them from the shells and strain off the cooking liquor. In another smaller saucepan, heat the olive oil and brown the onion and garlic lightly. Add the tomatoes and about half the clam liquor. Boil to reduce by about a third and add the clams, just heating them through. Season with salt and pepper and pour this over the well-drained spaghetti. Sprinkle with parsley and serve.

There is no reason why *cannelloni* should not be filled, or *lasagne* interleaved, with a savoury mixture of minced fish – such as that used for Mixed Fish *Quenelles* (see page 190), but omitting, of course, the *panada* – and covered with a Tomato Sauce or *Sauce Mornay*. Now I await only inspiration to announce the evolution of the fish *ravioli*.

I again go to Alan Davidson for a somewhat complicated recipe involving fresh sardines and the use of a very fine type of *macaroni*.

(For our purposes *vermicelli* or the thinnest kind of *tagliatelle* you can find will do.) It makes a splendid dish – though not, I fear, inexpensive.

**Pasta con le Sarde** (A Sicilian macaroni and sardine pie)
500 gr (1 lb) fennel bulbs (if in Sicily, use the mountain kind called *finocchielli*)
50 gr (2 oz) sultanas
500 gr (1 lb) fresh sardines (about a dozen)
2 wineglassfuls olive oil
a few shallots
3 salted anchovies
pinch of saffron
100 gr (4oz ) pine-nut kernels
salt and pepper
500 gr (1 lb) *maccheroncini* (a kind of pasta which is a little thicker than *vermicelli*, and may also be found under the names *bucatini* or *perciatelli grossi*)

'Clean the fennel bulbs, trimming off bits which are too tough. Boil them for 10 minutes in water. Take them out, drain them, and cut them into very small pieces. Save the cooking liquid. Soak the sultanas for 15 minutes in warm water. Drain them. Remove the heads and backbones from the sardines. Take one-third of the sardines and cut them up very small to go in the sauce. The remaining two-thirds are to be floured and then fried in olive oil.

'Heat some more olive oil and let the shallots take colour in this. Add the chopped up sardines and crush them in the pan with a spoon. Add the chopped fennel and let the whole cook for a little, adding if necessary a small amount of the fennel cooking liquid.

'Wash and bone the salted anchovies. Heat some more olive oil, then add the anchovies – but at the side of the stove, not over the flame. Help the anchovies to 'melt' by using a fork.

'Now add to the onion/shallot/fennel mixture the melted anchovies, the saffron (mixed with a very little water), the sultanas, the pine-nut kernels and salt and pepper, and let it all go on cooking for a few minutes.

'Meanwhile, cook the pasta: bring the fennel cooking liquid to the boil, supplement it if necessary with water, and cook the pasta in this with a little salt. Drain. Combine with the sauce.

'Finally, place a layer of the pasta in a greased oven dish, with fried sardines on top and more pasta on top of them and so on. Bake this dish in a hot oven [200°C/400°F, gas 6] for 15 minutes or so. This is the practice at Trapani. At Palermo you would be more likely to find that all the sardines had gone into the sauce, and that this last stage would therefore be omitted.'

## *Fish with eggs*

### Omelette Arnold Bennett

450 gr (1 lb) smoked haddock
3 dl (½ pint) milk
3 dl (½ pint) water
1·5 dl (¼ pint) double cream
4 eggs, separated
50 gr (2 oz) Parmesan cheese, grated
salt and black pepper
25 gr (1 oz) butter

The haddock should be poached in the milk and water for 15 minutes. Leave it to cool before removing any skin and the bones. Then combine the haddock with half the cream and season well. Beat your egg yolks and mix them and most of the Parmesan into the haddock mixture. The egg whites should be beaten until stiff and folded into the mixture.

Heat the butter in a large omelette pan, and add the mixture. Cook over a medium heat until the underside is lightly browned; the top should be slightly liquid. Place the omelette on a heated serving dish and fold it in half. The other half of the cream should be poured over and the remaining Parmesan sprinkled on top. The omelette should then be quickly browned under a hot grill and served.

### Fish Soufflé

225 gr (8 oz) cooked fish and cooking juices
1·5 dl (¼ pint) thick *Sauce Béchamel* (see page 64)
3 egg yolks
4 egg whites

First light your oven, set at a moderate heat (180°C/350°F, gas 4), and put a baking tin on the middle shelf to get hot. Pound the fish to a purée (or put through the blender) and amalgamate with the thick *béchamel*. Add the strained liquid from the pan in which the fish has been poached, reduced to a few tablespoons of *fumet*. Beat in the egg yolks. Warm and butter well a 16-cm (7-in) soufflé dish in readiness. Now beat the egg whites to a stiff froth with a metal spoon and *fold* (don't beat) them lightly and quickly into the mixture. Scoop the mixture out of the mixing bowl into your soufflé dish as quickly as you can, and shake level. Stand the dish on the heated baking tin in the centre of the oven. Cook for 25 minutes. For the quantities given, and provided the procedures have been correctly and quickly carried out, 25 minutes should produce a perfectly cooked soufflé. To open the oven door to 'take a peep' before 25 minutes are up is to court disaster. Bring to table and serve immediately on hot plates.

If individual soufflés are being made, these require cooking for only 15–20 minutes.

Any of the sauces based on the *béchamel* can be used for fish soufflés, and nearly every fish in the formbook can be called into service for them. The crustaceans (lobster, crab, prawns, shrimps, crawfish) are perhaps the best performers, followed closely by salmon, monkfish, trout, red mullet, sole, turbot, whiting, smelts and, of course, both smoked and fresh haddock – to name only my favourites. In fact the range of possibilities is so wide that a different fish soufflé for each week of the year should be common kitchen practice.

## *Fish salads*

Most white fish and shellfish can be made into attractive salads and cold dishes.

The following recipe for a mixed fish salad can be varied at will, and the vinaigrette-type dressing can also be altered to suit the particular fish chosen. Though some trouble to make at home, this is the sort of variable salad which should, as a matter of course, be a permanent feature of the menu of any fish restaurant.

### Mixed Fish Salad

1 small squid, cooked in stock until tender, and sliced
2 scallops, poached and diced
4 large cooked prawns

10 poached mussels
150 gr (6 oz) fillet of sole (John Dory, monkfish or dogfish will do), poached and cut into 8 pieces
150 gr (6 oz) eel (conger will do), cut into 5 or 6 pieces
4 thin slices cooked fennel root, diced

Distribute the shellfish and pieces of sole and eel on a dish. (Reserve the stock in which they have been cooked for a soup or for use in some other recipe.) Sprinkle with the diced fennel root. While waiting for all the fish to get cold, prepare the following vinaigrette dressing:
½ small clove garlic, crushed
1 teaspoon sugar
½ teaspoon salt
1 teaspoon made English mustard
1 tablespoon shallot and chives, chopped
3 tablespoons wine vinegar
½ teaspoon freshly ground black pepper
1·5 dl (¼ pint) olive oil
1 tablespoon parsley, chopped

Pound all the ingredients, except the oil and the parsley, with the vinegar. Pour in the olive oil, beat well and pour the dressing over the cold fish at least half an hour before serving. At the last moment, sprinkle the chopped parsley over the dish.

Serve at the table and offer thick chunks of real bread. (Served in small portions on side-plates, this salad makes an excellent first course.)

Vary the vinaigrette by substituting horseradish *or* 1 tablespoon Watercress Purée (see Glossary) for the mustard, and for the shallot 1 tablespoon pounded capers or red or green sweet peppers.

Of course, the fish used in your salad can be varied according to choice and availability – and it is unnecessary to use as many varieties as I have listed in the above recipe. A very pleasant salad can be made using only one kind of white fish combined with one kind of shellfish.

You can vary the type of salad you make, as well as the ingredients. See page 86 for a recipe for *Salade Niçoise*.

## Fish Mayonnaise

Cover a similar selection of ingredients to those used in the above recipe – which for this dish should be resting on a bed of chopped watercress – with mayonnaise (see page 69). Garnish with sprigs of parsley and thin slices of cucumber.

To achieve a *chaudfroid* effect with mayonnaise, fold into it 1·5 dl ($\frac{1}{4}$ pint) concentrated fish *fumet* (clarified, as explained on page 63 under *Chaudfroid* Sauce, by boiling with the beaten whites and pounded shells of two eggs and then straining carefully through a fine sieve). The fish *fumet* should be on the point of setting when added. Coat your fish with it, and put in the refrigerator to set firmly.

All the sauces based on mayonnaise (see pages 69–70) are suitable for use with fish salads.

## Chaudfroid Dishes

The *Chaudfroid* Sauce given on page 63 can be used to coat any cold fillets of poached white fish, salmon, salmon trout, grayling and many others. Coating should be carried out when the sauce is cold and just on the point of setting.

## Aspic

The addition of a knuckle of veal, or other veal bones, to the usual ingredients of a good fish stock made from skate, conger or turbot bones and trimmings will ensure that, after long cooking, the resulting much-reduced broth will set when cold into a stiff aspic. The broth should, of course, be skimmed of all fat and clarified at least once in the manner described under *Chaudfroid* Sauce (see page 63) and also above, under Fish Mayonnaise.

To give aspic a good colour, a teaspoonful of fine sugar, caramelized to the stage at which it takes on a reddish-amber colour, can be stirred into the broth before it is put to set. The addition of a tablespoon of red wine, sherry or Marsala also helps in this respect.

# Mediterranean postscript

We live in Limassol, a town which after the Turkish invasion of Cyprus in 1974 had suddenly to absorb and house tens of thousands of refugees from the north. We were therefore extremely lucky when we arrived here in 1977 to find an old house of noble proportions in the middle of the town, which with some modernisation and painting has been our comfortable home for the last five years. Othonian Greek in style, it has a lofty hall running the length of the house into a spacious courtyard – a citrus orchard of exceptionally tall trees, enclosed by walls on two sides and a wide 'dog leg' veranda on the other two. It is on this veranda that we live, work, laugh, and sometimes even sing and dance, for pretty well eight months of the year. Extending from the house down the longer leg of the dog are the spare room, the bathroom and a glorious kitchen and scullery, both sixteen feet high. As if all this were not sufficient blessing, the house is only five minutes away from a splendid market which fulfils, on a minor scale and all under one roof, the functions of those three London 'bygones', Billingsgate, Smithfield and Covent Garden.

It took me some time to get on terms with the market fishmongers here, but my first breakthrough came when I was making an attempt, in my long-unpractised 'kitchen' Greek, to find a John Dory (see pages 15 and 142). Nervously I approached the swarthy fishmonger and essayed my linguistic skill in pronouncing two of the names by which this fish is known in the Mediterranean.

'*Exeis*' ('have you') I ventured, '*Agios petros?*' There was no reaction to this whatsoever.

I ventured further: '*Exeis christopsaro?*' There was still no sign of comprehension, though the fishmonger signalled that he was in touch by cupping one ear with a hand and leaning towards me.

Rather more crisply I repeated my question two or three times, varying the stresses on the syllables. Still the words meant nothing to him. Suddenly I remembered the copy of Alan Davidson's *Mediterranean Seafood* in my pocket. I drew it out, found the right illustration and proffered it.

'Ah!' he exclaimed. '*Christopsaro*!' His pronunciation of the word was identical with my own. This is something that is always happening in Cyprus.

Thereafter we were on terms, Takis the fishmonger and I. The trouble with *Christopsaro*, I gathered, was that it did not sell well on the market. Few large ones were caught and the small ones (four to six inches) were tiresome for the housewife to prepare. As a result fishermen kept these for themselves and took them home to their wives. Takis, too, kept for himself small ones which came to market among the boxes of small fry. I indicated to him the size of Dory I was interested in (ten to fifteen inches) but did nothing to discourage him from producing small ones as well.

So began a slow and irregular supply of John Dory in every size between four and twenty inches, but never anything as large as those one can regularly obtain in London. However for flavour and texture I have never tasted better. Dealing with the infant Dorys, even if one takes the easy way out by using them for soup, involves painstaking and finicky work since it will take about twenty of these small ones to make a dish for four hearty eaters. I myself think it well worth the time and effort, and I am quite resigned to spending two hours or more in careful preparation for poaching and then filleting (each into four perfect fillets), prior to saucing and adding a final garnish.

I have singled out the John Dory because since I came to live here it has provided me with the pleasure and practice of making fine white seafood dishes. It is indeed an all-purpose fish which can be dressed with every sauce – and variation of it – given in this book, from the simplest of chameleon sauces to the richest of *veloutés*. But my admiration for it is also, I contend, justified by the wonderful 'presence' and structure of the fish itself. Gaze at it, with its fins extended, and you will see a cubist portrait in the intricately arranged bones of its prehistoric head. In the length and beauty of its fins, some webbed, springing like wings from the sharp, serrated edges at their base, it is, in all but colour, which is that of wet ashes, a very peacock of the sea. Note also the expression of utter surprise and disillusionment in the eyes. It is as if, at some early evolutionary stage, realization had suddenly come to its fishy brain that it had been duped into taking an irrevocable step in the wrong direction; originally designed to fly but now forever condemned to a liquid element. And then what of those mysterious black imprints on its sides? Icarus, touched by the fingers of the sun god and, with what was left of his burning wings, plunging into the sea? All of which makes the Dory no easier to prepare for the table.

In keeping up with my 'John Dory' commitment and in searching for other fish, my almost daily visits to the market, once my northern inhibitions had been removed, became a joyful settled habit and I was pleased to see that even my modest purchases were encouraging the more frequent appearance of both Dorys and other larger fish, such as the *rophos* (*merou* and grouper) and the *synagrida* (*denté* and dentex bream), which usually go direct to the hotels and restaurants in which Limassol abounds.

Habitually I leave the house at eight in the morning – no point in going earlier, as the incoming fish will not yet have been sorted out and I run the risk of becoming involved in the grim *paso doble* of the meat porters, their headless burdens clasped in their arms like macabre dancing partners, as they stagger in with them to the butchers' stalls. By this time, too, the motorized stampede to work from the outlying suburbs down to the narrow-streeted old town and port will have subsided. The Cypriot is a fine and always competent driver and wears his car as naturally as his clothes. With a cigarette in his right hand, which dangles limp-wristed out of the window, and two fingers of his left alternating rapidly between horn button and steering wheel, he provides too heart-quickening an encounter for any strolling fish cook, however adventurous.

As I go in by the main entrance to the market I turn left, averting my eyes from the big central island area, reserved for the butchers, where dismemberment and evisceration of carcases will be in the train on a daunting scale, and moving clockwise round it take in the scents and colours of mountainous slopes of – it seems – all the fruits of the earth. This rich display is kept up all through the year, new fruits and vegetables constantly arriving to replace those going out of season – in Cyprus, unlike northern Europe, we eat only home-grown produce. At the top of the main hall there is an opening into a smaller hall, set at right angles to it. On the right of this hall is another salad, herb and vegetable market with 'casual' stalls for villagers selling the fresh produce which they have risen long before dawn to dig up or pick and which they have brought down on the first buses from their mountain villages. On the left is the fish market.

Here two opposed groups of *ichthyopoleis* (fishmongers) preside over their long stone- and metal-topped counters. Of the two groups, the one on the right is by far the more prosperous, with an abundant display of stock. On the left, my friend Takis is in command of a meagre, widely dispersed display which suggests undercapitalization.

The frenzy of sorting out large crates of small fish is slacking off as I arrive and the first small cups of coffee are being sipped before the calls to 'come and buy' are sung and business begins. The coffee-seller goes round collecting empty cups and glasses (a glass of water always accompanies coffee), as the fishmongers begin to drum up trade, *fortissimo*, in a fishy antiphony.

'*Exo barbounia*' ('I have red mullet!') '*Exo maridha, kalamarakia, xifias*!' ('I have whitebait, baby squid, swordfish!')

These calls from one side provoke from Takis, on the other, an answering, all-inclusive, staccato '*Psari fresko exo*! *Psari fresko exo*!' ('Fresh fish have I!')

Beginning on the right-hand side, in the far corner against the wall, two counter-sunk basins contain octopus, squid and sepia. A small separate mound of tiny infantine squid is arranged between them. (These tiny cephalopods are a great delicacy, first brought from cold to simmering point in seasoned water, kept at that temperature for ten minutes, then drained, dried, dipped in egg and breadcrumbs and fried quickly in olive oil.) At the front of the counter, pride of place is given to a lovingly arranged display of *barbounia* (red mullet), hardly more than four inches long, perhaps the most sought after fish in this country and, weight for weight, almost as expensive as crawfish. (Large *barbounia* are now only a memory, as a result of the overfishing which has accompanied the growth of the tourist industry over the past fifteen years.) Behind these rises a tumulus of *maridha*, also in great local favour, but moderately priced. They are mostly picarel, more approaching the size of sprats than that of the whitebait most menus claim them to be.

Around and between these two mounds of small choice fish are usually arranged what I would call the 'round fish' of the day. *Kephalos* (grey mullet) and other handsome mullet, sea bream and sea bass, long fat *zargana* (garfish of the green bones), mackerel, *litsa* (pompano), a small *mayatico* (the large ones run to a couple of metres) and, with luck, a *rophos* (grouper) – all these, and their cousins, being of good size, are 'carriage-trade' fish. Although I list them all here, there will never be more than a few on display at any one time and even when there has been a good catch there will only be, at most, a choice of six different kinds. All these beautiful round fish are expensive and a rather dotty system governs their pricing when they are beyond a foot in length (around thirty centimetres). Though it is impossible to establish an exact calculus, take it that for every two-inch increment the asking price will rise by one third, up to say, two feet, and for every inch thereafter the price will be doubled, all measurements being ocular. This is an indication of the depletion of stocks of even half-grown fish in this part of the Mediterranean. One cause of this progressive impoverishment of the sea is not far to seek as we move to the next section of the counter and come upon a densely packed heap of small fish of all families and species in a decor of fragments of seaweed. In spite of stringent regulations as to the minimum width of mesh for nets, these hecatombs of infant fish appear to be a staple of the market and it seems to me that extravagance verges on hubris when the fry that would develop into several tonnes' weight when fully grown are so light-heartedly consumed. Friends tell me it has always been like this here: 'The fish, they always come, and always will, *o Theos boithos* – with God's help!'

Alongside this sad heap of victims cut off in their infancy are a medley of gurnards – several types of these, with differing colour schemes, but all with the same bulldozer faces – and a large jumble of rick fish of all kinds, including rascasse. All of these are good for my Kettle of Fish soup (see page 107) and, I need hardly mention, for *Bouillabaisse*. I interrupt to say that, in Cyprus, there is no tradition of Fishermen's soups (see page 105) such as the two just mentioned above, and even the concept of a fish pie does not exist, which surprises me after the island's near hundred years of British rule. However, the British had little influence on Cyprus cookery – with one unfortunate exception. How I wish they had introduced the fish pie with the energy they must have employed to achieve blanket coverage of the island with the good old fried-fish-shop chip. But back to the market. . . .

At our next *guichet* we come upon a restless mound, two feet high, composed of long-legged creatures which in the sea are invisible to their enemies under a superb camoflage of sea moss and weed. Here, alas, with their legs pedalling away, they are pitifully exposed as spider crabs, those pear-shaped, thorny-backed favourites of Italian gastronomes. I am in some difficulty about these crustacea, accustomed as I am to the sort of crab you buy at Margate or Blackpool. I give them full marks for flavour, which is all very well, but for cooking purposes I need meat as well. How best to come to terms with these, speaking cuisinologically, is part of work in progress – as are the tiny crabs, less than an inch wide, which are heaped next to the spider crabs and which are served in the better restaurants here with their legs removed, deep fried in a thin, seasoned batter – a delicious and crunchy experience. They also make a marvellous *bisque* (see page 101) but I have other fates in store for them as well.

Of other crustaceans, the flat lobster (*grande cigale*) appears occasionally on the market, the true lobster never – though of course I may have missed one, but I doubt it; after five years of hoping, it has become a myth. The flat lobster's flesh is just as good, but the unfortunate creature only has very stunted pincer claws, and how I miss that lovely fleshy clawmeat!

The crawfish never comes to market either – but crawfish can be found in tavernas around the coast, near small fishing ports. The specimens I have enjoyed have all been full-grown, which suggests to me that this wily crustacean has discovered a way of concealing its growing young from the keen-witted local fishermen. In the summer the motorized hunt for the crawfish is a serious sport.

Fresh prawns put in an occasional appearance on the market. The problem is much the same as with the John Dory: the prawn catch of individual fishermen is so small that they usually take it home to the family. By pressing Takis and putting him on his mettle I have eventually become able to obtain modest supplies. I now feel as if I were in the position of 'underwriter' of both these fish and feel guilty unless I buy a substantial amount of them each time they appear – which is not very often.

If the market is short on crustacea, it makes up for it with lavish catches of several varieties of skate, some of remarkable size, and various small sharks – dogfish, monkfish and Angler, and others of that cartilaginous ilk. Here they are skinned, cleaned and cut up and arranged for display. The skate dominates this section, but we may also find small flat white fish like the sole and plaice – I have never yet encountered a turbot or brill. The soles are so small that one needs about ten of them to provide a meal for two. They are easy to cook quickly *à la meunière* (see page 171), but where are the mothers and fathers of these hand-sized youngsters?

The last and longest section of display counter is reserved for two enormous frozen logs of flesh – the tunny fish and the pathetic sword-fish, shorn of its weapon. Here are scenes reminiscent of a forester's log camp, as first a massive cleaver is hammered an inch or two into the great cylinders of frozen fish before the two-handled saw is brought into play and wide, inch-thick steaks are sawn off as required. Small fresh tunny fish do appear now and again and are sold as fast as the fishmonger can cut them up.

Let us now move over to the opposing team of *ichthypoleis*, of which Takis is the undoubted captain. He is a handsome, thick, piratical figure, so weathered in neck and hands as to give the impression of being half bound in morocco, slightly rubbed; he has a Bourbon nose and a Hapsburg chin and a glint of gold in his mouth when he laughs. But today he is serious and brooding and his '*Kalimera*' ('Good day') is half-hearted. He has no *christpsaro* for me, but what he has got, I perceive, is a bulky, three-foot-long *synagrida*, its skin a glistening silver and pale cinder red. He has made no attempt to attract attention to this fish, has sung no elegiacs in its praise to draw the shopping housewives, for he knows that they will only want him – and in a flood of objurgations and '*Kyrie Eleisons*' force him – to cut it up into steaks. In fact, it was only as I approached the counter that he whipped away the sack with which he had covered it, for he thinks there is just a chance that I am a customer who might buy it whole – for, as we have seen earlier, the price of a whole big fish is higher that that of the sum of its parts. By this calculus, value is added in respect of the fish's beauty when entire and that value is increased by the amount of pride the possessor feels in its ownership, which, when selling it, he must surrender to the purchaser.

To begin with, Takis makes no move to sell the fish to me, but he watches me closely. He has some good fresh sardines and anchovies, two noble morays and a conger, and I inspect these, but it is impossible for me not to eye the charms of his *synagrida* on the sly. It has now become unthinkable – and it would be unforgivably rude – for me to walk away from the counter without making some congratulatory remark in praise of his splendid fish, which is now exercising its own hypnotic spell on me.

'*Ti thauma to psari!*' ('What a wonderful fish!') I exclaim, and I mean it. This is the moment Takis has been waiting for. He has watched me snuffling at the bait. Now he picks up the fish in both hands and pretends to fumble with it.

'*Zondano eine!*' ('It is alive!') he shouts, as he mimes the fish's attempts to escape his arms. Then he turns solemn, holds it out in both hands towards me. 'Look at it, touch it, see how fresh it is,' he says, as with one finger he lifts the opercal at the head to show the scarlet gills. I advance my hand and am anointed by the glistening lubricants that make the iridescent scales sparkle.

'*Touto to psari* . . . ,' he begins on a slow hieratic note. 'This fish. . . .'

Ten minutes later, during which a small crowd gathered round us to enjoy the solemnities, and during which Takis twice withdrew the fish from sale, throwing the sack over it to protect it from profane eyes, then snatching it off again . . . ten long minutes later, I felt the tug as I took the hook, and surrendered, 'Ah! Ah!' sighed the crowd.

It still remained for us to determine the price I must pay. 'Ah!' sighed the crowd again, anticipating the joys of a noisy second act.

But Takis would have no audience for this final and most important phase of our negotiation. 'Be off with you,' he said to them sternly and they scuffled off obediently, mumbling a '*Po! Po!*' here and a '*Kyrie Eleison*' there. By this time I had become too feeble-minded to put up much resistance and Takis seemed a little hurt when suddenly, after only his third reduction of price, I caved in and paid him the money. I could see him thinking, 'These British! No wonder they lost an Empire!' As I left the hall, burdened with my fish in a sack (the latter on loan), I could hear Takis, in good heart and better voice now, beginning a spirited *da capo*: '*Exo psari fresco. . . .*'

I will not describe in detail all the problems this fish created at home: how it had to be cooked in two halves, though kept whole and intact, because none of our pans or dishes was big enough; how a train-bearer was needed to support the tail section as it was carried from the kitchen on to the veranda for consumption by eight hurriedly assembled guests, to the music of Grapelli and Fats Waller.

It would be churlish of me to omit from this postscript some notes on the excellence of the regional cuisine of this lovely island. With its Balkan, Lebanese, Turkish and of course Greek influences clearly evident Cypriot cooking, which is best at its simplest, owes nothing to the traditions of *haute cuisine* and the *béchamel* hardly shows its face outside the four- or five-star hotels. This absence of enriched flour-based sauces is one of the main features of the *minceur* canon, and in this respect at least Cypriot cuisine may be said to have anticipated that 'modern' movement by several hundred years – so much for modern movements! Anyway, there is no doubt that it is healthy and invigorating and gives the Cypriot that demonic energy for work and play which he so wholeheartedly expends.

The humble '*mezé*' or appetizer (which needs no introduction from me since Greek and Cypriot restaurants and tavernas abound all over the world and have already crept, some say, into heaven), originally a free offering to encourage custom, provided by the management with any drink ordered, was always a pleasant aspect of Greek tavernas I used to know in the mid 1930s. When money was short one could surreptitiously dine quite well in this way. The Cypriots have expanded this concept into what is called a 'Full *Mezé*', an extravagant, long-running banquet which may include up to as many as twenty or thirty dishes. An officially sponsored book lists* and illustrates sixty recipes from an apparently inexhaustible repertoire.

As the 'Full *Mezé*' proceeds, with its succession of small dishes of savoury hot and cold fish, flesh, fowl and all the fruits of the earth, wine is liberally dispensed and a Dionysiac element will often enter into the occasion. It is then that the desire to dance and stamp around the tavern floor becomes irresistible, as a bouzouki strikes up and a strident klephtic ballad begins. . . .

A *mezé* does not have to include all the categories of food mentioned above. Sometimes – and to my taste ideally – it will be composed entirely of fish. This 'Full Fish *Mezé*', as some tavernas advertise it, will generally consist of the following items: small red mullet, grilled or fried; segments of octopus, stewed, pickled or grilled; squid – the larger ones cut into rings – egged and breadcrumbed and fried in oil; cubes of swordfish, marinated and grilled over the charcoal fire; *maridha* (picarel), sardines or anchovies, and prawns when available, marinated

* *The Cypriots at Table* by Marios Mourdjis. C. A. L. Graphics, Nicosia.

and grilled. Each dish will be dressed with some sort of relish – basically oil and lemon juice seasoned with salt and pepper and containing finely chopped herbs such as parsley, basil, coriander, *rigani* (marjoram) and thyme – all such dressings being variations on the chameleon sauce theme (see page 54).

Accompanying these fishy delights will be plentiful supplies of crusty bread and various dips: taramasalata (see page 87), houmous and tahina. There is also usually a great salad containing shredded lettuce or cabbage with rocca, tomatoes, cucumber, small black olives and fragments of white and crumbly *fetta* cheese.

During my stay here I have speculated increasingly on how this kind of entertainment might be adopted in other countries. In Britain, with the far greater variety of fish available, it could be enormously extended.

A cold *mezé* can of course be prepared in advance, with its accompanying relishes and sauces. A hot *mezé*, however, means a long evening standing at the stove engaged in non-stop cooking, saucing and serving – but what an opportunity it provides for the cook to display his or her skills! Obviously the *mezé* should be served in the kitchen – the modern kitchen-dining-room being perfect for the occasion. I would choose from the following fish: scallops, crab, mussels, prawns, turbot, trout, haddock, octopus, small squid, monkfish . . . but the possibilities are endless. No large quantities of the bigger fish are required, as the guests are only expected to have a small amount of each dish. It is the almost Chinese multiplicity of the fare which makes the success of these running feasts. Many of the dishes described in my chapter on hors-d'oeuvres and savouries (pages 82–93) will prove particularly appropriate – for instance fishcakes and fish dumplings (see page 87).

The possibilities are endless. For us in Cyprus most of the fish I have just mentioned are simply dreams of the past. Occasionally, as I chop and stir in my kitchen, I cannot help brooding on the fish I left behind me. Perhaps those I miss most are oysters, mussels, scallops and the crab. This is sometimes hard to bear, but then I realize that it is only a small price to pay for one of the finest climates in the world.

# Glossary

*Bouquet garni* A faggot of herbs tied together with thread for flavouring stocks, sauces, soups. Choose your own herbs, but parsley, thyme, bay leaf and celery are the usual components.

*Chine* The ribs and fine skeleton of the crab, etc.

*Clarified butter* The purpose of clarifying butter is to remove the salt; there is no need to clarify unsalted butter. The butter should be melted in a saucepan and heated gently while all the scum and impurities rise to the top; it should not be allowed to colour. Strain it through a muslin-lined sieve and allow any sediment to settle at the bottom of a small bowl. Then pour the butter into another bowl, leaving behind the sediment.

*Compound butter* This is butter blended with any seasoning, spice, purée of vegetables or herbs, or – for the purpose of this book – fish. The large variety of flavouring ingredients possible makes compound butters a valuable element in fish cookery.

*Court-bouillon* Savoury vegetable stock in which fish is cooked. A *court-bouillon* can be based on water, wine, wine vinegar or milk. See pages 57–8 for recipes.

*Duxelles* A 'chop-up' of mushroom stalks cooked in oil and butter with a little onion until all moisture is driven out. The mixture is then poured into a basin and covered for use when required.

*Fumet* A highly concentrated essence of fish and seasonings made by reduction of a strong fish stock from, say, 12 dl (2 pints) to 3 dl (½ pint). A good *fumet* should 'jell' when cold. For use in enriching sauces and soups, and for making *chaudfroid* dishes.

*Goujons* These are small strips of the fillet, either poached or lightly fried.

*Marinade* A mild pickling liquid usually containing vinegar in some strength, wine, herbs, spices and seasonings in which the fish is soaked for some hours to tenderize or to impregnate with flavour. A souse for mackerel or herring.

*Mirepoix* A 'chop-up' or dicing of ingredients – which might include celery, parsley, onion and carrot – to play a role in any fish dish. This mixture is stewed lightly in butter preparatory to its use in, for example, a braising recipe.

*Panada* In simple terms, a 'stiffener' for stuffings, forcemeats or *quenelles*; it is made with breadcrumbs soaked in milk and then squeezed dry and used as a dough. For recipes, see page 189.

*Purée* Doing it the hard way, a true purée is only achieved by passing the cooked ingredient concerned through a fine sieve. Today, when every kitchen has a blender, it is a simple matter to obtain a smooth and consistent texture. Although I myself tend to stick to old habits, the reader is naturally at liberty to use all the modern aids he has. Remember, however, that puréeing tomatoes in a blender will result in emulsifying the pips as well as the flesh, and that fish must be passed through a sieve to remove the small bones.

*Roux* A mixture of butter or oil and flour cooked together as the basis for thickening soups, sauces etc. (See page 56.)

# Index